OB Workbook Supplement

to accompany

ORGANIZATIONAL
BEHAVIOR

SIXTH EDITION

JOHN R. SCHERMERHORN, JR.
Ohio University

JAMES G. HUNT
Texas Tech University

RICHARD N. OSBORN
Wayne State University

JOHN WILEY & SONS, INC.

New York • Chichester • Weinheim • Brisbane • Singapore • Toronto

Copyright © 1997 by John Wiley & Sons, Inc.

Excerpts from this work may be reproduced by instructors
for distribution on a not-for-profit basis for testing or
instructional purposes only to students enrolled in courses
for which the textbook has been adopted. *Any other
reproduction or translation of this work beyond that
permitted by Sections 107 or 108 of the 1976 United States
Copyright Act without the permission of the copyright
owner is unlawful. Requests for permission or further
information should be addressed to the Permissions
Department, John Wiley & Sons, Inc., 605 Third Avenue,
New York, NY 10158-0012.*

ISBN 0-555-11679-4

Printed in the United States of America

10 9 8 7 6 5 4

Printed and bound by Bradford & Bigelow, Inc.

Preface

The OB Workbook Supplement to accompany Organizational Behavior 6E by Schermerhorn, Hunt, and Osborn was designed to supplement the cases and experiential exercises that appear in the text. There are 22 cases and 38 exercises, with topics ranging from Starbuck's Coffee to Negotiating Contracts for the National Hockey League. You will note that the cases do not have questions and answers; this was done intentionally to allow students to determine for themselves the issues and applications and to provide maximum flexibility for the OB classroom.

We are confident that this *Workbook Supplement* will be another valuable tool to help today's students become the leaders of tomorrow's organizations.

Table of Contents

CASES FOR CRITICAL THINKING

CASE 1
Mutually Uncommitted
· ·

By Sally Power, University of St. Thomas, Minneapolis

With the old social contract between companies and workers

dead and buried, what are our options for rebuilding the

employee-employer relationship?

Three years ago, Clarence Wilsen was abruptly laid off from his job as an analyst at a major West Coast financial services firm. The forty-five year-old took on low-paying day jobs and went to night school to brush up on his skills. After a year and a half, he found a job at another financial services company. Finally, he figured, his annual income would by year's end be back to where it had been in 1992.

That was before he learned last month that his unit will be "re-engineered," resulting in layoffs totaling 10 percent of its workforce, by September 30. "That's where I'm at," he says. "My job is in jeopardy—again." (Wilsen is an alias: Given his desire to keep his job, his identity was altered for this story.)

Wilsen's plight is just one example of a story that's become all too common in corporate America. The workforce is churning as wave upon wave of people are being let go due to corporate restructuring. Newspapers carry stories about layoffs weekly. Seventy-five percent of those polled in a 1994 *New York Times* survey reported they personally knew of someone who had lost his or her job in the last few years. And the American Management Association's annual downsizing survey found almost half of the companies polled in 1994 reported they laid off on average about 9 percent of their workforce in the past twelve months.

Most of us who are still employed work more, and worry more. Gone is the old social contract between employers and employees. And in its place is a system in which employees are loyal to themselves, rather than to a company, and in which employers view long-time employees as expensive burdens instead of valuable assets. Both sides have, for good reason, become mutually uncommitted.

The question is, how can businesses best manage employees in this new era? Continuing, as some businesses are, to tap and then toss away employees as if they were disposable raw materials, clashes with employees' needs for income stability, health care insurance, and overall security. In such an environment, anything, even the reinvigoration of the union movement, becomes a reasonable possibility.

Indeed, the parallels between today's labor situation and that of the 1920s are striking, according to Peter Rachleff, an associate professor specializing in labor history at Macalester College in St. Paul, Minnesota. The 1920s were a decade of technological change; racial, ethnic, and gender recomposition of the workforce; structural economic shifts; and employer and government anti-unionism that had severely depleted the union rolls. Financially, most businesses were doing well. Some companies even began providing benefits such as pensions and vacation time. With the Depression, however, those benefits were dropped and employee wages and security greatly decreased.

Then in the 1930s the argument was made that higher wages for workers were good for the American economy because turning workers into successful consumers would help American business. The argument prevailed, and so did the unions. From a membership of barely two million in 1932, the rolls exploded to ten million by 1938.

Business faces a similar situation today. Net earnings for the S&P 500 companies rose 40 percent overall in 1994—the fourth year of double digit increases. Other financial indicators are up as well, and have been for a number of years. Yet employees are feeling more and more insecure about their jobs and their futures.

As the twentieth century draws to a close, will workers find they must organize to respond collectively to companies that shortchange them in their business decisions? Is "mutually uncommitted" the phrase that will describe employee relations in the twenty-first century? Or can employers and employees work together to forge a new employment contract?

Faced with global competition, increasingly sophisticated automation, a compressed business cycle, and demands from shareholders to increase profits, business leaders say they must downsize and move to a more contingent workforce. Layoffs that reached a high of two thousand a day in the first quarter of 1994 continue. Forty-four percent of some 203 *Fortune* 500 chief executives polled last year said they expected to employ more contingent workers in the next five years.

"The attitude of management is, 'We'll get rid of them, cut costs, and hire them back if we need to'," says a disgruntled Wilsen. But as wrenching as this sounds, within the traditional business model, it makes sense. That model, born during the industrial revolution, sees employees as a cost just as computers or other capital equipment are. When costs can be cut, they should be. It's a well known formula for beating

Source: This originally appeared in *Business Ethics,* September-October 1995.

the competition: the work-harder-for-less, low-wage strategy.

While this is difficult for some employees, it's also hard on some of those executives who make the decisions. As Graef Crystal, a noted executive compensation expert, describes it, "Almost every executive-compensation package is oriented toward maximizing the shareholders' position. It often puts the CEO in a very awkward position, where he is being rewarded for others' misery."

But if these times are difficult for executives, they're excruciating for the hundreds of thousands of employees laid off in recent years. To them, the demise of the social contract between employee and employer has meant a demise of their way of life. Many have reacted to the change with fear, anger, and defensiveness: "You want to be uncommitted to me, I'll be uncommitted to you." If the company owes them no more than a paycheck, they owe the company no more than an eight-hour day.

To overcome this hostility and indifference, both employees and employers must change. Employees need to see their lack of job permanence more as an opportunity and less as a threat. They need to continue developing their skills, marketing themselves, and taking more responsibility for their own welfare. And they need to commit themselves to go the extra mile to help their current organizations to achieve their goals.

But employers also have to do more, mainly by addressing some of the most pressing issues on workers' minds today, including health care coverage, having a life outside the office, and the threat of being replaced by "contingent workers."

No plan for building a stronger, more respectful relationship between business and its workers will work, however, if employers don't walk their talk. The most glaring misstep by top management today is with respect to CEO pay.

Regardless of the extra effort and sacrifice they are asking of employees—many of whom will be lucky to see a pay raise of 3 percent or more this year—most CEOs are taking good care of themselves. Last year CEO salaries and bonuses advanced 11.4 percent over 1993 levels, according to a William C. Mercer study. Because of a sluggish market, CEOs did not exercise their stock options as much last year. But "mega grants," a type of compensation that involves gifts of stock ranging in value from one- to three-times an executive's annual cash compensation—increased. Thus the CEO compensation packages continued to expand in value at a significant rate.

Advocates of generous CEO compensation often hold that high pay is acceptable because corporations like buying "stars," and just like top athletes, CEOs should not be begrudged their stupendous compensation. "But wait a minute," says Ron Bosrock, a managing director at

Arthur Andersen International and a member of this year's Stakeholder Dialogues panel. "Aren't managers today taught that their work is to coach?" Taking the analogy further, he points out, coaches of sport teams hardly ever make more than their star players.

	1979-83	1987-91
Blue collar workers laid off	18.6%	14.1%
White collar workers laid off	7.3%	8.9%

Source: *The State of Working In America, 1974-1994,* By the Economic Policy Institute, Washington, D.C.

Some companies are making headway on this issue. Delta Airline's CEO and Chairman Ronald Allen, after announcing the elimination of fifteen thousand jobs, told his board in 1994 that he wanted to forego any pay raise or bonus for a second straight year. Gerald Grinstein, CEO of Burlington Northern, Inc., also took a pay cut in 1992 when things were hard for the railroad. He was quoted in the *Wall Street Journal* saying, "They're tough times, and I share the belief that these difficulties have to be" shared in the executive suite.

Meanwhile, employees continue to worry more about whether they'll be able to continue taking care of their families, especially on the health care front. While it used to be a given that family health care and pensions would be available to all working Americans, our current system is shifting into reverse. A study by James Medoff, a Harvard economist, showed that in 1988, 38 percent of all new jobs offered health benefits, down from 43 percent in 1979. Only 15 percent offered pension benefits in 1988 vs. 23 percent in 1979.

Lynn Martin, chair of the Council on the Advancement of Women for the accounting firm Deloitte & Touche, says one idea is to make health care insurance and pensions more portable, allowing employees to take them along as they switch employers. Devising such portable plans would prove a daunting task. But businesses might take a leadership role here—they have the experts who can deal with the complexity of this issue, and the clout to make it happen. It was, after all, businesses that first created workers compensation benefit plans in the early 1900s.

Even when there is ample insurance coverage, using it is another issue. Taking time off of work to take care of sick children is still viewed by many companies as unacceptable behavior, according to Felice Schwartz, this year's lead panelist for the Stakeholder

Dialogues. Schwartz has for more than thirty years championed the notion that corporations need to recognize the needs and strengths of women who work and also have children. The same applies to men, she says.

Another source of workplace insecurity is the apparent growth in the number of contingent workers. They now come in all varieties, from clerical workers to engineers to top managers; but most of them come with few benefits, no pensions, and reduced protections from exploitation or discrimination because they are not working full-time for their employers. And, there's a growing number of older, seasoned employees coming back to work part-time or full-time who don't look to their job as the sole source of income, but rather as a part-time activity that provides a second source of revenue. These employees have experience and proven talents, but also come with their own pensions and health care benefits from previous jobs.

It's hard to say just how many contingent workers there are. Temporary employees, who make up a major chunk of the contingent workforce, increased by an estimated 240 percent during the past ten years, according to the Bureau of Labor Statistics. Meanwhile, there's the previously mentioned poll of *Fortune* 500 CEOs that indicates even more contingent worker hiring in the future.

This month the Labor Department should be releasing its first-ever survey of contingent workers, according to Tom Nardone, an economist at the U.S. Bureau of Labor Statistics. This should provide a good starting point for looking at the costs and benefits of the contingent workforce.

While management touts them for the flexibility and lower costs they carry, others suggest that contingent workers, as more than an occasional occurrence in a company's workforce, introduce a class system among workers and encourage divisiveness and fear.

Think about it from the full-time employee's point of view: You constantly adjust to changes big and small in your work place, keeping your skills sharp and learning new ones. You recognize you may not be working this job for long, and you are constantly thinking about how you can market yourself. Furthermore, you're concerned with the potential financial risk to your family changing jobs might present. Your employer wants you to perform at your best. Wouldn't you be more likely to be able to give that extra effort if:

• You knew a contingent worker wasn't possibly going to replace you;
• Your family's health care and your pension would not cease if your job was lost;
• You were given all the information the company had about work changes and the skills that are and will be needed;
• You were being aided in

developing your skills;
• Your wages were at least adequate;
• And you felt mutual respect between management and employees was the norm.

"How can an enterprise build capabilities, forge empowered teams, develop a deep understanding of its customers, and—most important—create a sense of community or common purpose unless it has a relationship with its employees based on mutual trust and caring?" asked Betsy Collard and Robert and Judith Waterman in a *Harvard Business Review* article they wrote last year. "And how can an enterprise build such a relationship unless it commits something to employees and employees commit something to it?"

Thankfully, a growing number of companies are thinking about employee concerns. Instead of reacting with the same mechanistic response of the traditional business model, a few have started programs in "career-resilience" to tap their workforce as a source of renewable energy.

To the extent a company uses an employee's skills and knowledge but doesn't encourage growth or learning, "you are using them up," says Collard, program director and organizational consultant at the Career Action Center in Palo Alto, California. "We need to shift from looking at employees as a cost factor in manufacturing terms to thinking of them as investments based on intellectual capacity."

Raychem Corp. has been a pioneer in this area. Its career resilience program includes a

A Mutual Understanding
Ways Employers and Employees Can Better Work Together

Employers	Employees
Commit to providing employees with respect and basic security	Recognize and learn how to succeed with the increased insecurity in the workforce
Identify new skills and knowledge needed in the workplace	Constantly work on improving your skills
Advocate portable health care and pension benefits	Take on more responsibility for your own long-term security
Create new jobs and pay more people a living wage	Focus on achieving the organization's goals and giving extra effort when needed

process that pushes managers to specify exactly what "working harder" means and how it will be measured, as well as what new skills will be needed by employees in the future. It also has set up a continuous feedback system and a career center staffed by independent counselors from Collard's Career Action Center.

"We didn't come at it from the perspective of how can we save our people or how can we be more of an advocate for our people," says Steve Balogh, vice president of human resources at Raychem. "We were much more driven by the business side—what is the win/win situation for our employees and our business divisions."

These career-resilience programs focus on helping employees in two areas: periodically assessing their skills, interests, values, and temperaments so they can identify the work for which they are best suited; and benchmarking their skills on a regular basis.

In order to be effective, the programs require that the employers share much more of their management-related information, allowing all employees to better understand how they can fit in with the constant changes that take place within a business. Employers also show support, with time and resources, for employee learning and job changes.

Such ideas are a major change from the older, mechanistic paradigm because they recognize a need to treat human resources differently from other resources. They are more than a cost; they are people who created the entity which we know as the workplace. And they are people who need to have trusting, respectful relationships in order to do their best work.

This fall, Honeywell and twelve other corporate and nonprofit sponsors began a series of public discussions in the Twin Cities on these issues and more in a program entitled, "Rethinking Work in America." The programs came after a year of planning. "The hope is to be able to look at some new things that are going on—new practices, new arrangements—and encourage some of these companies who are participating in the forum to try them on an experimental basis," says Geri Joseph, former ambassador to the Netherlands and a member of the Honeywell board of directors until her retirement last year. She and Pat Hoven, the company's vice president for community and local government affairs, created the initiative.

"They all saw it as a critical issue," Hoven says of the sponsors. "The nature of work for their companies, their employees, and everybody is changing. It's not business as usual. They want to understand the problem."

Here's hoping that attitude spreads.

Interview: Howard Schultz

By Mary Scott

His dad was beaten down by the system. Today, the CEO of Starbucks runs a thriving business built upon making every worker feel respected.

When the Chicago-based U.S./Guatemala Labor Education project sought to publicize the near-slavery conditions on Guatemala's coffee plantations, it didn't go after such coffee giants such as Folger's or Maxwell House. Rather, the nonprofit advocacy group aimed its missives at Seattle-based Starbucks Coffee Company, the fast-growing specialty company that is fueling the coffee bar craze.

With more than five hundred company-owned stores throughout the country, Starbucks projects as a progressive business, touting its "Bean Stock" employee ownership plan, full medical and dental benefits—available to even part-time workers, and its annual six-figure donations to non-profit organization CARE.

Yet, according to the U.S./Guatemala Labor Education Project, workers toil in inhumane conditions in Guatemala to earn two cents a pound picking beans, while Starbucks sell the same beans for up to $8 a pound. Using that juxtaposition and others, the group last year targeted Starbucks in its campaign to improve working conditions for foreign coffee bean pickers.

Part of Starbucks' strength and influence is manifested in its partner-ships. Its stores feature the book *Starbucks Passion for Coffee,* the first in a series written with Sunset Books; and an exclusive jazz CD produced with Capitol Records, the first of a four-part series. And Starbucks New Venture Company, a wholly-owned subsidiary, has entered into a joint venture with Pepsi-Cola to develop ready-to-drink coffee-based beverages. The first, Mazagran, is being test-marketed in the Los Angeles area.

Suddenly, the upbeat yet tranquil scene of Starbucks coffee shops turned controversial. Activists started passing out anti-Starbucks leaflets to customers entering its stores. At headquarters, hundreds of impassioned letters began pouring in from customers and investors wanting action.

Starbucks management was soon being asked to adopt a "code of conduct" that would encourage Third World employers to ban child labor and to provide workers with increased wages, improved working conditions, and at least minimal health care.

At first, management balked, noting that the Seattle-based company's annual $100,000 plus donations to the relief agency CARE for programs in coffee growing regions was more than any other coffee company did to help people in such regions. By early 1995, however, it started writing a code that was released last month.

In doing so, Starbucks followed the leads of Levi Strauss & Co. in the clothing industry, and Reebok International Ltd. in the footwear industry, in establishing guidelines for its suppliers. It also broke the ice on an issue previously ignored by its peers.

The majority of specialty coffee firms previously had not considered working conditions in coffee-producing countries a top ethical priority. "Purchasing products without regard to their effect upon local environments" was ranked the thirteenth most significant ethical blunder, behind situations including, "Roasting beans with no formal training," and, "Fixing prices with competitors," according to a January 1995 survey of members conducted by the Specialty Coffee Association in Long Beach, California.

"Starbucks has gone a long way to deal with a very new situation," says Eric Hahn, the Starbucks Campaign Coordinator for the U.S./Guatemala Labor Education Project. "There's nothing else like this code of conduct in the coffee or agricultural industries."

Yet, pushing beyond the norm has been standard fare at Starbucks. The company has been in a constant state of growth since CEO Howard Schultz and a group of investors purchased it in 1987. From eleven Seattle stores and fewer than one hundred employees, it has since exploded into an empire serving nearly three million cups of coffee per week in six hundred stores around the country.

"Starbucks has created an incredibly powerful brand name in a relatively short period of time," says Michael Moe, a growth stock analyst for Lehman Brothers, a Manhattan securities brokerage firm. "It's now a half billion dollar company, and growing at rates hardly any company could match. I consider them the finest emerging growth company in America."

According to Moe, Starbucks' rapid growth did not come at the expense of its decidedly progressive corporate culture. "They're a bunch of idealistic people who believe Starbucks is their vehicle to contribute to society and accomplish a broader mission," he says.

And they realize that the only way to get anywhere is by treating employees well. In fact, Starbucks is widely considered the first large retailer to deviate from the age-old edict that "the customer always comes first." At Starbucks, the employee comes first, Schultz says.

The result: great benefits for workers and security for the employer—Starbucks' annual employee turnover rate is less than 50 percent. The industry norm is more like 400 percent a year. Less turnover means reduced training time and costs. And better benefits hasn't hurt the company any. Since 1989, Starbucks has reported a compounded annual revenue growth rate of 80 percent. Profit margins have improved each quarter since, as well.

And there's the other factor to consider: the enthusiastic, happy-to-be-working employees keep customers coming back for more. Same store sales in the 47 weeks ending August 27 were up 10 percent compared with earlier sales. Most retailers would celebrate reaching just 5 percent in such a category.

Starbucks' robust growth has left a bitter aftertaste in the mouths of some, who see it as nothing more than a chain store business dressed in glitzy, neighborhood-shop facades.

Three years ago in the San Francisco suburb of Mill Valley, locals accused outsider Starbucks of trying to bump off their local coffee house. Specifically, they claimed Starbucks offered the landlord of the Mill Valley Coffee Roaster double the rent—and a $50,000 one-time fee for an electrical upgrade—to take over the lease. Mill Valley Coffee eventually matched the offer and remained in its original space.

"The real estate part of our business is very, very competitive," Schultz admits. "But we've never acted in anything but an utmost ethical manner." Still, this was one of the well publicized times Starbucks left people feeling jittery. "It was a very aggressive technique, which resulted in a lot of negative publicity for Starbucks. They were depicted as the evil empire," says Matt Patsky, an analyst and senior vice president at Adams, Harkness & Hill in Boston. "But the real estate value for anything that can house a coffee shop has skyrocketed due to the explosion of this category."

Much of the anger toward Starbucks, says Patsky, is the general public's aversion to chain stores versus independents. For example, in Minneapolis' upscale Linden Hills neighborhood, residents and local businesses effectively blocked Starbucks from opening a store in its small downtown area. "We don't want our dry cleaner and our children's consignment clothing shop to be run out of business by the increasingly high rents trendy national chains can pay," says Debby Magnuson, chair of the Linden Hills council. "We also didn't want the traffic and we already have three coffee shops. How much coffee do we need?"

Source: This originally appeared in *Business Ethics*, November-December 1995.

Schultz, however, says he's only interested in going into areas where people want a Starbucks. If residents disagree with him, he sees it not as widespread public animosity against the firm, but rather one more reason to work even harder. "He's highly competitive and loves the game, and wants to win," says Howard Behar, president of the company's international division. "At the same time, he's a great boss. He's not afraid to bring strong people in, and he allows all of us to do our job as we see best."

For example, each Starbucks store is given the authority to work with a variety of local community groups, donating products for events and fund-raising. In Seattle, one store provides $50,000 a year to the Zion Preparatory Academy, an inner-city school that works to build self-esteem and leadership with its students.

Another sign of success is how comparable businesses view Starbucks as a role model. "We spend a lot of time talking about Starbucks' success internally," says Steve Finn, president and CEO of Brueger's Corporation, a Burlington, Vermont-based bagel franchise company with locations throughout the country. "We compete with them, primarily for real estate, and have found them in all cases to be worthy competitors acting ethically. I'm impressed with the passion they bring to their business."

Yet still, in many communities from San Francisco to New York, Starbucks creates good and bad feelings. Howard

Schultz recently took some time out to talk with *Business Ethics* about these and other issues.

Starbucks is known for its strong employee relations. Why such an effort in this area?

When we started the business we asked ourselves, "how can we build a company that is sustainable, that will withstand the pressures of growth." We recognized we had to build trust and confidence with customers and shareholders. But first and foremost, we had to build this trust with employees. As a result, we created unique benefits and mechanisms so the growth of the company would be extremely meaningful to all three constituencies. This is why we created the only employee stock ownership plan that offers stock ownership to all employees, including part-timers.

Also, I grew up in a lower middle-class family in federally subsidized housing in Brooklyn. My Dad was a blue collar worker who had worked many jobs, ranging from taxi driving to factory work. He was not valued as a worker; the system he was a part of beat him down and he became a bitter person who lost his self esteem. That image was firmly imprinted on me. I felt strongly that if I was in the position to affect a change in the workplace, I would, making sure everyone felt valued, respected, and part of the winning result.

But what good does it do a business to treat its employees well?

A lot of employers have

forgotten the vital importance of who represents them to the customer every day. The great and sustaining companies are the ones embracing employees. I took my family to Disneyland at the height of the Easter season last year. It was a mob scene. But the effort by employees to ensure every child and parent had a wonderful time was so apparent, at one point I turned to my wife and said, "can you feel the common thread of commitment here?"

How have you been able to maintain the practice of your core principles while growing sales at a compounded annual rate of 60 percent during the past five years?

The greatest strengths of our early years came from being in an intimate, small group. As we've grown we've had to redefine what intimacy is. We developed a system of delegating and realigning, so we all had more responsibility with less tasks. It's a situation that continues to challenge the company. Today we have twelve thousand employees. The greatest challenge we face is maintaining our uniqueness and "specialty-ness," while reaching a level of ubiquity.

Many view fast-growing Starbucks as an evil empire. It's almost as if popular perception sees growth at Starbucks' present pace as inherently bad.

Growth is not the driving force. Rather, it's the passion for quality and respect. Growth is the manifestation of a strong

level of success. Along the way, it would have been easy to say yes to so many opportunities which would have allowed us to grow all the faster. But we've taken the most difficult possible route to growth. We buy our own beans, roast our own beans, open and operate our own stores. We give a piece of the company to every employee, comprehensive benefits, training, and career advancement opportunities. We could have done it a different way and had higher earnings. But at the end of the day I wouldn't have had the kind of company we feel is built to last with the commitment to quality for the product and relationships we have today.

When you enter markets, you often set up in neighborhoods already well-served by local coffee companies. What do you say to the growing perception of Starbucks being a big, chain store-like outsider out to hurt the local player?

Starbucks coexists with a number of local players and has done a good job to enhance the specialty market. As far as I see, Starbucks is an anomaly to categorization of chain stores. The level of execution, and the commitment to quality, is unprecedented. We're also very involved in the communities where we do business. For instance, we donate to groups relevant to the local community.

You believe the benevolent side of the business is not something the press wants to report. Why do you think that's the case?

Generally speaking, when small companies become large, there is a dilution to quality, passion, and values. But in my view, our size and scale has enabled Starbucks to enhance the qualities that gave us the ability to grow the company— the gestalt of the business.

The press usually wants to talk about the size, the scale, and the growth level or stock price. Those are not relevant. What is relevant is the quality and integrity of the company's foundation, and how our people interact with customers.

What's unique about Starbucks' growth?

The level of growth has been sustained with a passion for coffee quality that borders on fanaticism. We only have company-owned stores, which is not consistent with many retail operations. Pride about our standard of freshness is why we don't franchise, opting to take on the significant cost and more arduous task of opening company-owned stores only. It would be too difficult for six-hundred-plus franchise stores to adhere to our levels of control of freshness, training, and quality of coffee.

While you speak of a responsibility to shareholders, as well as other constituents, your board of directors is made up of five white men, all of whom seem to have a vested interest in the company—they're major customers, suppliers, or debt holders. How is this responsibly serving your constituents?

We've recognized for quite a while that change is needed, and I will say that we are far from perfect. We've had a search on for more than a year with one of the most pedigreed search firms in the country. It's been taken seriously with diligence and pride. We just don't want Band-aid solutions, and we don't want to make mistakes.

We have been searching for two more outside board members and have found one thus far. The new members will be added at the end of the calendar year, and will both represent diversity. It's difficult because we are looking for board members who understand our mission and are available. It takes a long time to find the right people who understand our value system.

Starbucks has entered partnerships with some key companies, including Barnes & Noble and most recently, PepsiCo. How significant are these, and how do you determine what companies you work with?

You are the company you keep. We're very sensitive about what companies we conduct business with. Starbucks looks for alliances with other businesses which share a commitment to quality and focus on exceeding customers' expectations. But our associations with other companies don't dilute our integrity.

Our first alliance, with Nordstrums, has been great. Crate and Barrel in Chicago is testing having a Starbucks within its stores. We have a relationship with Barnes &

Noble and ITT Sheraton. And we've just launched a joint venture with Pepsi, which will bring Starbucks in a bottle to a much greater distribution. Both companies (Pepsi and Starbucks) brought important factors to the partnership. Pepsi has the core competency with distributors we didn't have.

Starbucks' Code of Conduct

In addition to upholding guidelines such as "we aspire to purchase coffee from people who share our commitment to treating employees with respect and dignity," the company has developed more concrete, measureable goals. They include a strategic plan for implementation of a "coffee mission" for each country in which it does business.

In fiscal 1996, Starbucks' focus will be on Guatemala, where it hopes to develop with Anacafe (the Guatemalan coffee producer organization) a set of industry standards. Starbucks also plans to work with other specialty coffee companies to identify actions that can improve the lives of coffee workers there.

Which companies have you looked to as role models in building Starbucks?

A number of business models served different purposes. The first company to recognize the relevance of building social values culturally which served as a model is Ben & Jerry's Homemade Inc. In terms of building a large company whose brand and product maintained relevancy and integrity, I looked to Nike.

Coffee Facts

• Coffee is the second largest internationally traded item.
• Coffee is the world's second cheapest beverage.
• In the early 1960s, 75 percent of American adults drank three or more cups of coffee per day.
• In 1995, less than 47 percent of American adults drink an average 1.5 cups of coffee per day.
• There are currently 4,500 coffee houses nationwide.
• The number is expected to double within five years.

Source: Specialty Coffee Association

Why have coffee shops like Starbucks become so popular?

There's been such a fracturing of American values as evidenced by a strong level of mediocrity in terms of service. There's a growing list of factors which reduce trust in institutions whether it's government, business or baseball. As a result we have a unique opportunity because coffee is a part of our personal habits. We drink it every day. As such, our stores are extensions of our homes, the third place after home and work where people gather to socialize, or enjoy quiet moments for themselves.

Rus Wane Equipment: Joint Venture in Russia

By Stanislav V. Shekshnia, Paris, France and Sheila M. Puffer, Northeastern University College of Business Administration, Boston.

"John, yesterday Lev presented me with a candidate for the human resource manager's position. Tomorrow he is going to ask the board to appoint Sasha Neresyan. What do you think?" Ronald Chapman, Wane Machines, Inc.'s country manager for Russia, was querying John Swift, deputy general manager of Rus Wane Equipment, as they discussed Wane's Russian joint venture on the eve of its third anniversary in November 1993.

The question came as quite a surprise to John, who had virtually given up hope that the human resource manager would be filled and would never have considered 30-year-old Sasha as a candidate for the job. Not that Sasha lacked desirable qualities as an employee. He had joined Rus Wane in June 1992 as a customs clearance officer and had subsequently earned a very good reputation in the company by skillfully negotiating with bureaucratic and often corrupt Russian government officials who could turn importing of crucial goods and components into a nightmare for the joint venture. Before joining Rus Wane, Sasha had retired from the Army with the rank of captain, having worked in the Middle East using his background as a military translator. His excellent communications skills and fluency in English had helped him build good relations with many local and all expatriate Rus Wane employees.

But being a good customs clearance officer, John thought, hardly makes one a qualified human resource professional. As Ron paused, John wondered aloud: "Will Sasha be respected by senior Rus Wane managers, even though he is at least twenty years younger than they are? And what does he know about HR practices?" John did not have the answers to these questions, but he knew Sasha was a smart and hard-working young man. What really bothered John was the fact that Sasha had been brought to Rus Wane by the general manager, Lev Novikov, who had been a long-time patient and friend of Dr. Neresyan, Sasha's father. This hiring proposal was the latest episode contributing to the strained relations between the Russian general manager of the joint venture and his American deputy general manager.

The U. S. Partner, Wane Machines, Inc.

During its 150 years of operation, Wane Machines, Inc. had grown from a one-person, one-invention workshop in New York City into a multibillion-dollar multinational corporation with manufacturing, sales, and service operations in dozens of countries. Wane had always remained in one industry, engaging in the manufacture, installation, and maintenance of large-scale heating and cooling equipment for office and apartment buildings. In the late 1890s, Wane began its international expansion by setting up operations in Europe. From the outset, its strategy had been to be recognized as a local company in every market it entered, and to establish long-term relationships with customers by providing a complete package of services, including product maintenance, repair, and upgrading. Following this strategy consistently for nearly a hundred years, Wane Machines became a global market leader with a network of more than 50 companies operating in 160 countries.

Wane Machines had four regional divisions: domestic (the United States and Canada), Europe, Latin America, and Asia. In the 1980s domestic operations lost its sales leadership to the European division, as the market for new construction in the United States dropped precipitously during the severe economic recession. After a decade of spectacular growth, the European market also declined sharply in the early 1990s a the United Kingdom, and later France and Germany, entered an economic recession. To attempt future growth, Wane management began to explore the markets that had begun to open in Eastern Europe and the Soviet Union. In 1989 Ronald Chapman was appointed Wane's country manager for the Soviet Union. Ron, who had a Harvard M.B.A. and 20 years' experience with Wane, was charged with studying the Soviet market and setting up Wane's operations in Moscow and St. Petersberg. Before this assignment, he had managed Wane's joint venture in Taiwan after working in Japan and Hong Kong for 10 years. In his new function, Chapman reported to the area vice president for Central and Eastern Europe who was located in Wane's European division in Brussels.

Source: NACRA. Faculty members in nonprofit institutions are encouraged to reproduce this case for distribution to their students without charge or written permission. All other rights reserved jointly to the authors and the North American Case Research Association (NACRA). Copyright © 1995 by the *Case Research Journal* and Stanislav V. Shekshnia and Sheila M. Puffer. The authors gratefully acknowledge the valuable suggestions of editor John Seeger, three anonymous reviewers, and Northeastern colleague Daniel J. McCarthy. This case was written solely for the purpose of stimulating student discussion. All events and individuals are real, but names and industry have been disguised.

Entering the U.S.S.R. Market

The Soviet market was not total terra incognita for Wane, as the company had been exporting its products to the U.S.S.R. through its Austrian company since the 1970s. During that period Wane sold its high-quality heating and cooling equipment for installation in several Soviet government buildings as well as an American-built hotel. However, it could not penetrate the huge domestic market for several reasons. The ruble could not be converted to hard currency to pay for imported goods, few Soviet enterprises had access to hard currency, and until 1988 all purchases of imports were controlled by government foreign trade organizations with whom enterprises were required to negotiate for imported equipment and other supplies.

By the late 1980s the market potential in the U.S.S.R. for Wane's products was the largest in the world, as 85 percent of the country's 290 million people lived in apartment complexes, most of which required upgrading of their large-scale heating and cooling systems. In addition, more housing was planned under President Gorbachev's "Housing 2000" program, announced in 1986 with the goal of providing every Soviet family with a separate apartment by the year 2000. This would be a massive undertaking, as some 25 percent of families lived in communal apartments in which they shared kitchen and bathroom facilities with other families. Because of

these conditions, demand for large-scale heating and cooling systems was expected to double through the remainder of the century.

According to the Ministry of Building Equipment Manufacturing, in the late 1980s annual demand for large heating and cooling equipment was approximately 100,000 units, while Soviet enterprises manufactured a total of 60,000 units. Production planning, resource allocation, and customer selection were all controlled centrally by government bodies such as Gosplan, the state planning ministry, and Gossnab, the government supply organization. The domestic heating and cooling industry was fragmented: manufacturing plants under the Ministry of Building Equipment Manufacturing, installation units were attached to the State Construction Committee, and maintenance services were operated by local civic authorities. The major cities of Moscow, St. Petersburg, and Kiev had their own manufacturing facilities and installation units.

For more than 20 years, Soviet factories had been manufacturing the same, unimproved heating and cooling products for the domestic market, having little incentive or ability to upgrade them under the system of central planning. Artificially low prices were established by state authorities with little regard to actual costs or customer demand. For their part, customers, who were construction ministries and building management organizations attached to local governments, paid for goods not with their own money, but with funds allocated by the government. They were usually glad to receive the scarce equipment, even though it was of poor quality and low reliability.

Formation of the Joint Venture

In 1989 the Soviet Ministry of Foreign Trade put Wane in touch with NLZ, a medium-sized factory located just outside Moscow that manufactured heating and cooling equipment similar to Wane's, but of lower quality. In February 1990, after what appeared to Wane's management as lengthy and sometimes frustrating negotiations, a joint venture called Rus Wane Equipment was formed, with the primary purpose of establishing a new plant to manufacture products virtually identical to Wane's European models. Registered as a Soviet-Belgian joint venture, the new company had initial capital funds of USS11.5 million. Wane contributed $8 million in hard currency and equipment for the new factory to built with the Soviet partner. The latter contributed use of the facilities in the existing plant to manufacture components, as well as the site for the new factory. Whether NLZ or the government owned the land was unclear, however, because of ambiguous legislation on property. Wane Machines had a 57 percent share of the joint venture, and NLZ, 43 percent. At about the same time, Wane signed a second joint

venture with a St. Petersburg partner to install and service Rus Wane's products in western Russia.

Wane's strategy for Russia consisted of three major elements. First, they did not expect to make money for the first three years. Second, they planned to develop export potential for Eastern Europe. Third, Wane hoped that the Russian ruble would become a convertible currency in the near future.

The highest governing body of Rus Wane joint venture was the board of directors. The chairman of the board was Wane Europe's area vice president for Central and Eastern Europe. The other board members were the legal counsel of Wane Europe; Wane's country manager for the Soviet Union, Ron Chapman; Rus Wane Equipment's general manager, Lev Novikov; and an official from the Soviet ministry of building equipment manufacturing. The board of directors met quarterly to review developments since the last quarter's meeting, to review business plans and the progress made toward achieving them, to approve capital expenditures, and to appoint direct reports. Organization charts depicting the Rus Wane Equipment joint venture and its relationship with Wane Machines are provided in Exhibits 1 and 2.

At the time of Wane's initial negotiations, joint ventures were the primary form of market entry into the Soviet Union. The Joint Venture Law of 1987 had opened the door for foreign investment in the U.S.S.R. and

accorded preferential taxation status and other privileges to foreign joint ventures. Initially, Soviet law restricted foreign ownership of joint ventures to a maximum of 49 percent, and the head of the operation was required to be a Soviet citizen. In 1988, these provisos were withdrawn by the Russian government, permitting greater foreign ownership and control.

Although Soviet law no longer required a Soviet citizen to hold the most senior position, Wane's policy throughout the world was to put local managers in charge, because they were believed to be the most knowledgeable and capable individuals to run local operations. Therefore, Lev Novikov, a 58-year-old mechanical engineer by training, was appointed general manager of Rus Wane Equipment. He also remained general manager of the Soviet partner, NLZ, a position he had held for 15 of the 25 years he had worked in the industry. His experience, enthusiasm, and strong leadership led Wane's management to view him as the driving force who could manage construction on the new manufacturing facility and see it through to completion under very difficult circumstances.

Construction of the Plant

In October 1990, shortly after the joint venture agreement was signed, Wane's management took the bold step of beginning construction of a plant in the Moscow area to produce heating and cooling equipment for the

Russian market. The multimillion-dollar investment was one of the first major commitments by a Western firm to manufacture products in Russia, since most companies were unwilling to take such a risk in Russia's highly unstable political and economic environment.

The state-of-the-art plant was built in full compliance with Wane's specifications, making it technologically comparable to Wane's European facilities. The plant was completed in June 1992, an extremely short period of time, especially in the Soviet Union, where such building projects usually took years, and sometimes as long as a decade. Furthermore, the external environment at the time of construction was marked by the breakup of the Soviet Union; severely deteriorating economic conditions in Russia, including monthly inflation exceeding 20 percent; disintegration of the centralized resource allocation system; and confusing and vacillating legislation on corporation taxation, business development, and the status of foreign operations. Inconsistent government policy on foreign direct investment, including taxation and ownership rights, along with erratic domestic policy concerning government subsidies, business law, and ownership of property, contributed to the external problems confronting international firms in Russia.

Rus Wane Equipment's plant was designed to manufacture Wane's European models of heating and cooling equipment, with minor modifications for the Russian market. Product characteristics, such as length of service and number of callbacks per unit, showed that the quality of Wane's products was more than four times that of Russian competitors', requiring half the energy to operate. Wane maintained a pricing policy not to exceed twice the price of the grossly inferior Russian models. The first product was scheduled to be shipped from the new factory in June 1993, and full capacity of 5000 units annually was projected for 1995.

In August 1993, only 6 weeks behind schedule, Rus Wane Equipment celebrated its first shipment with toasts of Moet champagne and Stolichnaya vodka. By September the factory was fully operational, with an available production capacity of 85 units per month. Most of the joint venture's office employees and factory workers came from NLZ, the Russian partner. A select group, they were full of enthusiasm for working on the joint venture and looked forward to excellent working conditions in the new plant as well as democratic and participative Western management methods.

Sales and Service Operations

While the plant was under construction, Rus Wane also set up an organization to sell, install, and maintain Wane's imported and locally produced equipment. Field personnel, who numbered 150, were recruited from various Moscow installation and service agencies. This part of the business was quite successful, offering Western-style maintenance service to numerous foreign organizations and some Russian companies that could afford it.

Early Obstacles

Construction of a state-of-the-art manufacturing facility and establishment of a sales and service network were achievements that few joint ventures had accomplished in Russia up to that time. However, reaching these goals by no means guaranteed Rus Wane's success. Among the obstacles confronting the firm once it became operational were an unexpected downturn in demand, difficulty in securing reliable suppliers, and an unpredictable legal and economic environment.

Despite the Soviet Union's vast market potential, much of Rus Wane's production capacity sat idle in the initial months because of weak customer demand. As a result, only 17 units were manufactured in September, 12 were completed in October, and 15 were planned for November. As Russia and other countries of the former Soviet Union entered a severe economic crisis, new construction declined dramatically and demand for heating and cooling systems plummeted. No one had exact data, but Rus Wane's management estimated annual domestic sales in Russia to be 6000 units, while total combined capacity of domestic manufacturers was 30,000 to 40,000 units.

Under this tremendous supply pressure, aggravated by

the extremely difficult financial position of most of their customers, price became a major factor in the purchase decision. Rus Wane's product, sold even at zero profit margin was still nearly twice as expensive as domestic equipment because of small production runs and costs associated with the sophisticated design. Prospective Russian customers, primarily state- or municipally-owned construction and engineering enterprises, were caught in a squeeze. They suffered a cash shortage resulting from sharply reduced government subsidies of their operations, and hyperinflation had eroded their purchasing power. A limited number of price-tolerant and quality-sensitive customers, such as commercial banks, foreign hotels, and joint ventures, appreciated the quality of Rus Wane's products. Even those, however, often preferred to buy competitors systems manufactured in Western Europe, considering the foreign origin to be more prestigious. High inflation of the ruble, along with its devaluation against foreign currencies, eliminated virtually all cost advantages of manufacturing in Russia, and did not allow Rus Wane to sell profitably to customers outside the country as it had planned.

Developing relationships with reliable domestic suppliers was an objective that proved challenging to implement. The company carefully sought out enterprises that had produced for the military sector because they had been held to higher quality standards and stricter delivery schedules than other enterprises under the former central planning system. Such enterprises also often had idle capacity and faced layoffs resulting from drastic cuts in government orders, and hence were eager to find customers. However, even these suppliers were not easily able to meet Rus Wane's standards, and they required a considerable amount of Rus Wane's time and energy for training and monitoring.

Like other companies operating in the Russian market, Rus Wane had to struggle with a constantly changing legal framework and unpredictable government policy. For example, in 1992 the Russian government froze the company's bank account for 6 months. The State bank had run out of cash and arbitrarily withheld payments owed to Russian and foreign enterprises. In another unfortunate financial incident, Rus Wane was forced to pay $1.5 million in taxes on their new factory building when the Russian government introduced a value-added tax, even though the building had been completed well before the introduction of the tax.

In spite of such problems, the company was growing and its management systems were being developed. With significant cash flows from its sales and service field operations compensating for the losses in manufacturing, Rus Wane was a profitable organization overall, with 320 employees and monthly revenues of $600,000.

Staffing Key Managerial Positions

According to the joint venture agreement, Wane Machines was responsible for sending three experienced executives to serve as Rus Wane's deputy general manager, manufacturing manager, and financial manager for the first 2 to 3 years. Russian nationals would take over the positions at the end of this initial period. The major objectives of this policy were to provide "assistance in technology and management skills transfer, management systems and processes development, and local personnel coaching." Two other senior management positions, sales and service manager and human resources manager, were to be filled by local nationals from the beginning because they involved regular contact with Russian customers or workers at various levels, thus requiring a thorough knowledge of local culture and employment practices.

An experienced local manager had been found to fill the sales and service manager's position, but the remaining key managerial positions had been harder to fill. Wane fell behind schedule in sending its expatriates to Russia, and Lev Novikov, the general manager, delayed hiring a local for the human resources position, preferring to administer that function himself.

John Swift, a 35-year-old American, was appointed as Rus Wane's deputy general manager in late 1991. For nearly 10 months, while seeking suitable accommodations for his family, he commuted frequently from European headquarters in Brussels; he finally settled in Moscow in September 1992. John had joined Wane in 1989 after graduating from business school. He then completed the corporate management development program and worked for 2 years in Western Europe as a field operations manager. Before 1991 John had never been to Russia nor, he said, had he ever had any intention of going there. He was, however, ambitious, and readily accepted the job offer, seeing it as a valuable career move. As deputy general manager, he reported to Lev Novikov, the joint venture's general manager, and was responsible for supervising technology transfer, sales, pricing, and personnel. He also served as the liaison between the joint venture and Wane's European headquarters, and reported to Ron Chapman, Wane's country manager for Russia.

Jean-Pierre Dumont, Rus Wane's manufacturing manager, had 15 years of engineering experience with Wane Machines in his native France, but the Russian appointment was his first management position. Like John Swift he had little prior knowledge of Russia, yet he was equally eager to take the job. He explained: "It's very rare these days that an engineer gets a chance to work in a factory created from scratch. I am lucky to get this chance and I'm not going to miss it."

Convincing an experienced financial manager to relocate to

Russia was not an easy task. After an intensive and lengthy search, Jeff Nichol, a 27-year-old Englishman who had been working at Wane for 2 years as a corporate auditor, was selected in October 1991. Because of Jeff's limited experience, Ron Chapman sent him for training in Brussels for 6 months before going to Russia. In the meantime, Lev appointed Katya Karaseva, NLZ's chief accountant, to head Rus Wane's finance department. Katya had worked in the industry for 24 years, 17 of them with Lev.

Wane's Russia country manager, Ron Chapman, worked out of Wane's European headquarters in Brussels, but flew to Russia at least once a month to visit Wane's St. Petersburg joint venture as well as Rus Wane Equipment in Moscow, where he would review the joint venture's situation with the general manager, Lev Novikov, and his deputy, John Swift.

Tensions in the Finance Department

When Jeff Nichol arrived at Rus Wane in the spring of 1992, Lev suggested that he be a consultant for a while rather than immediately assuming the duties of financial manager, citing his young age, his need to adjust to the local culture, and his lack of Russian language abilities. Ron accepted the arrangement because he wanted Jeff to spend some of his time at the St. Petersburg joint venture. For a while, Jeff traveled between Moscow and St. Petersburg,

spending most of his time learning the Russian language, becoming acquainted with Russian accounting systems, and developing financial procedures for both joint ventures.

Early in 1993, when a financial manager had been recruited for the St. Petersburg operation, Jeff decided it was the right time for him to become financial manager at Rus Wane. John Swift fully supported him. By that time Rus Wane had eight employees in the finance department: Jeff, Katya, and six accountants, most of whom came from NLZ. Unfortunately, this small group was unable to work smoothly together. As John explained to Ron: "We've got total confusion in the finance department: people don't know who's the boss, Katya does what she wants, and Jeff is running out of patience. His contract expires in March and I don't think he's looking forward to staying any longer. Ron, we can't allow this situation to continue—the company needs a financial manager."

To compound the problem, the accountants expressed their disappointment to John that Western management practices that they had hoped would give them greater participation in decision making had not been implemented. They also complained about not being rewarded on merit, and the fact that the Westerners, whom they considered to be doing comparable work, were receiving substantially higher compensation.

From the beginning, communication between Jeff and

Katya had not been easy. The language barrier—he did not speak Russian and she did not speak English—was not the only problem. Several times Jeff had organized training sessions for Rus Wane's finance personnel, yet each time Katya had found excuses not to participate. When, after a year at the joint venture, Jeff had become conversational in Russian, communication between him and Katya failed to improve in any meaningful way. Even though they worked virtually side by side, with Katya in a private office and Jeff in an adjacent common area, they communicated only through interoffice mail.

Jeff made a number of appeals to Lev to try to get his point across. He wrote several memos, with copies to the vice president of finance for Wane Europe, in which he described Katya's mistakes, but the general manager never replied and continued to show his full support for Katya. In addition, the finance staff had been expanding, yet Jeff had never been involved in the selection process. When he raised the issue with Lev, the latter responded that hiring was his problem, not Jeff's.

Discord over the General Manager

In February 1993, John Swift sent a memo to Lev suggesting that he propose Jeff's appointment as acting financial manager to Rus Wane's board of directors for approval, as required by company policy.

Lev did not respond. A month later John raised the issue again and received the categorical reply: "He cannot be a financial manager." Without challenging that conclusion, John forwarded his suggestion to Ron Chapman who had shown full understanding of John's viewpoint. The subject of the financial manager's appointment was put on the agenda for the next board meeting. However, the day before the meeting, the item was withdrawn from the agenda. Ron later explained to John that Lev had convinced him not to be in a hurry to appoint Jeff to the position.

Meanwhile, tensions in the finance department continued to escalate. The joint venture experienced some delays in consolidating its first business plan, as well as difficulties in cash management and inventory control. On several occasions Jeff openly expressed his low opinion of his Russian colleagues' professional qualifications. These problems deeply concerned the deputy general manager, but the country manager did not take the matter seriously. Nor did Ron seem to be concerned about other signs of poor morale. For example, the first Russian hired as a salesperson, who had been trained in the United States and Western Europe and was highly respected in the company, left to work for a Russian trading venture. In addition, turnover in the factory was 5 percent a month.

In a discussion the two had about the finance department, Ron assessed the situation quite

differently from John: "I think you're dramatizing the situation, John. Rus Wane has an excellent cost accounting system, our corporate financial software has been successfully introduced, and the skills of the finance people have improved tremendously."

"Yes, but Jeff has done it all himself," John replied.

"That's because he doesn't know how to delegate. He needs to work at improving his management style. I am beginning to understand why Lev can't see him as a financial manager. Jeff doesn't know how to manage people and he is becoming paranoid about Katya. I'm afraid that if on a Saturday night his girlfriend doesn't show up for a date, he'll find a way to blame it on Katya. By the way, John, Lev is looking for a financial manager from the outside. It could be a good solution."

John was unpleasantly surprised to hear about the proposal. Lev had mentioned nothing about it to him. "You know, Ron, it's always very difficult to communicate with Lev. First, he doesn't like to share any information with me and he prefers to make all the decisions himself. And second, he is simply never there. The last time I saw him was ten days ago."

Although Lev had officially become a full-time employee of Rus Wane Equipment in January 1993, he had never resigned from his position as general manager of NLZ, which was still manufacturing its old product next door to the joint venture's new plant. Some people at Rus Wane were concerned about the situation; their perception was that their general manager was also their competitor's general manager. There had been rumors about the old plant being in a difficult financial position, but no one had reliable information. Yet it was well known that NLZ had been going through the process of privatization, as mandated by the government, and Lev had been leading it. A major task would be to determine what percentage of shares would be owned by various managers and other employees.

John thought that there was a clear conflict of interest between Lev's role at the old factory and his position in the joint venture. He tried to raise the issue with Ron during one of his monthly visits: "Lev is preoccupied with his own interests, not Rus Wane's. When you are not here, he spends all his time at the old factory trying to turn it into his private property."

Ron angrily interrupted: "Let's drop the subject. This is not your responsibility, John."

Hiring a Human Resource Manager

John suppressed his instinctive response, feeling his anger growing. On several previous occasions he had tried to raise the subject of Lev Novikov's management style with Ron, but the latter never wanted to discuss it. Now, totally frustrated with personnel management issues at the joint venture,

John shifted to another sore point: "As you know, Ron, we still don't have a human resource manager here at Rus Wane. I believe Lev hasn't filled the position on purpose. He wants to continue to do things the old Soviet way—to run the company like a tsar."

Ron looked up sharply: "That's a pretty strong statement, John. You've got to have facts to prove it."

John was sure he had the facts. A human resource manager was supposed to have been hired 3 years ago—just as soon as the joint venture was official—in order to organize the selection process for other positions. However, Lev had decided to manage this function himself. As a result, all of the joint venture's senior managers other than the expatriates, and most of the lower-level managers, had come from NLZ. John considered this move a dangerous mistake. What was worse, he believed, was that quite a few senior managers' relatives had also been hired. The most notable, Lev's son, had already built an astonishing career within 12 months, starting as an assistant, becoming purchasing manager, and then going to Western Europe for 18 months' practical training. John had strongly opposed the decision to send Novikov junior abroad, arguing that there had been better candidates and that Rus Wane's reputation among its employees for fairness and democracy would suffer. Ron had ignored these concerns, and, just as he had anticipated, John began to detect silent but strong

disapproval and disappointment from employees.

Unhappy with Lev's hiring practices, John championed the introduction of selection and hiring procedures that had been developed for Russian operations by Wane's European headquarters (Exhibit 3). The procedures for implementing Wane's standard corporate practices—preparing job requisitions, advertising vacant positions, evaluating candidates' resumes, and having human resource and line managers conduct interviews—had been approved by Ron Chapman and were supposed to be mandatory at Rus Wane. However, the Russian managers ignored the procedures. For instance, a week before John's meeting with Ron, an angry Jean-Pierre Dumont told John that a new machine operator had been hired for the factory without his knowledge. It took John some time to find out that the 18-year-old new employee was the son of a local customs officer who often cleared shipments for Rus Wane. The young man had no manufacturing skills and was eligible for the army draft the following spring.

When John described the incident to Ron, he got a rather philosophical reply: "Well, you've got to remember the specifics of the country you are operating in. Russia has an Asian culture and European faces should not mislead you. American standards do not always work here. If hiring people you have known for a long time, and therefore trust, is a local custom, you can't change it overnight. And you probably don't need to change it."

John didn't challenge his boss, but he saw no reason to change his mind about hiring practices. He strongly believed that hiring friends and relatives was equally bad whether one was in the United States, China, or Russia. Now Ron was telling him that Lev was going to appoint his doctor's son as human resource manager. John has always regarded a human resources manager as one of the primary business officers responsible for enforcing high ethical standards in the company. Would Sasha be able to fulfill such an important responsibility? How much credibility would he have? And how independent would he be from his boss and likely mentor? These were some of the questions for which John did not have a ready answer.

Prospects for the Future

This latest hiring decision only added to John Swift's growing frustration over the management of the joint venture. He had been appointed to provide expertise in Western management systems and to coach local personnel. Yet his attempts had been foiled at virtually every turn. He didn't know who was more to blame—Lev, for sticking to his former Soviet practices, or Ron, for letting Lev get away with such seemingly counterproductive behavior.

All of these issues contributed to John's worries about the future of Rus Wane Equipment. With the prospect of privatiza-

tion turning NLZ into more of a competitor than a partner, and the advantages of joint ventures declining as a result of changing governmental legislation, John wondered whether Rus Wane had the right organizational structure and management systems in place to be a viable player in Russia's rapidly changing business environment. And not the least of his worries was whether there would be a place for him at Rus Wane that would allow him to be taken seriously.

EXHIBIT 1
Rus Wane Equipment's Organization Chart

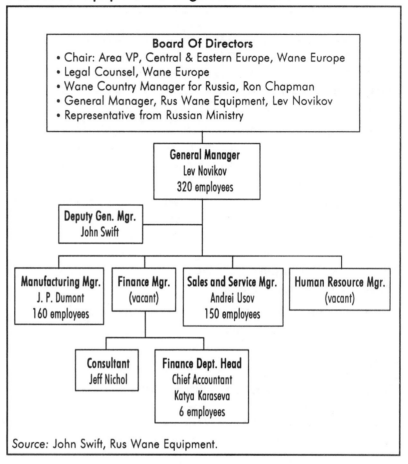

Source: John Swift, Rus Wane Equipment.

EXHIBIT 2
Wane Machines, Inc. Organization Chart (Abridged)

Source: John Swift, Rus Wane Equipment.

EXHIBIT 3
Wane Machines, Inc.'s Human Resources Policies for Rus Wane Equipment

Recruitment and Selection Process

The following recruitment and selection principles have been established in order to assist company management in hiring the best qualified employees. It is the responsibility of the Human Resources Department to manage and facilitate recruitment and selection in collaboration with line management, with the final decision on selecting and hiring candidates made by line management. It is also the responsibility of company management to ensure that these principles are followed and to maintain their effectiveness.

1. Identification of job openings. The number of positions to be staffed in the company is primarily determined by the workforce forecast established every year as part of the business plan. Input is then provided by line management throughout the year with necessary adjustments to the plan made in order for the HR Department to take action in recruitment and selection. Any vacancy or opening due to resignation, termination or other reasons will be filled according to line management's request. A final list of job openings is then established and updated as necessary. A job requisition form must be signed by line management and the General Manager before every recruiting action.

2. Determination of job requirements. In close collaboration with line management, each position to be staffed is documented as follows:

• A list of professional and technical requirements as well as a list of personal traits required to do the job (strengths, personality, background experience, etc.)
• A written job description outlining the basic responsibilities of the position, and the main tasks to fulfill position responsibilities and deliver the expected results.

These two documents will be established jointly with the HR Department and approved by line management.

3. Attracting applicants. A list of possible human resources outsourcing options is presented below. One or several sources listed may be used with consideration given to availability, costs, and likelihood of success.

• Spontaneous, unsolicited candidacies are examined and acknowledged. A curriculum vitae and letter of intention are necessary documentation.
• Advertisements for jobs may be inserted in local or national newspapers: they advertise not only the content of the job through a short description, but also the required profile of the candidate. A description of the company is also recommended.
• State employment agencies: Contracts to conduct employee searches can be used with recognized agencies. Company needs are specified in a job requirements position description.
• Educational institutions: The company should develop and maintain regular and frequent contacts with local and national technical and nontechnical institutions considered as potential sources of job candidates. Background on the company should be presented to students. Job postings may be sent to these schools.
• Private employee search firms: Restricted to managerial positions, private employee search firms may be used for candidate searches and screening interviews. The search must be cost effective, with conditions of the services rendered clearly stated in the contract.

The use of one of these options should result in a list of candidates for consideration, as well as detailed information about the candidates recorded on forms.

4. Prescreening. The Human Resources Manager establishes a final list of candidates by eliminating applicants whose profile does not meet requirements. At this time, the Human Resources Department informs candidates who are not selected for interviews that they are no longer under consideration.

5. Screening interviews. The Human Resources Manager contacts the eligible candidates for interviews to assess:

- Their knowledge of the company (product, service and culture, as appropriate). Additional information may be given to answer candidates' questions.
- Their background (education and experience) to determine whether it is consistent with their application. This step helps answer the question, "Can the individual perform the job?"
- The motivation of the applicant to perform the job in the company and to develop within the company's culture. This step helps answer the question, " Will he/she do the job?"

6. Level of approval for recruitment for senior positions. The General Manager will be involved in any recruitment for a position reporting directly to him/her, and will make the final decision. The General Manager will also interview candidates for positions reporting to his/her direct reports. Approval by the General Manager will be necessary before filling such positions.

7. Preselection. The interviews will be reported in a written evaluation of the candidate by the HR manager using the appropriate forms. These forms are reviewed with the line manager involved in the recruitment process, and a list of candidates to be interviewed is then established jointly.

8. Interviews with line management. The preselected candidates are called for interviews with the line manager. The purpose of the interview is to determine again whether professional aptitude based on experience and skills (technical and nontechnical) will enable the applicant to perform the work. Also, the interviewer assesses the candidate's motivation to work for the company and to meet the company's overall requirements (personal fit with the culture, etc.). At the end of these interviews, evaluation forms are filled out by the interviewer.

9. Evaluation of candidates and hiring decision. A joint evaluation of the candidates by the line manager and the human resources manager is conducted using evaluation forms, and a ranking of the candidates is completed.

10. Hiring decision. The line manager makes the final decision to hire one of the candidates interviewed based on an assessment of their capabilities and potential for development in the company. At that stage, the HR manager informs the unsuccessful candidates by letter of the company's decision. The selected candidate is also informed by the HR manager.

11. Offer to the candidate. A formal offer is prepared by the HR manager in cooperation with the line manager. The offer (including the contract and conditions of employment, etc.) is extended to the selected candidate. At the same time, administrative documents are given to the future employee to begin the employment registration process.

12. Integration in the company. The human resources manager assists the line manager in facilitating the newcomer's integration into the company.
A welcome guide is given to the new employee upon his/her arrival in addition to all necessary documents, identification badges, punch cards, safety brochures, internal regulations, etc. Mandatory employee training (e.g., safety) and any special training are coordinated by the HR manager in the new employee's first few days.

13. New-employee feedback meeting. Six weeks after the starting date of employment, the human resources manager invites the new employee for a feedback meeting to determine how well he/she is adapting to the work place. Any obstacles are addressed in accordance with company policies.
The HR manager provides feedback to the new employee's supervisor and follows up on any decisions made to ease the newcomer's integration into the company.

CASE 4
Beauty Classics, Inc.
By Peggy C. Smith, Kathy Kargel, and Lester A. Neidell, the University of Tulsa.

Preparing for the Internship Debriefing
Sabrina Hill was elated but concerned as she reviewed her notes and diary. Tomorrow, December 14, 1992, she was to make a presentation to the internship committee; her goal tonight was to prepare herself for the 15-minute oral session. All exams were completed and this was the last course requirement for graduation from Nashville University. Professor Williams assured her that the committee was sympathetic, but she was apprehensive that the committee really wouldn't understand why her internship had failed. Although she felt confident that her diary (Appendix A) was adequate as an activity report, she worried that it didn't explain satisfactorily why the internship into which she had so positively ventured had turned so negative in such a short time. She had always considered herself an able communicator, ready and willing for the business world. Now she had her doubts. She had never before experienced such a humiliating incident.

True, she had been over-committed, embarking on an internship at the same time she was working as a part-time waitress and completing the four additional courses necessary to finish her marketing degree program. However, she had known she needed the business internship experience for her resume. In fact, she had eagerly anticipated the challenge of the Beauty Classics, Inc. internship because it was an opportunity to put her creative ideas to work.

Although Beauty Classics, Inc. (BCI), was founded and operated by African-Americans, Sabrina did not recall any great apprehension because she had always believed people should be judged based on who they were, not on their race. Since Sabrina had not attended an ethnically and racially diverse high school, and her college experience so far had been only moderately diverse, she had been excited by the prospect of learning about people with different ethnic backgrounds from her own while simultaneously obtaining valuable work experience. Coming from an upper-middle class background and attending a relatively expensive private university did not mean that her limited exposure to other peoples and cultures was synonymous with intolerance.

Internship Requirements

The internship requirement that she spend 15 hours per week at the company had not at first appeared onerous. Her tasks were to (1) keep a weekly diary; (2) develop a company history and brief marketing prospectus; and (3) complete a project for the company.

Before the semester began, Beauty Classics management and Professor Williams had discussed three potential internship projects. These were: (1) reviewing distributor programs and incentives; (2) analyzing sales to the company's largest customer, Wal-Mart; and (3) managing a Christmas party for needy minority children in the immediate neighborhood of the BCI factory. Which project she would work on would depend on how the first few weeks of the internship proceeded. Professor Williams assured her that if none of these projects seems to fit her needs and those of the company, his relationship with the principals of the company was such that a mutually rewarding project could be established.

The Company

Sabrina's first three weeks of her internship were devoted to discovering how Beauty Classics had achieved its magnitude of success. Her initial meeting with the company founders did not impress her. The situation seemed quite chaotic. A number of people interrupted Professor Williams as he introduced her to the company founders, Dr. and Mr. Exeter. Moreover, the company's facilities did not reflect, in her opinion, a successful business enterprise. Her report of the company history and the company's marketing prospects (Appendix B) was, however, incomplete due to the abrupt termination of the internship on October 27.

Sabrina leafed through her report. She jotted some additional notes in the report's margin, quoting from a 1985 press release:

Edward Exeter [according to press clippings] flamboyant and jovial, model for black entrepreneurs.

Then she reviewed her preliminary evaluation (Appendix C), which she had shown Professor Williams earlier in the week. The evaluation was based on her diary and on her opinions of what had happened. At the meeting at which she gave the evaluation to Professor Williams, he had given her a partial transcript of a debriefing session

Source: NACRA. This case was written with the cooperation of management, solely for the purpose of stimulating student discussion. Data are based on field research in the organization and on the student diary developed as part of the internship requirement. All events and individuals are real, but names and locations have been disguised. Faculty members in nonprofit institutions are encouraged to reproduce this case for distribution to their own students without charge or written permission. All other rights reserved jointly to the authors and the North American Case Research Association (NACRA). Copyright © 1993 by the Case Research Journal and Peggy C. Smith, Kathy Kargel, and Lester A. Neidell.

he had conducted at Beauty Classics, Inc. (Appendix D).

Sabrina knew that her final internship grade depended on tomorrow's oral presentation. Could she adequately explain what she had learned from the experience? She recognized that the postpresentation question-and-answer session would be critical. "What types of questions will the Internship Committee ask me?" Sabrina wondered.

Appendix A
Excerpts from Sabrina Hill's Diary— September 2 to November 2, 1992

September 2

I went to Dr. Williams' office this morning to explain why I missed his night class, the opening class of the semester. I had to go into work at Pepper's; hopefully they aren't going to be inflexible with my schedule this coming semester. Anyway, something good came out of the whole deal. We discussed what I was going (or wanted) to do after I graduate in December. I've been kind of worried about getting a job since I basically have no experience. He asked what I would like to do and I told him I could see myself in the fashion industry.

It turns out that there is an internship available at Beauty Classics, Inc., an ethnic fashion accessories company. Professor Williams explained that Beauty Classics, Inc. is the largest minority-owned business in

town, and that it manufactured and sold fashion accessories, such as scarves, hairpins, and costume jewelry, aimed primarily at the black and Hispanic markets. He said they wanted a marketing intern to work on one of several projects. Professor Williams asked if I would like to take it. Of course I would! He explained it is going to take up a lot of my time and might be difficult to schedule since I already have a job. I know I can do it though, plus the experience will be worth it. Oh yeah, one more thing—I think I am going to be the only white person in the company. I am not too worried about that since I see people as who they are not by the color of their skin. I am kind of nervous about how they will accept ME, though.

September 4

Dr. Williams took me out to Beauty Classics, Inc., this afternoon. It was strange because I had a hard time deciding what to wear. I wanted to dress nicely, but not too nice. I felt that a business suit would be out of place. I wondered if I worried about it because it was a black-owned company. I don't think I have a negative attitude toward working out there but I am afraid they will have negative feelings toward me.

Beauty Classics, Inc., is located in a neighborhood known for its high crime rate. I am glad to have a beat-up car so I won't have to worry about leaving it there. I also think it will be good because it fits in with the rest of the cars on the lot. I don't want the people who work here to think I am a spoiled rich college student out here slumming or something.

Once we arrived at BCI I could not help but wonder at what I had gotten myself into. It seemed to me that the "factory" looked like an old bowling alley. Dr. Williams said that it in fact was that. Once inside I could not help but stare at the walls and interior of the place. It was like going into a time warp, back to the 1960s and 1970s. Everything was dated—the pictures, the carpeting, the furniture. There was also advertising posters on the walls and photographs of a handsome black couple with different celebrities from that time, such as Aretha Franklin and Tina Turner.

Dr. Williams pointed out one of the ad posters and told me that the model was Alexis Exeter. She is absolutely gorgeous! Dr. Williams also gave me a little more background about the company as we waited. Mr. and Dr. Exeter started the company, and their adopted daughter, Alexis, works with them. Mr. Exeter is in a wheelchair and he uses the company conference room as his office.

Finally we got to go into the conference room and I met the people who were going to be my new employers. It was awkward, I'm not going to deny it. Mr. Exeter is quite a character. He is a big man with long, slick, curly hair. He wore a jump suit and a lot of gold. Not at all what I expected, but he did seem excited at the prospect of me working there, and I have to

admit that I am excited too. His wife, Dr. Daisy Exeter, is going to be a tough one to figure out. She didn't say much to me and I caught her looking at me in a way that made me feel very uncomfortable. I would guess that the Exeters are in their late sixties. Alexis, on the other hand, appears to be pretty normal. In person, she is not as beautiful as in the poster, but she is extremely attractive. She's a little taller than me, about five-seven, and I would guess about 32 or 33 years old. It seems I will be working mainly with her. She has a bunch of different ideas for a project, but they seem to be mostly short term. She did not mention any of the projects that Dr. Williams had discussed with me. I'm not sure that any one of her projects will fulfill my internship requirements.

Mr. Exeter offered to pay me. Dr. Williams said that it's strictly up to the client. Interns are not required to be paid. I was offered $5.00 per hour. I wonder if it would be better if I did not get paid because they would have less control over me. It's hard to turn the money down though, especially since I am so poor, so I don't think I will.

One thing that kind of gave me the creeps was when Mr. Exeter mentioned my looks. I guess he thinks I am attractive, but it seemed out of place for him to say something about it. Maybe that's why his wife put up a little attitude in front of me. Who knows?

September 8

I am going out to BCI five mornings a week from 9 a.m. until noon. It will be all right for me to take one morning off and make up my time on Friday afternoons. That little leeway will be nice when I need time off during the week to catch up on school. So anyway, I went out there this morning and Alexis showed me around the building. The place is in a run-down condition, and the people seem kind of run-down as well. No one in the manufacturing area even looked at me as I went through. Alexis introduced me to people but they would not look me in the face. It was the strangest feeling. I felt that they all had cast an immediate judgement on who I was and what I was like. It made me mad because I did not feel that I should be judged based upon the color of my skin any more then they should by theirs. But I walked through and acted like I did not notice any of the undertones. I wonder if that is how black people feel when they are with all white people. I guess I got my first taste of what it must be like to be a minority.

Thankfully, the people in the front part of the building treated me much differently. The three salesmen and the secretary made it a point to be friendly to me. I appreciated it more than they could imagine. My desk is back by the salesmen. It is the first cubicle and desk that I have ever had! I like the feeling of having my own phone and place to put my stuff. Even if it is old and small, I can consider it my own.

Week of

September 14

My duties so far are not very clear to me. Alexis had me read up on the company. I looked through some magazines, at advertising and articles, to get a better understanding of what the industry is and how BCI does business. The magazines that hit their black target market are *Ebony, Sophisticate, Jet,* and *Essence,* and a trade publication, *Shop Talk.* I brainstormed some ideas for advertising and wrote down some questions I had about their products.

One of their key product lines is hair-care fashion accessories, including combs, hairnets, hair ribbons, and hair clips. The products used by their customers are much different from the ones Caucasians use. I did not realize just how much. Even the terms used to describe how they style hair are different. When Blacks straighten their hair they call it a perm: I am used to a perm being used to curl hair. Black hair gets damaged because of the chemicals used to style their hair, so heavy oils must be used for conditioning. This then requires special clips and combs. My hair is as opposite as it can be from black hair—bone straight and fine.

Alexis asked me if she could touch it so I asked if I could touch hers. It felt like something out of a movie, two people experiencing something new that is so common to each other. I am going to like Alexis. I do feel sorry for her because she has so much work to do all of the time.

Everyone in that place brings things to her to get done. She is also the mediator between Mr. Exeter and the rest of the company.

Week of September 21

It has been a while since I put an entry into this journal. I am so frustrated out at that place. Mr. Exeter has been "using" me to do things simply because I am white, and I do not appreciate it at all! I spend a lot of time in the conference room. His wife, whom he always addresses as Dr. Exeter, doesn't say much. Mr. Exeter has me call places because I have a "white" voice and he wants me to try to get accounts that he feels he hasn't been able to get because he is black. I am not a salesman—I have not been trained to do that type of work and it is ludicrous for him to think that I can get accounts because of the color of my skin.

He even had me try to call Ross Perot. I felt like the biggest idiot, trying to get a presidential candidate on the phone for my boss. I am seriously beginning to doubt the mental stability of Mr. Exeter. Yesterday he broke out in song during the meeting. He also recited a poem and a prayer. I had to write down what he was saying and then type it up for him. The looks being passed across the table should have been on videotape. No one changed facial expression but the eye contact among all of us was very descriptive.

There was an all-employee meeting today. I tried to hide in the back but it didn't work. Everyone in the company attended—an hour and forty-five minutes of wasted time! Nothing was accomplished, nothing except an embarrassing moment for me. Mr. Exeter wanted everyone to go around the room and introduce themselves. So much for me hiding in the back! When it got to be my turn he had me come up front and announced that I was going to be their new international model. I was shocked, and I didn't say anything—at all. But it seems preposterous that he would want me to model because I would not attract the market he is after. Honestly, it was flattering, but I don't think I would want my face associated with this product. That may sound like a harsh thing to say but it is how I feel about it. Their product line is low-quality and the advertising they use is poor. Not that I have ever modeled and have some type of image to uphold, but I still don't want to do it.

I think I made a huge judgement error today. Alexis was out for the day and she did not leave me anything to do. So I walked into the conference room to get something to do, or to be excused for the day. Well, Mr. Exeter decided there and then that Alexis was not doing her duty with me, and he was going to "take me under his wing." Uh oh! I guess I will be attending the daily production meetings from now on.

Every morning the senior people meet in the conference

room to discuss production and sales issues. The three Exeters are almost always there; other managers join them as different issues arise. I do believe that these meetings are a waste of time in most aspects. Granted there is a need for them, but not every day for three hours! Mr. Exeter likes to ramble on and on. I do think he just likes to hear himself talk. It is a power trip for him, something to build up his ego.

Week of October 5

It is interesting to talk to the salesmen. Walter is flashy and outspoken. He has a daughter my age and is very opinionated about how she should act and whom she should date. I am outspoken towards him too, and I don't think he knows how to take it. I think deep inside he likes that I am not afraid to tell him how I feel about situations. He believes that since he is male he is superior. He is beginning to get the idea, however, that I was raised in a similar (male chauvinistic) household and do not want any part of it now. He understands my position on certain situations, and I understand his, but we agree to disagree. We do have friendly, heated debates on topics like women in executive positions, men in the home, women in politics, etc. It is fun to get his perspective on issues.

Monroe is a lot different than Walter. He more or less goes with the flow, doesn't take a side, but pipes up on everything. He is very sincere and always willing to help me. If I have a question about anything I ask Monroe. His answers are usually longer than I would like, but he does explain things well. Monroe is full of questions for me, too. His questions are more personal, mostly about how I feel about black issues. I tell him truthfully, and he respects that. I believe a friendship is building between the two of us.

Albert is kind of a strange one. He is very quiet and, well…odd. He appears to be nervous all of the time, fidgeting and not looking in my eyes. He asked if I have any friends that he could go out with. I said no, and I hope he doesn't take it personally. It is just that I do not think any of my friends would date a black man. I would not either. Which might be a bad thing to say, but I think it is honest. Monroe asked if I would or have ever dated a black man, and I said no. My reason is that it would cause problems if the relationship developed. I also brought up the fact that many, if not most, black people would not date a white person. It is not that I think there is anything wrong with it, but it would not be a personal choice of mine.

It is neat how Walter, Monroe, and Albert treat me. They think I am helping the company, and I really want to. There is so much potential to be reached, but right now the barriers are too high. It seems that the salesmen like that I am working there. Does that make sense? I think they look at me as a symbol of white people, and that since I accepted the job it gives them hope that others may feel the way I do.

I do not think I am prejudiced. I do not want to be judged, nor do I feel it is my place to judge. This may come from my upbringing, but where I lived there were not too many people different from me. In fact, there was just one black person in my high school. I do worry, though, that I may appear to be prejudiced. Therefore, I worry about how I act or what I say, which may give the appearance of prejudice. It is kind of Catch-22. Although, I must say that I can already feel that I am more comfortable around black people, mostly because I think they will accept me as well. I think a lot of racial separation comes from a fear on both sides of not being accepted. But people should be intelligent enough to know that there is more to a person than the color of their skin. It's time to put stereotypes aside. It is interesting to me, though, that at BCI, some of the stereotypes do show. Many of the employees are lazy. But I think that some of it comes from poor management as much as anything else. I do believe that if those people were challenged to do more, and had an incentive to do more, they would. Right now they are paid minimum scale and do not receive any additional compensation or awards for excellent performance.

Week of October 12

I have been playing secretary to Mr. Exeter for the past couple of weeks. It is driving me insane. I have to go to the production meetings and take minutes. Mr.

Exeter also has me get his coffee and juice. I don't mind doing it, after all, he is in a wheelchair. But I can't help wonder why he is doing it? Is it because I am white? He has a secretary whose job it is to do these things, but he insists I do them. I do not want to rock the boat so I do not say anything about it. I did ask if I could be excused from the production meetings twice a week in order to work on the Christmas party project. Mr. Exeter took this quite personally. He felt that I did not appreciate being allowed into his "inner sanctum." In all honesty, I did not feel that my time was being spent well. I explained that it was simply that I had other projects to complete, but it was impossible when I spent every minute in the conference room. He agreed that I could have two mornings a week to work independently. Hurrah!

One thing that I cannot handle is his breakfast. Every single morning he has his secretary microwave a Polish sausage in a hot dog bun. Every morning! But he does not eat it very quickly, and when it gets cold I get the honor of heating it up—about three times a day. When he eats I almost get sick. He smacks and talks with his mouth full even as food flies out. It is the most disgusting thing. I have to turn away and tune out when he takes bites out of that thing.

Week of October 19

Mr. Exeter told me he was dropping my Christmas project, but he changed his mind again in about fifteen minutes. I am glad he reconsidered because it is something I really want to do. I have been in touch with area businesses to donate toys and I have arranged to have some kids to the factory for a Christmas party. I want each of them to send a letter with their "wish list" and I will make sure each gets a gift from their list. The day will include a Santa, breakfast, games, a matinee, and toys. Hopefully, I will be able to enlist enough help from people within BCI. Dr. Exeter suggested that Alexis help me get other business support because the area's black businesses may be more willing to work with her. It amazes me that every aspect of their life and business dealings revolve around being black or white!

October 27

I am still in shock over what happened today. I called in to say that I could not come in and that I would make up the time on Friday. This is something that I have done since the start of the internship, and is part of our initial agreement. Well, Mr. Exeter decided today that it was not acceptable. He started yelling at me through the conference phone where I knew the entire staff could hear both sides of the conversation. I tried to explain, calmly, why I could not make it in. He was very upset. He told me he was going to show me how he did business in his part of town, and not to forget that he was on Ross Perot's side. Crazy talk! He said some other cruel and insensitive things, and I got extremely upset. Mr. Exeter screamed at me to get in there right now, and hung up the phone. I was stunned.

I called Dr. Williams and asked what I should do. He told me to wait until tomorrow and he would handle it. I should have listened. Instead, I tried to pull myself together and handle it on my own. I do not know what it was that Mr. Exeter said or what he did that caused such a reaction in me, but I wanted to fight him on my own terms. Bad idea, because at that point I couldn't stop crying. Which is the most frustrating thing for me to admit because I believe that women should have every opportunity to reverse the stereotype that they will break down and cry when something goes wrong. It was a very humbling experience. I hope I have learned how to handle myself better in the future.

Anyway, I went in to BCI as Mr. Exeter ordered. As I entered the conference room where the production meeting was taking place, Mr. Exeter had everyone give me a round of applause for making it in. I think they were in shock, as was I. Based on what I had rehearsed on my way over, I said, "Good morning, Mr. Exeter. I cannot be here this morning." He proceeded to announce that I looked hung over. I explained that I had been up most of the night completing a paper, and did not shower before coming in. He told me to leave, and then said something else, but I did not hear him because I was walking out. I was so frustrated! I think that all of the pressure of two jobs and my last semester at school, together with the "uniqueness" of my situation at BCI, finally caught up with me. I did not realize how much I was being drained.

I went to a side room and hand-wrote a letter to Mr. Exeter. Mistake number two! The letter basically said that I was sorry if there was any misunderstanding, but it was my belief that it was okay for me to make up missed time later in the week. I could not resist writing that I thought he handled the situation poorly and cruelly. I also explained, in detail, why I couldn't work this morning. I also expressed my opinion that I was doing a good job for him and his company—that I did everything expected of me and more. I wrote, "This is only an internship for me; school is still the most important thing to me." I also told him I felt that a letter was the only way he would listen to what I was saying because whenever I opened my mouth he told me to be quiet.

I learned a valuable lesson. Never write (or never send) a letter because it is there in black and white. A letter can be read over and over to many people. Mr. Exeter was furious. He called my poor professor and chewed him out for about a half hour. He said he couldn't understand why a white person had been sent out in the first place. Slap!

Needless to say, my internship is no longer. I am going to miss the people I worked with, and I am worried that I won't have a successful internship to bolster my resume.

November 2

I waited almost a week before going back to BCI. I was worried that I wouldn't even be able to get my personal possessions from my desk. But I was amazed at the turnaround Mr. Exeter had taken. He apologized and said that I could use him for a reference. He said I did a good job in his company and wished me every future success. I didn't know how to take it, and wondered about his motives. It may have been genuine sentiments, but I suspect it was because he did not want to lose contact with the university. I guess I will never know.

It was very special to me though, when I went in that last time, that people were sad to see me go. Sandra, the secretary, gave me her phone number and asked if I would like to get together sometime. Albert came out and asked if I would come back and say "hi" to the guys. I did, and they were sincerely sorry that I was leaving. Monroe said that I could have done a lot of good for the company; Walter said it was definitely BCI's loss. That made me feel so good. It was one of those situations where you do not realize how much people like you until you leave.

My experience being the only nonblack person in a company taught me many things. I realized that even though I believe everyone is equal, I acted differently at first because I did not know if they thought the same. I was incred-

ibly intimidated, but after a couple of weeks it didn't matter anymore. They didn't care, and neither did I. Hopefully, I left that company with a better understanding of how little difference there really is between black and white people because I know that I learned that out there. I also learned things from a business standpoint that related to my college course. All in all, it was an experience I will never forget.

APPENDIX B
Internship Report by Sabrina Hill for Professor Williams

Beauty Classics, Inc. (BCI) is a manufacturer of fashion accessories whose principal target market is ethnic blacks. The company produces a variety of products marketed for use solely by professional hair and beauty consultants as well as products sold to consumers through retail channels. Products are marketed nationally, using national magazine advertising and regional and local television and radio spots. The company actively participates in national and regional trade shows and workshops for beauticians.

BCI was organized as a Tennessee corporation in October 1969. It began as a beauty supply house that purchased manufactured products and distributed these in Nashville and the surrounding region. Initial shareholders were Edward Exeter and Daisy Exeter, husband and wife. (Background information for these two founders are [sic] contained in Exhibit 1.)

Shortly after beginning business, the Exeters began manufacturing products, using their own brand name, in their home. Company sales the first year were $24,000. The peak sales year was 1985, with gross sales of over $13 million achieved. In 1986 the Exeters invested large sums in other ventures, including cosmetics, better jewelry, and African clothing and art. None of these businesses were successful; the dilution of BCI's financial and human resources led to BCI losing sales and market share. BCI's sales forecast for the year ending December 31, 1992 is $4 million.

BCI has a unique "window of opportunity" to capture market share in the ethnic fashion accessories market within the next decade. The 1992 sales projection was to capture a 1 percent share of this market; the company has products with a strong brand name, and a doubling of sales within a 3- to 5- year period is possible. This is particularly true since the company recently added Wal-Mart stores to its customer list.

The primary target market, ethnic blacks in the United States, contains approximately 31 million persons. A potential secondary market of Hispanic Americans currently has 22 million people. Combined, the two markets have over $435 billion in purchasing power. These markets are younger and growing more rapidly than the majority population. The average black per capita expenditure on fashion accessories is $23 to $25 annually. Hispanic consumption is somewhat less, but sociological and economic factors suggest this will increase. Both markets exhibit strong brand loyalty and a predisposition to purchase products produced and sold by their respective ethnic business-people. These markets are concentrated in urban areas which permits the focusing of marketing efforts.

Three distinct sets of competitors exist:
1. Black-owned companies whose efforts are directed primarily at the ethnic population
2. White-owned companies with the same targets
3. Large fashion products companies with specific product lines targeted at ethnic markets. While black-owned companies in total dominate the market, as a group they have proven to be inferior competitors. Many have severe financial problems. The larger fashion products companies apparently did not achieve projected results, and seem to be reducing their ethnic marketing efforts.

Three style or fashion submarkets currently exist. Competitive products are slightly different to address different perceived consumer needs for these styles. BCI management believes that its products are in several ways superior to those of its competitors and that these differences are noticed by consumers.

EXHIBIT 1
Brief Biographical Sketches of the Two Principals

Edward Exeter
Mr. Exeter graduated from Pennsylvania State University in 1962 with a B.S. degree in Business Administration. He served 15 years in the U. S. Army, and was promoted to the rank of Captain before leaving the service to start Beauty Classics, Inc. Mr. Exeter has received numerous civic and business awards, including Small Businessman of the Year and Manufacturer of the Year, and was recognized for outstanding achievement by *Black Enterprise* magazine. He is listed in "Who's Who among Black Americans" and is a member of the NAACP.

Daisy Exeter
Daisy Exeter is a graduate of several prominent fashion programs in the United States and France, and studied at Temple University. She received an honorary doctorate from Atlanta University. Dr. Exeter was a sales representative with Johnson Beauty Products (a prominent manufacturer of ethnic health and beauty products) for years prior to founding BCI.

APPENDIX C
Sabrina Hill's Assessment of the BCI Internship

My internship work became increasingly demeaning and

condescending. I was constantly embarrassed by Mr. Exeter's remarks, especially ones that I considered racial. The "production" meetings were a means through which Mr. Exeter exercised control, not only over me but over the entire staff. I was not the only one who was the butt of his cruel remarks; perhaps my skin was too thin.

I will never forget "the event." As usual, Mr. Exeter was on the speaker phone when I called in, and the entire staff KNEW what he said to me and my responses to him. When I walked into the conference room, and Mr. Exeter had those present give me a round of applause for showing up, I was incredibly angry at those "turncoats," those who had been my friends. I realize now that they had no other choice.

It is foolhardy to suggest that I was objective about what happened. What perplexed me the most was trying to decide if I felt like an outsider because I was only an intern, or if it was more a racial and/or sexual issue. Dr. Williams asked me specifically if it was my lack of socialization to the company, or were there really racial and sexual difficulties. I just don't know.

I'm sure I didn't handle Mr. Exeter with any great skill, but I'm not sure any intern could have handled it better. I think a black student would have fared even worse.

Mr. Exeter, despite any previous success, is currently a poor manager. All decisions in the company had to be approved by him; he took days, even weeks, to approve even the simplest request. Maybe his leadership abilities were once outstanding, and he deserved the awards he had won. But now his actions are nothing more than a struggle for power and control. His employees do as they are told, and have an appearance of respect for Mr. Exeter, but I am convinced that they tolerate his moods because they need the jobs. I'm sure they all agree that someone else could more capably run the business.

I am concerned that I haven't met with Alexis. I don't know what she thinks. I felt hurt that Alexis seemed to ignore me after the first couple of weeks, but looking back on it, she was just overwhelmed with work. She provided me with all the company background material, and encouraged me to follow through on the project. But Alexis was really the mediator between Mr. Exeter and the rest of the company. Did I undermine her?

APPENDIX D
Transcript of Debriefing Meeting Notes (Transcribed from Audiotape)

The debriefing meeting was held on November 20, 1992, in the Beauty Classics, Inc. Conference Room. Present were Edward Exeter, CEO; Dr. Daisy Exeter, Executive Vice President; Alexis Exeter, Director of Marketing; and Professor A. Williams, Professor of Marketing, Nashville University.

Professor Williams: I wish we were able to complete the internship, but it is unlikely that Sabrina wants to do it.

Edward Exeter: She was doing a good job for us. I'm sure the Christmas party is going to be a big success. Is there anyone else that could help Alexis?

Professor Williams: I don't think it's possible to get anyone at this late date. Even if there were a student that could assume the internship, it's not possible that this person could come in and take over. There's just not enough time.

Alexis Exeter: I still can't figure out what happened. She was right in the thick of things, privy to all the decision making.

Edward Exeter: She just didn't understand how hard we work. We were paying her $5.00 per hour, which is more than we start our production line at.

Professor Williams: Perhaps that was one of the problems. As I mentioned way back in August when we discussed the internship, it's not usual practice to pay an intern. In fact, our experience is that paid internships are usually less satisfactory because the company treats the intern like an employee.

Daisy Exeter: Excuse me! We don't ask for charity. Whenever someone does something for us they get paid.

Professor Williams: Well, that's just the point. Interns usually take up an awful lot of company time. Most companies get a completed project, but the cost to them is a great deal of time spent.

Edward Exeter: She had tremendous privileges here. Learning how our system worked. The production meetings are the way we run this company.

Professor Williams: As I explained several times, the intern has certain requirements that the college imposes. Sometimes completing these seems to interfere with what the company expects.

Edward Exeter: But we had great plans for Sabrina. She and Alexis were to model our new international line.

Professor Williams: Sabrina felt that recording the notes of the production meeting wasn't productive.

Edward Exeter: That's gratitude! I put her in a position very few people are privileged to see—what our concerns are and how we make decisions—and she's ungrateful.

Daisy Exeter: Young people just don't seem to want to work nowadays.

Alexis Exeter: No, I don't think Sabrina…

Edward Exeter: Well, it's over and done with. We sure could use some help around here. I hope Sabrina learned a lot, and that she understands how difficult it is for a minority business to exist. But, she'll probably be happier working in an environment without blacks.

Professor Williams: I don't think…

Edward Exeter: It's over with. But we'd like an intern for the spring. This time we want a black.

(The discussion continued over spring internship possibilities. No further direct mention of Sabrina Hill's internship occurred.)

CASE 5
Kate Cooper
· · · · · · · · · · · · · ·

By William E. Stratton, Idaho State University; David Efraty, University of Houston—Downtown; and Kim Jardine.

My name is Kate Cooper. I am 31, a registered nurse with a bachelor's degree in nursing and 6 years of supervisory experience. I was charge nurse and then house supervisor in the medical/surgical wing of a large regional medical center and was in-service director in charge of continuing education and staff development in a geriatric nursing setting. In addition, I have been teaching nursing courses in the night program at a local technical school.

Ready for the next step in my career, I obtained the position of Manager of Adult Services for the twenty-bed adult psychiatric wing at Green Meadows Hospital. Green Meadows was a newly constructed forty-room community hospital for the care of acutely ill psychiatric patients. It was the twenty-third facility owned by Southern Hospitals Corporation (SHC), the largest chain of acute-care psychiatric hospitals in the country.

I felt excited about my new position. I saw it as a fine opportunity for career development in nursing, and the possibility of transferring to other facilities in the chain was a definite benefit in my eyes. I had many projects to complete before the planned opening of the hospital in 2 weeks, and I started my new position with high energy and enthusiasm.

My supervisor, Alan Jones, who hired me, was assistant administrator of the hospital. He had 1 year of previous experience as director of nursing at a fifty-bed acute-care psychiatric hospital. On my first day he encouraged me to "just dig right in and get started" organizing my department. I asked to see my job description and the hospital policy manual to become familiar with the organization employing me. Alan gave me a job description and explained that I was part of the "start-up" process. At this time there was no personnel handbook for employees.

One condition of employment I stipulated in accepting the job was that I be able to continue my schooling as a part-time graduate student working on my master's degree in nursing education. Alan Jones readily agreed to this condition, stating that he was a strong supporter of continuing education for all managers and staff.

In my opinion the first week I worked for Green Meadows consisted of many wasted hours. I learned on my own that my main task prior to the opening was to hire the patient care staff for my twenty-bed unit. I tried to line up interviews for nurses and mental health workers, since

Alan Jones had told me to "go ahead and hire the personnel you need for your unit."

Peter Smith, manager of the eighteen-bed chemical dependency unit, had previously worked with Alan Jones at a psychiatric hospital 50 miles from Green Meadows. Peter had been hired by Alan along with two other managers from that location who had not yet arrived at Green Meadows. Peter was hiring staff for his unit, and he told me he wanted to interview the nurses and mental health workers also, since those employees would be working on his unit as well.

This request surprised me. I tried to find an organization chart and asked the hospital administrator, Doug Anderson, in passing one morning if he had one I could see. He jokingly asked me if I was serious. "After all," he said, "I think it is changing every day." I laughed at first, but my amusement was short-lived when no chart was forthcoming. Eventually, I came to visualize the organization chart as presented in Figure 1.

Doug Anderson had served as office manager in a small hospital in California. His wife, an occupational therapist, was also a part-time employee at Green Meadows. Two of Doug's hires were a personal friend

Figure 1
Green Meadows Hospital management staff—partial organization chart

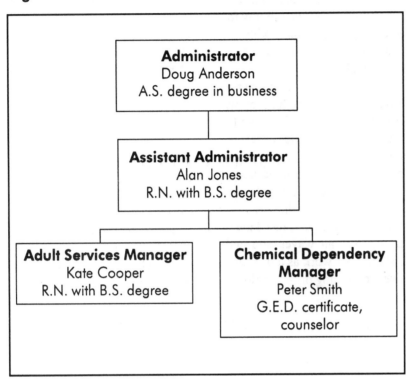

from California, Leonard Snare, and Leonard's wife. Leonard's sole job qualification was certification to be a psychiatric technician, earned by attending workshops. His wife worked in the business office.

Construction work had progressed, and Green Meadows was ready for staff occupancy 1 week before the planned hospital opening. Although much remained to be done and things were still confused, I was excited about moving into my new office.

During the previous week Peter and I had hired our initial staff. I was worried my unit would not be ready to receive patients and had written a 5-day orientation program specific to

the unit that included information I thought my patient care staff would find beneficial. I shared the orientation outline with Peter, who informed me that he would need 2½ days to teach the new staff members *his* program alone.

I was shocked and angered that he had planned this commitment for my staff. With one week left, both orientation programs could not be completed prior to opening. I asked Peter if his plan had been cleared with Alan Jones. Peter replied with a grin, "Of course. It was his idea." As a result, I sought out Alan and asked if he could meet on some neutral ground with the adult psychiatric and chemical dependency units. I told him that the orientation to my department was just as important as orientation to Peter's department. Alan told me that Peter had his program all ready to go and would only need "a couple of days" to present it. All of this left me feeling very frustrated.

I had other problems with Alan. Despite his having told me to go ahead and hire staff nurses and mental health workers, I later discovered he was hiring those people at the same time I was interviewing prospective employees. In addition, Alan had instructed me to assume the role of in-service director and write the staff orientation program. He told me that I would have to be the unit head nurse for the chemical dependency unit, although I told him that I thought the responsibilities would be too great due to my duties as the adult services unit manager. Alan's response to my doubts was his standard one in such situations: "You are tough, and I know you can handle it."

As a result of these and similar interactions with Alan, I became confused and frustrated by his lack of support and his behavior, which seemed inconsistent with directions he had given me. I was overwhelmed with the amount of work and responsibility. I was most frustrated and angered when additional tasks were "dumped" on me because I felt I had to complete the extra work as soon as possible in addition to doing my own work on the unit.

Alan apparently had difficult relationships with some other employees as well. Other female managers complained almost from the start that Alan needed to be "put in his place" for his sexist remarks and behaviors. Doug Anderson received reports indicating that Alan's behavior had been inappropriate on several occasions. Doug also heard second-hand that Alan was overstepping his responsibilities as assistant administrator and making policy statements contrary to Doug's positions.

This general employee dissatisfaction continued. Three months after the opening of the hospital Alan Jones strongly implied that I would have to quit school. He explained that he expected people to be there, saying that "to be a good manager you should be here all the time." I took issue with this and sought Doug Anderson's assistance. Doug had never been informed about my going to school and was unaware that I was even taking classes. Alan alone had approved my return to school to continue my education. Doug's response was simply to encourage me to speak with Alan again and "communicate better with him."

Feeling pressure on several fronts, I reached the limit of my tolerance with Alan Jones and handed him my notice of resignation. Alan Jones subsequently refused to speak with me. The manager of the chemical dependency unit told me that my timing was lousy, accused me of trying to create waves, and said I should put work as a priority over continuing my education.

CASE 6
TANDEM BROTHERS: THE COCHRANE TREE-PLANT

By Sam Moorcroft and Professor James A. Erskine

Thursday, May 26, 1994, near Cochrane, Ontario:
"You have no way to get us to work Tom. The tractor is useless and you know it. The planters are tired of walking to work. We've put up with too much. We aren't budging from that tent unless you pay us to walk!" Neil Thompson, senior planter, was forcefully representing the crew's position.

Tom Johnson, tree-plant Supervisor, listened in disbelief before responding. "But Neil, we're so close to finishing! You can't let me down now! You know that I don't have the money for that!" Neil stared straight ahead. "Sorry Tom, we just aren't taking this any longer."
Tom was gasping for the right words. "Listen, Neil…"

REFORESTATION IN CANADA

Each year in Canada, the provincial ministries of natural resources, together with various forest companies, initiated the planting of hundreds of millions of young seedlings, in order that areas harvested on public lands were reforested. Some planting was performed by the ministries themselves, but the vast majority was contracted out to companies that specialized in reforestation.

The planting season could start as early as January to March, depending on the weather and location, and would continue until late autumn. The bulk of the tree-planting oc-

curred in May through August, when weather conditions were the most favourable.

Each contractor was assigned ministry assessors, whose job it was to ensure that the contractor fulfilled its obligations to the ministry. The emphasis tended to be on the use of various sanctions rather than rewards to enforce compliance. Payment was primarily based on the results of random quality assessments of planted trees, performed by these assessors, and was on a sliding scale. For example, in some parts of Ontario, an assessment that 93% or higher of the trees were satisfactorily planted resulted in 100% payment. A 92% assessment resulted in 99% payment, and so on. An assessment below 85% resulted in no payment.

Because contracts could be worth hundreds of thousands of dollars, a few percentage points below full payment could seriously affect a contractor's profitability. The methods of assessment were meant to be as "scientific" as possible; however, field conditions were such

that a judgement call on the part of the assessor was often required. Not surprisingly, relations between assessors and contractors could vary considerably, depending on the personalities involved and the nature of the particular contract. Complications developed because different districts within and between provinces had different standards and methods of assessment. Contractors used to working in one district or province could run into trouble if they assumed that similar conditions existed elsewhere.

Many contractors had come to realize that relations with the ministry assessors had a "political" element to them and employed various strategies to ensure that they received as close to their bid price as possible on their contracts. For the most part this was within the bounds of acceptable conduct; however, some less scrupulous contractors had been known to engage in bribery and other illegal activities. For this reason, there was sometimes an element of distrust on the ministry side, especially with contractors new to their district. Some assessors believed, rightly or wrongly, that contractors would try to get away with anything.

Tree-planting

Tree-planting was very hard work. More energy was expended by a tree-planter at work than on any other labour-intensive occupation. Planters had to carry their trees in planting bags that were strapped around the waist and supported by shoulder straps. Fully loaded bags could weigh 20kg or more. The terrain varied considerably, ranging from flat, open areas with deep, exposed soil, to mountainous, thickly populated areas consisting of species that were left uncut because they were undesirable to the forest company that logged the land. Dense undergrowth could be evident, and blocking the way could be fallen branches, up-rooted trunks, and over-turned boulders.

Contracts usually stipulated a consistent spacing standard; that is, the contractor had to ensure that a certain number of trees, say 2000, were planted per hectare. In areas that had no site preparation after being

Source: This case was prepared by Sam Moorcroft under the supervision of Professor James A. Erskine solely to provide material for class discussion. The case is not intended to illustrate either effective or ineffective handling of a managerial situation. Certain names and other identifying information may have been disguised to protect confidentiality. This material is not covered under authorization from CanCopy or any Reproduction Rights Organization. Any form of reproduction, storage or transmittal of this material is prohibited without written permission from Western Business School. Permission to reproduce or copies may be obtained by contacting Case and Publication Services, Western Business School, The University of Western Ontario, London, Ontario, Canada, N6A 3K7, or by calling (519) 661-3208, or faxing (519) 661-3882.

logged, planters had to space off their own planted trees, or use landmarks to follow rows they had already planted. Exhibit 1 provides a glossary of terms related to reforestation. In some instances, the planter had to scrape away the root mat and duff layer to expose the underlying soil with his/her foot or planting shovel, to a foot-by-foot standard, and plant the tree in the middle of the scraped away area. Other contracts had been site prepared, but although the intent was to provide rows to be planted, often the treatment was a few years old, and/or was hard to follow.

The physical planting of the trees was the least difficult. The hard part was being able to move from spot to spot quickly and with a minimum of effort. It was this movement that separated "high-ballers" from "ordinary" planters. Experience, as well, counted for a lot, because such planters had trained eyes and could pick out planted trees quickly, even in dense foliage, and knew how to "work a block" efficiently and effectively.

Compensation was on a per-tree basis and could range from four cents to fifty cents, depending on the terrain, location, company, etc. Good tree-planters could earn $100-200/day and "high-ballers" could average over $300/day.

Contracts were usually situated in wilderness areas and were sometimes remote (although commuter-type plants from motels were also common). Entire crews would be situated on or near the planting site, and

planters were required to have their own tents and supplies. Usually, the contractor would supply a cook and set up mess tents, outhouses, and portable showers (subject to ministry guidelines) to service the crew. Some camp set-ups were very elaborate, consisting of under-ground plumbing, water towers, water pumps, generators, radio phones, various all-terrain vehicles, and even helicopters. Professional chefs were hired, and planters could order in personal supplies, consisting of just about anything.

Contracts ranged from small (fewer than 10,000 trees) with a few planters, to huge (between two million and five million trees, or more) with over 100 planters. The work force was made up of a mix of summer students and seasonal or tran-sient workers. Crews could be quite rough, and some supervisors were reluctant to let them "loose" on nearby towns on days off, for fear of violence and vandalism resulting from excessive consumption of alcohol and general stress relief. Planters worked hard and played hard. It was a rough life, but could be financially (and personally) rewarding if you were with a good contractor and had good land.

In addition to planters, there was the support staff, involving crew-bosses, tree-runners, quality checkers, cooks, mainte-nance-people, equipment operator/drivers, and a supervisor (depending on the contract size). Generally, these positions were filled by ex-planters, who had performed very well, and demonstrated managerial ability. See Exhibit 2 for a description of the various job responsibilities.

The intensity of the work and the close living conditions made it necessary for everyone to get along, or at least be civil. Supervisors sometimes found themselves mediating disputes and ensuring that certain workers were kept apart. Everyone in the camp had a distinct personality and a good supervisor knew how to motivate individual planters and staff, as well as the whole crew.

Maintaining morale was a big factor in ensuring that contracts were successfully completed with a minimum of turnover. Training new planters took time and effort, and retaining them for future seasons was a high priority. When contracts were good; that is, planters were making money and conditions were favourable, things ran smoothly. But when contracts were not good, a supervisor's job would become very difficult. Experienced planters formed the backbone of any crew, and they knew it. Keeping them happy was a high priority, but not to the point of rookies sensing any sort of favouritism.

TANDEM BROTHERS FORESTRY SERVICES

Tandem Brothers (Tandem), based in Lethbridge, Alberta, was founded in 1984 by identical twins, Paul and Rupert Tandem. They had started with a small, 80,000 tree contract with the Ministry of Forests, and together with a friend, had planted the trees themselves over an eight-week period. In subsequent years they had expanded slowly, drawing their recruits from various colleges and universities and providing these students with summer employment. The company was active in other areas of forestry, including brushing, thinning, and timber cruising, but its main source of income came from its tree-planting operations.

Tom Johnson

Tom Johnson first worked for Tandem in the summer of 1989, following his third year towards a politics degree. He had joined as a crewboss, having planted for a company in British Columbia the previous two summers. It was unusual for a tree-planting company to hire an "outside" crewboss, but Tandem was expanding that summer and did not have enough planters suitable for promotion. Tom had come with solid references and had been an exceptionally good planter, so Paul and Rupert had hired him.

Since 1989, Tom had become somewhat of a fixture with Tandem, working in various positions during the next four summers, including quality checker, tree-runner, planter, crewboss, and contract supervisor, to gain broad experience in the business. During the "off-season" he would use his earnings to travel and/or perform volunteer mission work overseas and various other activities that he wanted to do before settling down.

In September of 1993, he returned to university to start MBA, drawing upon his management experience with Tandem as part of his application. Tom wanted to obtain some corporate experience in the summer between MBA I and MBA II. He had risen as high as he could go with Tandem and thought that the company was not expanding fast enough to further utilize his talents. However, in March of 1994, Paul Tandem offered him a job that he could not refuse. Tom knew the job would challenge his abilities as no other in his seven seasons of tree-planting.

THE COCHRANE CONTRACT

Tandem had submitted a bid for a tree-planting contract in Ontario, its first outside Alberta. Tandem had heard that Ontario was a lucrative market and wanted to obtain some experience there. The particular site was situated in an area that had lots of muskeg swamp, and access was extremely poor, both to and from as well as within the site. It would be necessary to use helicopters to fly the crew in and out, and require a special vehicle called a muskeg tractor to transport trees and planters to the work-sites from a base camp. All-terrain vehicles (quad-runners) would also be required. This type of contract was completely new to Tandem (see Exhibit 3 for a comparison between a "typical" Tandem contract and the Cochrane plant, and Exhibit 4 for a map of the area).

Paul had indicated to Tom that he was nervous about the project, but Tom had told him not to worry. "You've seen my work in the past, Paul," he had said. Paul had agreed, saying, "Yes, Tom, we bid on this for you because you've been telling us to expand, so here you are!"

Tom had asked Paul to fax him a copy of the budget (see Exhibits 5 and 6). Tandem was the low bidder by only a slim margin. Competition was intense this season, due to the recent recession and Ministry cutbacks in seedlings tendered. Tom was concerned at the relatively low profit figure; $9000 could be used up very quickly in the event of unexpected expenses. In addition, $6600 seemed like a lot of money to rent a muskeg tractor for only three weeks. However, Paul had told him that this was the going rate in Alberta, at least, that was what the equipment operator in Lethbridge charged, where the tractor was to come from. Paul himself had never rented such a machine. Tom was also concerned about having to fly in the planters. This was very expensive, considering that the site was only a few miles from the nearest highway. Paul indicated that the Ministry did not want the existing trail torn up, because it was used in the winter to haul logs out of the bush.

Tom and Paul had agreed to split the task of hiring a crew, and during his spare time that spring, Tom had attended job fairs at nearby universities, and interviewed and hired share of the crew. (See Exhibit 7 for an organization chart.) Rupert travelled to the site in late April with a skeleton crew and moved in the initial camp supplies and equipment, including two quad-runners and the tractor. Since the ground was still frozen, Rupert was able to use the existing trail into the camp site.

Tom was apprehensive about the plant even before it started. He had some feelings that this might be a difficult assignment. In spite of his past experience in supervising tree-plants, there were so many unknown variables that could adversely affect this job. It seemed to Tom that the successful completion of this plant was highly dependent on a smooth operation with few mishaps.

As was his habit, Tom maintained a diary of events, so that he could look back and reflect on a job once it had been completed.

Tom Johnson's Cochrane Diary

Wed, April 20 - Fri, April 22

It was so nice to finish MBA I! I'm happy with the way my final exams went, but I don't have time to think about that now. I have to prepare for the upcoming tree-plant. I flew to Lethbridge on Wednesday, and over the last few days I have been in the office with Paul, organising the plant and finalising the hiring. Paul mentioned that it may be possible to send the crew in by boat, if the ice on the lake has melted sufficiently. That would really be great, because any money I can save now can be used as contingency money for the plant.

Mon, April 25 - Mon, May 02

Paul sent me to Prince George, British Columbia, to supervise a small contract of 65,000 trees, with five planters. He figured it would get me warmed up while he takes care of co-ordinating the arrival of the Cochrane crew at the Cochrane Inn, near the site.

Wed, May 04

My five planters and I have been driving for the last 36 hours or so to get to Cochrane in time to meet up with Paul and the crew. I am exhausted from the trip, but Paul wanted me here because he had arranged for the helicopter to fly the crew in tomorrow. Fortunately, the helicopter company has had to delay its arrival by a day. I now have a day to find an alternative, because I really do not want to incur this expense.

Thurs, May 05

Paul and I went out to the lake early this morning, but there was too much ice, so boating is not an option. Paul and Rupert then left for Alberta to start their contracts there. While I was sitting in the bar at the Cochrane Inn contemplating my options, I met a local equipment operator, Miles Shaw, who said he has a permit to use the winter trail with his own muskeg tractor. He said to forget the helicopter, because he would transport the crew in under his permit for only $250! When I radioed the assessors at the site they said that I would be in violation of the contract if I did. When Miles heard this, he phoned Ministry headquarters and said that he had the right to take us in because of his permit. The Ministry reluctantly agreed, and over-rode the assessors. I hired Miles to transport us in and will try to smooth things over when I meet the assessors tomorrow.

Fri, May 06

I met the assessors, Ron Small and Ken Blake, today. They are full-time foresters, unlike the summer students I usually deal with. Ron said that they would be dictating how things will be done. That's not the way it was done in Alberta. Assessors should assess quality and that's it!

Sat, May 07

What a horrible day! It seemed like everything went wrong. The water pump on the muskeg tractor broke down, and the crew walked the seven miles to work! It turned out that patches of the ground were still frozen, so I had to stop the planting and send the crew back to camp.

Mon, May 09

I can't believe what's happening! Some ground is still frozen and it will take a few days to get a replacement part for the tractor. Miles's machine is down for an unknown reason, so I basically have no transportation! Ron gave me a dressing down,

as he can't believe I don't have a contingency plan.

I split the crew and sent the experienced planters to the South blocks to set up a satellite camp. I have to keep these planters happy, because they're the backbone of the crew. I'd move the whole camp, but there's no water supply for food, drinking, and bathing. I'll have to make daily trips in the quad-runner to supply them.

I want to start the rookies at the North end near camp, but the trees have to be dug out of the snow-caches four days in advance, to thaw out. Ron is being totally inflexible and insists that the South end be planted first. It doesn't really matter which areas are planted first! I told Jim to start digging out one of the North-end caches. I have to plan for possible set-backs. I asked the crew to walk for two days and promised them that the tractor would be ready by Thursday.

Tues, May 10

I think this plant is jinxed! While I stayed back at camp to phone around for parts for the tractor, my crew bosses managed to misread their maps and put the crews in areas other than those Ron and Ken had picked out. Ron started yelling at me when I arrived at the South blocks. He said I was defying him, and waved a copy of the contract in my face. He does have the right to choose the areas, but what gets me is that it doesn't matter where we start planting! It all has to be done anyway, and I've been at this for

seven years, so I know what I'm doing!

Thurs, May 12

Well, the tractor was up and running until Dave [whose job it is to drive the tractor] managed to burn the clutch out on the way home by jamming the gears between third and fourth and not stopping. He said that he didn't want the crew to walk. The tractor broke down a mile from camp. I was furious. I didn't hire Dave, Paul did, and I wasn't told that he has never actually driven such a machine! These things aren't the same as trucks!

Fri, May 13

Fortunately, the trees were ready at the North end, so the crew only had to walk for five minutes to work. Ron wasn't pleased that I had done this, but he's starting to realize the pressure I'm under. Miles's tractor is back, and he hauled my tractor out to the highway, but charged me $800. That's actually a lot cheaper than calling in a professional company. It's going to cost over $2500 to fix the tractor! This machine is well worn, so it's not entirely Dave's fault. I've hired Miles at $250/day to be on hand whenever I need him.

Sat, May 14

Things were going well for a while today. The rookies are learning fast, and quality is excellent. Ron seems happier and we are starting to get along better. The South crew arrived for a day off. They aren't happy with their living conditions. Each planter is charged $20/day for food and the price of the cooks, but I reduced the South crew's costs in half to keep them happy. I have $250-300/day less revenue coming in. My radio-phone quit on me today, and the local rental company said it will take a week to get a replacement!

Mon, May 16

Miles's tractor overheated today on the way home. Miles is proving to be very unreliable. He said it would take him a day to repair. Production is running behind and I don't think we will finish on time. Every day I go over will cost me about $1000/day in staff wages, plus Ministry fines of $500/day.

Thurs, May 19

I thought things couldn't get any worse. Boy, was I in for a surprise! On Tuesday a small fire was started at the South end when swamp moss on a quadrunner manifold heated up and fell to the ground. It has been very dry lately. The fire quickly spread out of control and I had to halt all planting. It took firefighters three days to put it out with water bombers and 12 work crews. Fortunately, the local fire warden called to say they had ruled the fire an accident. It cost about $1-million to put it out! I reduced camp costs by half to keep the crew happy while we waited. There goes another $1000 or so!

Fri, May 20

I boated out to the nearest phone (as I have yet to see a replacement radio-phone) and phoned Paul to request that he send experienced planters immediately. He said he could spare six. Gas, food, and lodging on the way will cost me another $750. None of this is budgeted for!

Mon, May 23

Fortunately, our muskeg tractor is back, so that I don't have to pay Miles anymore. The six planters arrived today, and were most unimpressed with the working conditions. They planted a lot of trees, but are grumbling openly. That is the last thing I need. I've worked out that it will take us about five extra days to finish. All told, that will set me back about $7500 in wages and fines. I pride myself on running profitable contracts so this is really upsetting me!

Wed, May 25

I am not sleeping anymore because I am worrying so much! The drive shaft on the tractor failed today. Fred says that it was never designed to carry more than 40 planters! I can't get a hold of Miles because he's off on another job with his tractor. I don't know what to do!

CRISIS!

It was overcast when Tom go up early Thursday morning, May 26. He was getting ready for the day's planting when he looked at his watch. It was 7:00 a.m. The crew should have been outside the mess tent by now, and heading off to work. He started to head over to the tent, and when the crew saw him, everyone went silent. Just then Neil Thompson, one of the six Alberta planters, came out to meet him.

"What is happening, Neil?" Tom asked.

"You have no way to get us to work, Tom," said Neil. "The muskeg tractor is useless and you know it. The planters are tired of walking to work. We've put up with too much. We aren't budging from that tent unless you pay us to walk!"

Tom listened in disbelief before responding: "But Neil, we're so close to finishing! You can't let me down now!" Tom's mind was racing. The contract stipulated that if the plant was not completed, the company would be fined $30,000! "You know that I don't have the money for that!" Neil stared straight ahead. "Sorry, Tom, we just aren't taking this any longer."

Tom was gasping for the right words. "Listen, Neil…".

EXHIBIT 1

Glossary of Terms

Brushing	Involves cutting down brush and shrubs along right of ways and hydro-line towers.
Duff Layer	A layer of inorganic or decaying material that has yet to revert to soil. It has no nutrients and trees that are planted in it will usually die.
High-baller	A planter who is exceptionally fast and who outperforms most other planters. Such planters are indispensable to a crew, as they plant a disproportionate share of trees in a contract and are counted on to keep a contract on track, with regards to production. They are often an inspiration to the rest of the crew.
Muskeg	A type of swamp or bog that severely restricts mobility and which requires special machinery to navigate through.
Muskeg Tractor	A special all-terrain vehicle which can be used to haul trees and transport planters in very rough sites not suitable for trucks or other all-terrain vehicles, such as quad runners. It bears a resemblance to a pick-up truck on tank treads and effectively navigates through muskeg, bogs, mud holes, etc.
Quad Runner	A type of all-terrain vehicle that has four wheels and is meant to carry one rider. It is used by tree-runners or crew bosses, etc., to transport trees to difficult-to reach sites and to get around areas quickly and efficiently, when using trucks is not an option.
Quality Assessment	Assessors check trees in planted areas at random to ensure that they have been planted in accordance with Ministry guidelines, and to ensure that they have a good chance for survival.
Root Mat	A layer covering the forest floor consisting of roots from various types of under growth. It is hard to plant through this mat, and trees do not stand a very good chance of survival, due to the roots interfering with the establishment of the planted tree and airpockets being created.
Seedlings	Very young trees, usually less than a year old and ranging in height from 2.5 cm. to 60 cm. (They can be larger, but this is the exception, rather than the rule.)
Site Preparation	After trees have been logged from an area, the logging company will sometimes "plow up" the land by various methods, e.g., by dragging barrels connected to chains behind a skidder, a machine similar to a farm tractor that is used to navigate rough terrain. The point is to expose mineral soil in rows-of-sorts that can then be planted with seedlings.

EXHIBIT 1 (continued)

Glossary of Terms

Snow Cache	Sometimes seedlings are brought out from the nursery directly to the site in the autumn prior to the planting season and placed in winter storage. They are placed in boxes in cells and covered with snow, which is then covered with hay or sawdust for insulation so that the cache does not thaw out prematurely in the spring.
Thinning	A process of removing some trees in a forest area to allow and promote the growth of other trees.
Timber Cruising	Marking off with paint lines which forest areas are to be cut.

Exhibit 2

JOB RESPONSIBILITIES

Supervisor	Has overall responsibility for a contract. Organizes and executes a tree-plant. Specifically, organizes tree-planting crews, meal times, working hours; directs staff and planters in training and quality programs; allocates areas to be planted and the order in which they are to be planted. Assumes all liaison with Ministry or logging company personnel.
Crew Boss	Is responsible for a specific planting crew, usually consisting of five to fifteen planters. Trains rookies, provides sections of land to be planted, ensures that planting quality is acceptable, delivers trees when necessary, works with the supervisor and tree-runner.
Tree-runner	Responsible for tree handling and delivery, in accordance with the supervisor's direction and planters' needs. Works closely with crew bosses.
Tree-removal	Digs trees out of snow caches, opens boxes to hasten thawing, works with the tree-runner to ensure that an adequate supply is available each day.
Maintenance	Is in charge of overall camp maintenance. Makes regular trips to nearest town for food and supplies. Repairs and services all equipment.
Cooks	Prepare all food and ensure that costs are in line with the budget.
Planters	Form the backbone of the crew. They do the actual planting, in accordance with company direction.

EXHIBIT 3

COMPARISON CHART

PAST TANDEM PLANTS	THE COCHRANE PLANT
- access poor to excellent. Usually able to navigate logging roads with 4x4 vehicles, use quad-runners to access poorer sites.	- extremely poor access to and within site. Have to use muskeg tractor, specially designed to traverse muskeg, and quad-runners, only.
- trees delivered near to site by Ministry in refrigerated tractor-trailers, or buried in snow caches, accessible by 4x4 trucks.	- trees buried in snow caches, on site access only by quad-runners or muskeg tractors.
- bush camps off main highway or logging roads, easy access to nearby towns for supplies, etc.	- bush camp accessible only by boat, muskeg tractor, or helicopter. Contract with Ministry stipulates that route from camp to highway be used once in and once out only. Therefore, accessible only by boat during plant.
- planters transported to and from bush camp by company bus, trucks, personal cars. Can travel to nearby towns on days off.	- planters to be flown in and out by helicopter, and remain in camp throughout contract.
- planting areas in close proximity to bush camp, i.e., within 1-3 miles. Further sites readily accessible by bus or truck.	- planting areas part of narrow, long blocks, spread over 7 miles. Bush camp to be at north end of block, because only water source for drinking, cooking, bathing is at north end.
- contracts are between .5 and 2.5 million trees, spread over 6-8 weeks, with crews of 15-35.	- 1.3 million trees to be planted in 3 weeks, therefore requiring 50-60 employees.
- crews are predominantly experienced, have high rate of returning planters each season.	- contract to be in addition to normal work in Alberta, so will require 75% rookies, including staff.
- bid prices generally good, allow for good wages for crew, profit margin of 10% or more for company.	- low bid price to obtain work, lower wages to crew, net profit of 4-5% for company. No contingency money budgeted.
- communication from camp to headquarters sometimes by radio-phone, but can always drive to town if necessary. Distance to headquarters 0-500 kilometers.	- radio-phone to be only contact with outside world, besides trips to town by boat once or twice weekly. Distance to headquarters over 2000 kilometers.

EXHIBIT 4

MAP OF THE COCHRANE TREE-PLANT SITE

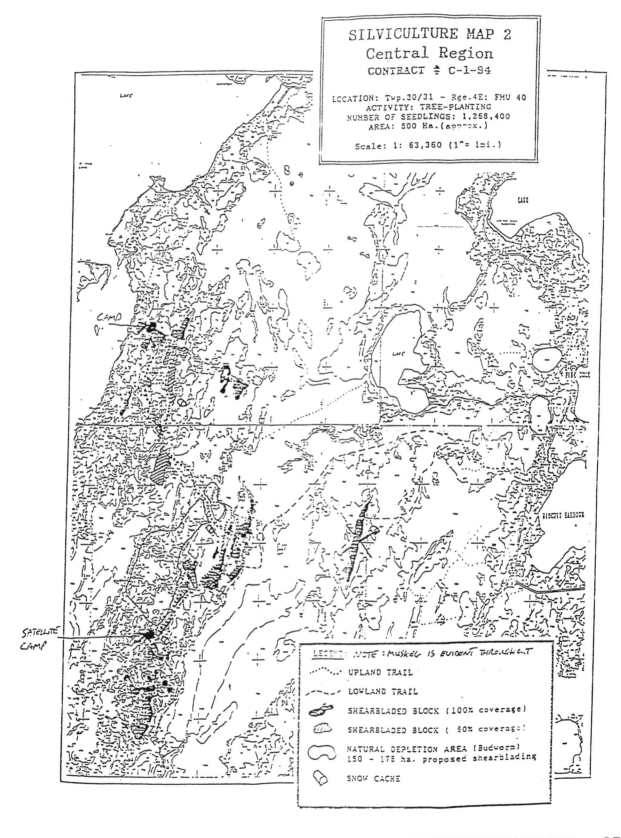

SILVICULTURE MAP 2
Central Region
CONTRACT ‡ C-1-94

LOCATION: Twp.30/31 - Rge.4E: FHU 40
ACTIVITY: TREE-PLANTING
NUMBER OF SEEDLINGS: 1,268,400
AREA: 500 Ha.(approx.)

Scale: 1: 63,360 (1"= 1mi.)

LEGEND: NOTE: MUSKEG IS EVIDENT THROUGHOUT
⋯⋯ UPLAND TRAIL
— — LOWLAND TRAIL
SHEARBLADED BLOCK (100% coverage)
SHEARBLADED BLOCK (50% coverage)
NATURAL DEPLETION AREA (Budworm)
150 - 175 ha. proposed shearblading
SNOW CACHE

EXHIBIT 5

CONTRACT

ONTARIO

Natural Resources   Forestry Branch

_____

_____

_____

April 13, 1994

Tandem Brothers Forestry

_____

_____

_____

Attention: Paul Tandem

Dear Paul:

RE: CONTRACT C-1-94

Further to your inquiry on the above contract, please be advised that your company was low bidder at .15772 per seedling. The contract was tendered for approximately 1,268,400 seedlings totalling $200,055.00.

I have received authorisation to prepare the contract in your name and it is currently being approved by our department. Once received, I will forward 3 copies for your signature and include instructions for you on submitting the required performance monies.

Trust the above information will suffice until the contracts are mailed to you for signature.

Yours truly,

_____

Contract Administrator

EXHIBIT 6

BUDGET

Cochrane Plant

May 9-May 29, 1994   Total number of trees: 1,268,400

Revenue	
Bid price	$200,055
Camp costs	20,680
Total revenue	**220,735**
Less wages	
Bareroot stock	52,380
Container	51,450
Supervisor	3,600
Foreman 1	3,240
Foreman 2	3,240
Foreman 3	3,240
Tree-runner	3,330
Tree-removal	1,800
Maintenance	2,730
Cooks	7,050
Misc.	2,200
Camp setup	2,000
Shop/office	2,000
Sub total	**138, 260**
Health, WCB, UIC, CPP*	23,504
Total wages	**161,764**
Less expenses	
Food	12,055
Fuel	4,000
Truck depreciation	3,500
Truck repair	3,500
Forestry, camp, shop, supplies	3,500
Kitchen	500
Shop rent	500
Helicopter	5,000
Boats	500
Travel, meals, promotion, view	1,400
Office and administration	2,100
Muskeg tractor	6,600
Equipment dep/repair (quad, camp, etc.)	3,000
Insurance	2,000
Interest	1,200
Radios	600
Sub total	**49,955**
Total wages and expenses	**211,719**
Net profit	**9,016**

*WCB: Workers' Compensation Board; UIC: Unemployment Insurance Commission; CPP: Canada Pension Plan.

EXHIBIT 7

ORGANIZATION CHART

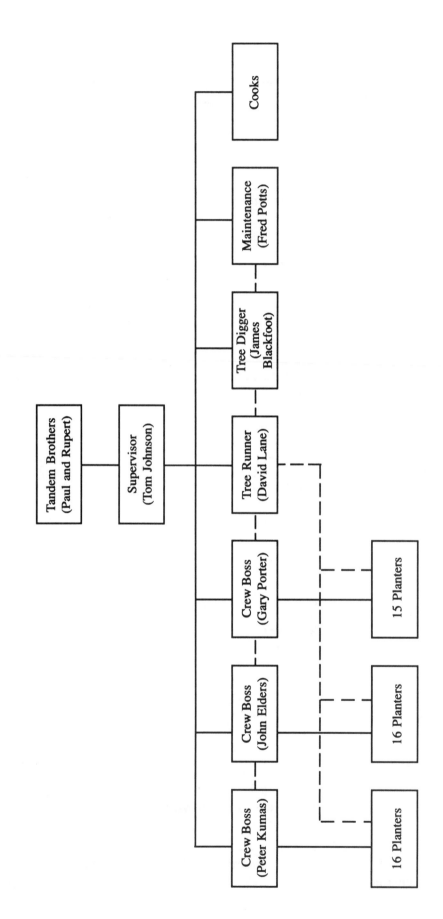

Who's Navigating?

By Julia Pool

The fourth time's a charm. That's what United Airlines labor leaders were saying a few months back, reminiscing about how only one year ago in July they pulled off the largest employee stock ownership deal in history. The lessons they've learned offer a compelling look at the challenges of creating a genuine employee ownership culture.

It took seven years and three failed attempts before the Chicago-based airline's eighty-thousand employees wrapped up an agreement that insures no layoffs for six years, employee presence on parent company UAL Corp.'s board, and control over 55 percent of UAL's common stock. The cost to employees was $4.9 billion in concessions and work rule changes over six years, a wage freeze that lasts at least three years, and other changes. According to both management and labor leaders who helped structure the deal, the employee stock ownership plan (ESOP) is a smashing success.

But some rank-and-file workers complain that this ESOP represents anything but "employee ownership," claiming management has yet to put into place a significant employee involvement structure. The largest group of employees at United, the flight attendants, refuses to take part in the ESOP; two pilots and a mechanic filed a class action suit in April claiming workers are grossly overpaying for their shares—about $40 a share more

than its trading price the day the deal was signed; and the FBI is conducting a criminal investigation into whether pilots union advisers engaged in conflicts of interest when they agreed to accept a total of $45 million in special bonuses if they successfully talked union members into voting for the ESOP.

UAL officials are quick to admit there are plenty of problems yet to be addressed when it comes to integrating employee ownership into the culture of United, the nation's second largest commercial airline. "With a mere nine months under our belts, it is too early to be able to claim that we have achieved an ownership culture," Eileen Sweeney, a UAL spokesperson, told *Employee Ownership Report* earlier this year.

But progress *is* being made. After years of top-down dissemination of information, UAL has established more than one dozen task teams to pull employees into the decision-making process. "Employees have tangible input into the way the company is changing," says Joe Hopkins, a company spokesman. Task forces have thus far

studied issues of employee dependability, communications, fuel conservation, and employee empowerment. And some union members—even a few who originally were against the ESOP—now support it. What's significant, they say, is the genuine effort by both employees and management to work together. In the U.S. airline industry, there has never been anything else like it at a major, unionized airline.

All said, it appears United is off to an impressive start, according to Corey Rosen, executive director of the National Center for Employee Ownership in Oakland, California. "By far, the critical factor in making an ESOP work is how well a company succeeds in getting employees involved in making decisions about their own jobs," he says.

While the jury is still out on UAL, several companies have become quite successful by doing exactly what Rosen is talking about. Take for example Life USA Holding Inc., a life insurance company based in St. Louis Park, Minnesota.

Eight years ago, industry maverick Robert MacDonald started Life USA as the nation's first employee-owned life insurance company. "The real value of employee ownership is direct participation in the company," MacDonald says.

Employee's of Life USA's operating company, Life USA Insurance, own 35 percent of the company. But they're not technically part of an ESOP. Upon joining the firm, employees agree that 10 percent of their salary will go toward buying shares of stock that they would then possess (after an initial public offering of stock in May 1992, new employees put their money toward stock options rather than shares of stock). Traditional ESOPs involve trusts that hold stock on behalf of participating employees.

Regardless of its formal structure, employee ownership has been key to MacDonald's success because he takes it beyond the accounting statement and into actual practice—in small and big ways. Smaller things include an employee entry that has above it the sign "Owners Entrance" and regular "Brunch with Bob" meetings, where non-management owners meet in a boardroom, have lunch, and talk with MacDonald about the company. Larger initiatives include "Owners Month," a recent company-wide event celebrating employee ownership, and the sharing of financial information with employees (something done even before the company went public).

Springfield ReManufacturing Co. takes a similar approach when it comes to involving employees in the management process. Employees of the Springfield, Missouri-based engine rebuilding company are taught by upper management what it means to own and financially maintain a company. Business classes are

offered so everyone can see how each employee plays a role in generating a profit. "In order for us to survive, we all need to be able to think and act like owners," says Jack Stack, president of Springfield ReManufacturing.

Springfield's ESOP began twelve years ago when fourteen employees bought the business from International Harvester Co. in an attempt to save their jobs. Since then, they've hired 716 additional workers and opened 16 more plants.

Through its ownership plan, the company contributes shares of stock to an ESOP plan on behalf of employees after each year of their employment. The ESOP owns 34 percent of the company. In return, all employees are encouraged to share ideas on how to make the company more efficient, and if the idea is beneficial, they receive a cash bonus.

Another way to gauge the success of a company's employee ownership plan is to take a gander at its financial results. UAL, for example, has shown significant improvement in its financial results since it started its ESOP last July. Its stock price has gone up nearly 50 percent, profits have increased and costs and debt have decreased. But the airline industry overall has seen a tremendously strong year, in large part due to low jet fuel prices and the ability in recent years to refinance existing debt at new, lower interest rates.

Roughly 25 percent of the financial gains at UAL this year is attributable to the company's

ESOP, says Paul Karos, an airline analyst with the securities firm of CS First Boston. The ESOPs influence is reflected in tangible changes that have been made in the efficiency and quality of service UAL is providing, he adds. "It has not made or broke them yet."

On the other hand, Life USA wouldn't have grown as quickly as it did without its employee ownership plan. Today, the company employs four hundred people at its main office and works with sixty-five thousand agents in the field. It generates more than $275 million in annual revenue and expects to net a profit in excess of $20 million in 1995. Springfield reports the same type of success. Since its ESOP began in 1983, the company's annual revenue has grown from $16 million to about $104 million.

Stack says he owes his firm's financial success to the fact that most of his employees understand Springfield's finances, and want to use that knowledge to make more money for the company, and thus, for themselves.

Source: This originally appeared in *Business Ethics,* September & October 1995

Estella Rios:
Performance Problems at the Toll Authority

By Michael Thompson, Brigham Young University

When the personnel director of the Toll Authority (TA) asked Estella Rios to take the position of supervisor in the accounting unit, she was delighted. Rios had just finished her fourth year with the TA and was pleased with her progress. She had spent her first two years on a computer aided design project, and had subsequently moved to a design unit team where she helped the deputy commissioner of the TA handle all the intergovernmental transactions necessary to issue bonds for financing new state road and bridge construction. Rios work had brought her into contact with many people in other state agencies and private firms in the northeast. She had even worked with people in the governor's office. The new offer was concrete evidence that her career was taking off.

Rios was 31 years old. A second-generation Hispanic whose parents emigrated from the Dominican Republic to New York City when she was 10, Rios was bright and ambitious. After earning a degree in civil engineering from a state university in New York, she worked for two years in the design unit of New York State's Department of Transportation (DOT), where she made good use of her recent training in computer aided design. She loved the technical side of things, but also had ambitions to become involved in management. The work force at DOT was mature (average age 49) and 81 percent white male. Rios knew she would have to earn further credentials if she wanted to move into management, and she had completed half of an executive M.B.A. program at a college in Albany when she was offered the toll authority job in another northeastern state. Although Rios had felt some misgivings about leaving DOT and going to a different state government, and had not been happy about interrupting her work on the MBA, she had felt that the move would be a step up.

Rios didn't take long to say she'd be happy to transfer to the TA's accounting unit. The promotion meant a 13 percent pay increase and a little more flexibility in her schedule. Rios would now be on the Financial Division's management team, which would give her a bigger window on the organization and its environment. At 31, Rios was eager to do and know more. This new job looked like a solid opportunity.

A Sketch of the Toll Authority

The TA was created as a nonprofit, financially self-supporting organization by the state legislature to serve the public. It collected all the revenue from state toll roads and bridges and used its revenue to build and repair roads and bridges and supplement federal and country funding for infrastructure projects within the state. Through a legislative quirk, the TA also handled the retirement funds for all 960 of its employees. The retirement funds alone exceeded $230 million. TA employees earned slightly more than their counterparts in state agencies and slightly less than their counterparts in the private sector. Most TA employees felt that job security was good and that benefits were excellent; in addition most regarded their jobs as acceptable in terms of workload and quality of work life.

The accounting department kept track of the TA's money, held the retirement funds in high interest-bearing accounts, and occasionally embarked on a bond issue to raise funds for capital investment projects. The

TA also audited the local toll offices across the state. The TA was frequently under fire from the state legislature, which believed the TA should hand the management of its revenues over to the State Division of the Budget, an organization that the legislature could influence directly. Thus the work of the accounting unit was vital to the TA's success not only financially but also politically, since internal financial problems could result in a loss of political legitimacy.

Rios would be supervising the work of fourteen accountants and auditors—seven in the central office, four in the northern regional office, and three in the southern regional office. The accounting unit kept track of all revenue and expenditures and made sure the TA's money was invested to ensure a maximum rate of return. Some

Source: NACRA. The author thanks Daniel Hecht for assistance on an early draft of the case, which was written solely for the purpose of stimulating student discussion. Data are based on field research; all events are real, although the names of organizations, locations, and individuals have been disguised. Faculty members in nonprofit institutions are encouraged to reproduce this case for distribution to their students without charge or written permission. All other rights reserved jointly to the authors and the North American Case Research Association (NACRA). Copyright 1994 by the *Case Research Journal* and Michael Thompson and Daniel Hecht.

of the small "accounts," the little toll bridges in the state's southern townships, were the hardest to manage. Rios was told that some of those townships had, over the years, been known to skim a portion of the revenue by keeping it off the books. Field audits conducted by TA accountants were supposed to detect problems and prevent irregularities, but the audits were not always effective. The local field offices were protective of their turfs, and auditors from the central office were not welcomed with open arms. Joanna Rice, personnel director at the TA, hoped that Rios would be able to improve relations with the field.

Although Rios had confidence in her abilities (her previous job with the TA had made her familiar with the TA's accounting and auditing procedures and she had a strong quantitative background), she knew that a few eyebrows had been raised when she was brought in to supervise the accounting unit. In the past, the promotions had always come from within, and a seasoned accountant had been rewarded with the supervisor's position. Rios, who was not an accountant, knew that many would feel she had gotten the job because she was a female minority. It was no secret that the TA had been criticized by the Governor's Office of Employee Relations for having a workforce in which minorities and women were underrepresented. She knew she would have to earn her legitimacy with good performance.

Enter Ted Barlow

After about a month on the job—in early January—Rios faced her first real challenge: Glenn Streck, director of the financial unit at The Dunns Memorial Bridge, called Rios to complain about the way the team leader for the annual audit of the Bridge's offices had conducted the audit. The team leader's name was Ted Barlow, a name that would surface often as the months went by.

Barlow's Background

Barlow, who worked as field auditor and funds accountant in the central office, had joined the Toll Authority during a time of expansion. Because salaries in the private sector were slightly higher, competition for qualified accountants and auditors had always been difficult for the TA. For entry-level accountants, the state required a bachelor's degree, with at least 18 hours of credit in accounting courses. Most of the accountants in Rios's unit were field auditors, and most had secured their jobs by going to night school and studying accounting. Barlow, who had graduated from the state university system with an accounting major, came to the TA with four years' experience with a manufacturing company. He was very bright, and fundamentally competent.

Despite his credentials, Barlow was the most controversial and talked-about person in the unit, and he had a reputation for being to being close to controversial issues. Even his friends in the agency said that his work had sometimes suffered in the past because of all the union issues he became involved with. Four years before Rios came to the TA, Barlow had been elected as an officer in the Public Employees Federation, the union that represented most TA employees. Barlow served in that position for two years. In his first year, the TA set a new record for the number of grievances filed by employees: 26. The annual average was 16. No one accused Barlow of being directly responsible for the high number of grievances, but he was heavily involved in some of the hearings that took place as part of the grievance process. Some colleagues complained to the Personnel Department that Barlow was leaving agency work unfinished because of his union-related activities. The Personnel Department tried to deal with the issue diplomatically, not wanting to upset the already strained relationships between union officers and the agency's management. Eventually, the storm passed, without anything having been said to Ted Barlow or other members of the union committee. Although some TA workers regarded Barlow as a champion of employee rights and interests, others were highly critical, claiming that he was sometimes "disloyal" to the agency. At the time of Rios's promotion, Barlow was no longer an officer of the union, but he remained closely connected to the union leadership and was frequently consulted on labor-management issues.

The Dunns Memorial Bridge Incident

The general thrust of Streck's complaint about Barlow's handling of the Dunns Memorial Bridge audit was that he was guilty of "insensitivity and pushiness." Specifically, Streck claimed that Barlow had given the unit insufficient lead time to prepare for the audit and then he asked for almost random information, giving Streck's people little opportunity to explain themselves.

The day after hearing Streck's complaint, Rios talked to Barlow about the incident:

Rios: Ted, I received a call yesterday from Glenn Streck at Dunns Memorial. He had some concerns about the way the field audit was handled. In fact, he was pretty unhappy about it. He said that your team had given his people very little notice and then pushed them through the audit. He didn't think you had given him enough opportunity to answer questions and explain things. I was pretty concerned about his call.

Barlow: Well, let me help you understand what's happening. Streck's office isn't covered with glory to begin with. He has been written up twice in three years for being out of compliance with some basic stuff, and, yeah, he gripes about not having enough notice. We go out of our way to not give those people much notice, because they will cook the books if they have time. We like to come in fast and hard and find out what's going on. I let him answer our questions. He oughta buy me a beer

for not writing him up. We found some stuff. The books looked better this year so we gave them some verbal advice and reprimands and let it go. Gee, talk about getting off easy. Streck should have called you and said me and my team were the greatest.

Rios: Well, OK. I just hope we weren't out of line in any way. We're under heavy scrutiny, and our personnel director keeps asking me what I'm doing to improve relations with the field offices.

Barlow: It's going OK. We have to keep a grip on these characters or we'll have real scandals on our hands. Believe me, it's not all bad when the field offices complain about the way we treat them. We get too cozy and we're not doing our jobs.

Barlow's responses seemed reasonable and intelligent to Rios, and she felt reassured.

The Queller Turnpike Incident

In mid-February Barlow's name came up again, this time in a memo from the office of the state controller. Barlow was in charge of revenue management for the Queller Turnpike. An audit by the controller's office showed that funds had been left in lower interest-yielding accounts and had run up a shortfall of $34,788 in a 2-year period compared with what an optimal investment policy would have returned. The memo included a reprimand for such "negligent handling of the public trust," and, of course, a copy was sent to the TA's commissioner, Hyde Randall. Fortunately, this incident escaped the notice of the local media; however, by the end of the month, the problem had cost Rios more than one sleepless night. Rios again called Barlow in and had a chat about the Queller account. Barlow responded that the TA must take some responsibility for the problem. The workload of the accountants was too heavy, and their responsibilities too diverse. Barlow put it this way:

> You have to realize that this kind of thing has happened before and it'll happen again. We have too many things to do. We do the field audits on all the offices in the state, and at the same time, they keep a gun at our heads and tell us we have to manage the retirement funds. The financial markets are volatile. It would take a couple of full-time fund managers to stay of top of where the money ought to be each minute. If I didn't have access to some pros in New York City who give me free advice, we would do a lot worse on where the money should go when the markets change direction. Listen, I'm not the one that could be left out to dry on this issue. The TA isn't exercising "due diligence" in managing retirement funds. If you want details, I can supply them.

Rios's instincts told her that the Queller incident might be symptomatic of deeper problems, so she decided to keep careful records. She felt strongly that Ted might be trying to cover up for his own poor perfor-

TO: Ted Barlow

FROM: Estella Rios

DATE: February 20, 1993

SUBJECT: Notification of Substandard Work

I have talked with you previously about problems with your work. Again, your work has caused problems with our audits and reports with the state. Your work on the Queller account has caused a $34,788 shortfall in interest revenue.

If there are any more troubles with your work, as one who must account to the citizens for their money, I will have to take action to protect those resources. Please take more care. If you are having any problems with your workload or assignments, please come in and talk to me about them.

mance. He always seemed to have reasonable explanations about complaints or problems, but Rios was becoming uncomfortable. Immediately after her conversation with Barlow about the Queller funds, Rios sent a follow-up memo to him and put a copy in the file. She also made a note to herself to pursue the issue with various managers at the TA. The memo, the text of which follows, did not mention any of the points Barlow made in his defense. Rios was not convinced that his defense was valid.

The Whistle Blower Incident

Rios decided to do some research on Barlow's history. She began talking to people and looking through the files. The personnel file on Ted Barlow recorded an incident Rios had heard about, but never understood. About a year earlier, the TA had received an unfavorable

report during an audit by the State Controller's Office. Some money in the employee retirement fund had been mismanaged, resulting in an estimated loss of $160,000 of potential interest revenue. No funds had been stolen. As in the Queller case, the loss had resulted from keeping funds in low interest-bearing accounts for too long. Before the organization had time to react, the story was leaked to the press.

There were strong indications that Ted Barlow was responsible for the press leak. The journalist who had written the article about the mismanagement of funds was a good friend of his, and Ted had been quoted as making some "very critical comments" about the situation. Of the employees with knowledge of the information that had been leaked, only Barlow had continual access to the facts of the case as it developed. All of the others had been on vacation at least part of the time.

The personnel file contained a report by one of Barlow's coworkers claiming that the day before a newspaper report appeared revealing some of the facts of the case, Ted had been overheard talking on the telephone about those same facts. This sequence, as well as the knowledge that Ted was the only one with full access to the facts, were enough to convince Ted's supervisor that there was a strong case against Ted. Although the supervisor never confronted Ted about the situation directly, he wrote a memo to file in which he stated his belief that Barlow was the source of the leak. When someone from another unit asked Ted about the rumors, Ted neither confirmed nor denied them. He simply said, "Whatever you think is fine, but you can't prove anything in a court of law, and you and I both know that the law protects anybody who makes this kind of stuff public anyway."

Even if Ted's responsibility for the press leak could be substantiated, he would probably be shielded from any disciplinary action by state and federal legislation protecting whistle blowers. In fact, Rios suspected that the report of the press leak incident included in Barlow's file was illegal and that Barlow could take action against the TA for the material in the file. Rios was not even sure how the documents got there. She learned by talking to people in the legal office that top management had told people to "stay away from Barlow and take no recriminating actions."

She made a note to discuss the issue with the Toll Authority's chief counsel. She also had some frustration about the TA's role in the situation. Commissioner Randall was outraged that the problem had been made public before he had a chance to investigate it, but Rios felt that such problems probably *should* become public before all the damage could be controlled by internal management. She also had the impression that the TA, while not "punishing" Barlow, probably shunned him, at least unofficially. That behavior was hardly professional or helpful. It provided support for Barlow's apparent opinion that the leadership of the TA could not be trusted.

Barlow and the Toll Authority System

Rios, however, was more worried about Barlow's use of information than she was about the TA's use of information. Barlow had been heard to say that he knew "where the bodies were buried around here," implying that if some kind of action were taken on his performance, he could retaliate because he knew where people were vulnerable. This threat concerned Rios, whose knowledge of the TA's history was so limited. Barlow seemed to Rios to take a very political view of issues. For him, controversies seemed reducible to who had power. Those who had power would prevail over whose who did not.

Rios also wondered about the truth of Barlow's charges that employees in other units were "milking their jobs" and doing substandard work. She wanted to make her unit more results-oriented, and she wanted to reward merit. But how did her standards compare with those of other departments? She wasn't sure. When she looked at Barlow's work, he did seem to have real performance problems, but when she talked to him about his performance, he blamed the system for most of his difficulties, saying that the system set people up to fail or make mistakes. The other accountants had neither Ted's problems nor his strengths. They seldom discussed the big issues he brought up. They audited the field offices, managed the funds, and turned in their reports. They made fewer mistakes, and were more positive about the system, but Rios felt they had fewer ideas on how to improve the process.

Apparently, Barlow really did know a lot about state government and the informal network of relationships and information that people used to get work done and make decisions. Some of his claims might have been bluster, but some had been substantiated by the homework Rios did. People stepped lightly around Barlow. He intimidated them with his technical knowledge (most people, even in the accounting department, were only slightly computer literate) and he had an uncanny memory for details. He also seemed to know at least half the people in the state legislature. In the spring of 1992, the TA's legal staff was officially reprimanded by the Division of the Budget for their handling of a suit brought against the TA by a private contractor. While working on a new bridge, the contractor's son had been killed by a car. (The TA had responsibility for traffic control on all toll road and bridge construction sites.) When the suit was filed, the response from the TA's Legal Department had been slow, which only made matters worse. During this time, Barlow had told several people in the TA about conversations between the contractor and staff members in the attorney general's office. From all Rios could determine from her own sources, his reports were accurate and current. Ted Barlow had an effective information network.

Barlow and Routine Job Performance

As the weeks and months passed, Ted Barlow continued to be a challenge to Rios. More performance problems surfaced. Rios, a stickler for deadlines, didn't like getting work handed to her at the last minute. During her first month as supervisor she had shortened the deadline for monthly audit reports by two days. She wanted more time to review them before passing them upstairs. Barlow, however, continued to get his reports in at the last minute, usually only one day before Rios had to send them on. In addition, although

Barlow's reports were usually insightful and provided helpful recommendations and posed thought-provoking questions, they were quickly written and sometimes lacked basic details. Rios had a strong personal reaction to what she considered "inconsiderate and unprofessional behavior" on Ted's part. She spotted Ted one afternoon by the water cooler and told him he had to be more careful about deadlines. Ted put the blame on people from the field, claiming that they were often late in giving him the information he needed to complete the reports. Rios became irritated and impatient.

In January, her first month on the job, Rios had met with Barlow to discuss his "insensitive, pushy" work on the Dunns Bridge audit. Rios recorded the date and subject of the meeting in her planner. The Queller case hit the fan in February. In March, another monthly audit report had prompted a phone call from the controller's office complaining that a small section of the data was missing. Later in March, Ted had missed an important meeting with people from the accounting office of the Jameson Turnpike. Rios covered for him. Ted also missed a March meeting with a productivity team from another agency; his excuse was that the team had not set up a definite appointment time with him. Rios noticed that he was clearly unprepared for a monthly briefing in early April. In addition, Ted could be disruptive in meetings. Always talkative and verbally aggressive, recently he had been even

more aggressive, trying to dominate discussions more often and growing impatient when decisions did not go his way. Rios often agreed with the positions he took, but was frustrated by his lack of diplomacy.

Barlow's performance record was not totally negative; it also contained some pluses. In his file was a February letter from Grace Hendricks, a manager at the State Insurance Fund, thanking Ted for his "very professional handling" of an audit conducted on another state agency, an audit that required special cooperation from the TA. When the governor's office sent a consulting team to interview people in public agencies and identify new ideas for streamlining work and improving services, Barlow, according to the team leader, came up with better suggestions than anyone else interviewed at the TA.

Another plus concerned Ted's training of a new accountant during the first quarter. Rios's brief chat with the new employee revealed a positive assessment of Barlow's work and his knowledge of accounting and auditing procedures. No one disputed Barlow's technical proficiency. He had been one of the first auditors to take a laptop computer into the field to conduct an audit, and he was often the person audit teams conferred with on technical problems.

Rios had no doubts about Barlow's abilities, but she felt that he was currently running on intelligence and experience, not on consistency and motivation. The accounting unit had recently added three people to its staff, and Rios had been instrumental in getting the new hires. The new employees often conferred with Barlow on technical issues, and Rios was worried about his influence on them. She knew his advice and expertise were solid, but feared that the negative effect of his example and attitude would outweigh any positives.

Insights from the Field

In April, Rios was faced with the task of submitting her unit's performance evaluations, due at the end of the month. The other thirteen ratings were not going to be too difficult, but Ted Barlow's was. Rios decided to get some input from Barlow's coworkers, and chose the five who knew him best, the members of his audit team. Following are the points made by Barlow's coworkers that Rios thought most relevant to the case.

1. Ted was a "knowledgeable guy" and "very bright," but his work was "spotty." Sometimes his audits were thorough, and sometimes sloppy. As one coworker said, "On a good day, Ted is as sharp as anyone in the unit; on a bad day, he would help everyone by staying home. Fortunately, he still has more good days than bad days." (Three of the five team members were surprised that

Ted had not had some kind of disciplinary action taken against him.)

2. The past supervisor was nice, but not strong-willed enough to try to change Ted's habits, which had been developed over years under weak supervision. It was easier to look the other way, at least in the short run. People *had* looked the other way, and as a consequence, the unit seemed to have lost a sense of mutual accountability. One employee said, "I don't think we care enough about each other and our work to really hold one another accountable."

3. Rios was clearly perceived as more "results oriented" than the former supervisor had been. Three employees said that they sensed pressure was mounting in the organization to improve performance and prevent costly errors, but this new emphasis would require better management and lots more feedback on how people were doing in their jobs.

4. Everyone agreed that Ted had been a good contributor "at times" to the TA and that he frequently provided valuable technical information, but that over the past 6 months his work had been noticeably weak.

5. Ted had never raised the issue of personal problems, but the word in the department was that he was going through an ugly divorce and custody

battle. Ted was known as a guy who liked to have a drink after work, and sometimes at lunch. Two people volunteered that Ted had recently returned pretty "high" from a birthday luncheon for a friend in another unit, and that the other times he seemed to be "under the influence" while at work.

6. Shortly before Rios's arrival, Barlow had taken all of his accrued sick leave over a 2-month period, but several people reported that Barlow had been seen around the community during that time "functioning well."

Time to Decide

Although Barlow's coworkers had not explicitly said so, Rios had the impression that Barlow was drinking heavily on a regular basis. The drinking issue was a particularly troublesome one. Substance abusers in the public sector had more protection than those in the private sector. For example, the Supreme Court had ruled that federal employers can only dismiss an alcoholic "who refuses treatment, or repeatedly fails in treatment." No one, to Rios's knowledge, had ever broached the issue with Barlow. She suspected that if drinking were affecting Barlow's performance, she had a legal, as well as ethical, responsibility to take the initiative and offer help through the Toll Authority's employee assistance program. On the other hand, she was wary about how to approach Barlow. He knew the law and the TA's culture better than she did. If she handled things wrong, Barlow might be able to take legal action.

Very soon Rios would have to submit formal performance evaluations on all the workers under her supervision, including Barlow. The TA's policy was to dismiss employees who received overall ratings of under 2.3, unless there were extenuating circumstances. Unit managers, such as Estella Rios, had the authority to set up short-term periods of probation for employees who received unsatisfactory ratings, but these arrangements had to be approved by the division manager. Unit managers were not allowed to dismiss permanent salaried employees. They could recommend dismissal, but the action had to be taken by the director of personnel. Barlow had just completed his fifth year with the TA. His performance ratings for the previous four years are listed in Table 1. (The TA hired new employees in May, which meant that they were not given a performance evaluation until they had been on the job for a year.) Average ratings for TA employees correlated with their tenure are given in Table 2.

Not only did Rios have to decide what rating to give Barlow, but, as required by the TA, to write a memo to him explaining the rational behind the rating given. The performance evaluation for Ted Barlow was the most difficult task that Rios had faced in her new position.

TABLE 1
Summary of Ted Barlow's Performance Ratings for the Years 1989-1992

| | Categories | | | | | | |
Year	#1	#2	#3	#4	#5	#6	Avg.
1989	3	3	4	3	2	3	3
1990	3	3	3	3	3	3	3
1991	3	3	4	3	3	3	3.1
1992	3	3	4	3	3	3	3.1

Scale: Rating of 1 = unacceptable
         Rating of 5 = ideal
Categories:
1. Level of knowledge in required field
2. Effectiveness in working with others
3. Degree of initiative and self-directedness
4. Consistency and dependability in doing quality work
5. Willingness to share skills and information
6. Overall effectiveness

TABLE 2
Average TA Employee Ratings Correlated with Number of Years with Company

Year	Average Overall Rating	% in Unacceptable Range
10	4.2	0
9	4.1	0
8	4.2	0
7	4.1	0
6	4.1	0
5	3.9	2
4	3.6	0
3	3.5	4
2	3.3	17
1	2.9	26

Trading Places: A New Way to Break Down Old Barriers

by Marty Duhatschek, Simmons Juvenile Products. Member ASQC.
and Dan Stoelb, Simmons Juvenile Products. Member ASQC.

During a recent team meeting at Simmons Juvenile Products, members turned to the subject of justifying an additional truck driver for the third shift. One team member responded, "I'd like to see the superintendent try to drive on third shift for a while. I bet we'd be getting another trucker the next day." The idea of trading places fired up the team's imagination, and it spent the remainder of the meeting coming up with a plan that incorporated a dream almost every factory worker has had at one time or another—a chance for the boss to walk a mile in his or her shoes.

This team meeting wasn't the typical complaint session that might be heard at some organizations. The cornerstone of the total quality management (TQM) program at Simmons has been teams, and they have accomplished several significant projects for this London, WI, furniture manufacturer: designing and implementing a computerized racking system for parts staged between operations; cutting drying time from 12 hours to four hours on finished products by adding a kiln in the packing department; and eliminating time-consuming manual operations in the repair department by purchasing a new detail sander. Because of their winning track record, the teams' ideas are taken seriously.

The program begins

A simple program was mapped out. Every month, several managers and shop employees would be randomly selected to trade places for one day. The first half of the day, the shop employees would train a manager to work on a shop-floor position. The second half of the day, a shop worker would be shown the other side of making the business work.

The team anticipated three benefits that would occur with the trading places plan:

1. Mutual understanding would increase on both sides of the labor pool.
2. Managers would gain hands-on experience in day-to-day problems and see how shop policies work.
3. Shop employees would understand the reasons behind management's decisions.

The next month, the plan began. The vice president of operations inspected case goods before they were boxed, the vice president of manufacturing checked lumber for defects on the cutting line, and the second shift paint-line workers trained the plant manager as a booth sprayer. Shop employees sat in on meetings and became more aware of how and why decisions were made.

The team believed it was important for the plan to begin with top management's participation in the first month. This made a big impression in the shop. It also set an example for the rest of management.

Positive results

Six months later, office and shop employees have had enjoyable and even profitable experiences from trading places. Both sides have said, "This job is a lot harder than it looks." One manager, who rarely spent time in the plant's rough mill, now has a working knowledge of how things operate and feels comfortable asking questions when he visits. An assembler in the crib department has a computer-aided design drawing of a crib hanging on the wall near his station; he designed it while working in the design department for a day. While laying up dresser tops to be glued, the purchasing agent found a bill of material that didn't look right. His discovery of the error resulted in substantial savings.

Although barriers will occur, a trading places program is easy to adapt to most work environments. The following recommendations will help it succeed:

• Don't force employees into the rotation if they do not want to participate. They may choose to take part later after discussing the results with co-workers who have participated.

• Don't trade places for more than one day every four months. It is difficult for managers to take a full day "off" from their daily responsibilities.

• Don't expect employees to learn everything about another job in four hours. Some jobs are very complicated. In some operations, it might be better for the workers to just explain to the employee what they are doing or have him or her do a quality check of their work.

• Get feedback from both participants. They can offer useful suggestions.

Although implementing a TQM system can be difficult, it was easy for Simmons to put together the trading-places program. And it has been successful: Bonds between management and shop personnel have been created that could not have been formed otherwise. Learning about another employee's responsibilities and working with that person, if only for one day, reminds employees that they are on the same team and that the work of all employees is necessary to serve the customer.

Plans for the future

Where will Simmons go with this program in the future? There are plans to offer the trading places program to suppliers and customers. Several operators on the cut line are already looking forward to bumping elbows with the sawmill suppliers.

What other benefits has Simmons experienced since implementing the trading places program? There is another trucker on third shift now!

Source: This originally appeared in *Quality Progress*, February 1996

CASE 10
INTERNATIONAL INFORMATION LTD.

By Craig Robbins and Professor James A. Erskine

It was July, 1994, and Craig Robbins, founder of International Information Ltd., was back in his hometown of Bogota, Columbia, following his first year of MBA studies at the Western Business School in Canada. He spent his first three days reviewing the company's operation and listening to key employees. He was surprised and disturbed by what he found: declining sales, weakening financial health, and a number of key people poised to leave the company.

COMPANY BACKGROUND

International Information (I.I.) was located in Bogota, a city of 6.5 million people, and the most important financial and industrial city in Columbia (see Appendix A). I.I. handled subscription sales and distribution of a number of foreign publications to both subscribers and newsstands throughout Columbia, and in some cases acted as an advertising sales representative. In 1994, I.I. represented The Wall Street Journal (WSJ), The New York Times, The International Herald Tribune, USA Today, The Financial Times, as well as a well known weekly magazine. Recently, I.I. had successfully introduced a second widely read American weekly magazine by selling bulk subscriptions to major corporations. The company also distributed approximately 500 different magazines and newsletters for a British dealer.

Although the core of the business was subscription sales, for which the company earned a commission or a spread, distribution fees were expected to become an important revenue-generating item.

When possible, I.I. protected itself from competitors by signing contracts with major publishers. Although very few of these contracts guaranteed I.I. exclusivity, it was common practice amongst North American and European publishers not to sign more than one contract per geographical area.

Relations with the Columbian government were very important. Every four years, special advertising sections promoted Columbia's image to foreign investors through the patronage of public companies and major private corporations in key publications like WSJ. Since this effort took only six to eight months and advertising rates for these types of publications were high, the 10% to 25% commission on all ads placed in the supplements was a fundamental part of I.I.'s long-term revenue planning.

The subscription business consisted of companies that provided subscriptions for their executives, as well as personal subscriptions delivered at home. Another important market segment was the newsstands, which included drugstores, hotels, and bookstores. Some publishers' agreements specified certain acceptable percentages for returns. In other cases, particularly when publications were obtained from international distributors, returns were not allowed and I.I. needed to keep careful track of sales statistics by newsstand, or lose money. The company paid distributors an established fee per magazine/newspaper delivered, and since the price of a magazine in a newsstand could represent as much as 60% of a delivery person's daily salary, strict inventory and distribution controls were required.

When I.I. acted as a representative for advertising sales, its role was the same as an advertising agency's. This role included knowing the editions, ad prices and potential customers, as well as helping design the ads if needed (usually the client had the art work created by its ad agency), and splitting the commissions with the advertising agencies, when the clients were brought by them. This side of the business would have no overhead assigned and would become possible only after a change in government occurred in the fall of 1994. Publishers' statistics showed that average advertising expenditures in foreign publications were significantly higher in other Latin American countries than in Columbia.

The market for I.I.'s products was restricted to those who read English, estimated to be less than 10% of the Columbian population. Although more than 70% of I.I.'s customers were located in Bogota, cities like Cali, Medellin, Cartagena, and

Source: This case was prepared by Craig Robbins under the supervision of Professor James A. Erskine solely to provide material for class discussion. The case is not intended to illustrate either effective or ineffective handling of a managerial situation. Certain names and other identifying information may have been disguised to protect confidentiality. This material is not covered under authorization from CanCopy or any Reproduction Rights Organization. Any form of reproduction, storage or transmittal of this material is prohibited without the written permission of the Western Business School. Permission to reproduce or copies may be obtained by contacting Case and Publication Services, Western Business School, The University of Western Ontario, London, Ontario, N6A 3K7, or by calling (519) 661-3208 or faxing (519) 661-3882. Copyright 1995 The University of Western Ontario. Revision date 1995/04/21

Barranquilla also had enough industry and business activity to be attractive markets. All I.I.'s direct employees, including telemarketers and sales people, were located in Bogota.

Competition was virtually non-existent for foreign, English newspapers, since I.I. was the only company that guaranteed reliable subscription deliveries just one day after publishing date. Some bookstores had people who eventually sold them newspapers, but not daily. Magazines represented by I.I. faced traditional competitors who represented other publications. In general, competitors representing magazines had stronger, better trained and more permanent sales forces. Some had also established a presence in the four major cities and were already moving into the smaller ones, using franchise agreements with local dealers. The local magazines, some of which used second copyright agreements with foreign publications in order to translate their articles to Spanish and publish them, had gained many subscribers in the last five years. Very recently, The Wall Street Journal had signed an agreement with a major Columbian newspaper to publish three pages of translated articles daily in a section called The Wall Street Journal Americas.

Specialized magazines were another market trend. A former I.I. sales manager had quit his job and had gone into business by himself importing specialized publications. Although his company sales were significantly lower than I.I.'s, figures

showed that there was a potential market for those publications, which required a highly skilled sales force.

News summaries were also sold via fax to big companies and multinational corporations. These summaries contained news clips from local newspapers and international news agencies and were sent early in the morning from Monday to Friday, to the subscriber's fax machine.

Electronic information systems such as Reuters and Dow Jones Financial Services were also being aggressively introduced in the Columbian market. I.I. had recently failed in representing one of Reuters' major competitors, which had decided to go into the market independently.

CRAIG ROBBINS AND I.I.'S EARLY YEARS

Craig Robbins had started the business as a part-time activity in January, 1981 when he was 19 years old. At that time, his father Oscar had operated a development company in the country for many years, and was approached by The Wall Street Journal to represent them in Columbia. Since it was not in line with his main business, he was not particularly interested. When he was about to refuse the offer, Craig told him that he would do it. He borrowed a desk, a chair and phone at his dad's office, and began to work.

The initial agreement was for 30 copies of the WSJ to be delivered Monday through Friday at the El Dorado International airport in Bogota. Since Craig was still attending his first year of university, he would attend classes in the morning, drive the 40 km from downtown Bogota to the airport and return downtown with the papers, usually by 2:30 p.m. At his father's office, Craig wrapped and labelled the papers and then distributed the 20 subscription copies by foot to his first customers. He left the remaining 10 copies with prospective customers, along with a letter inviting them to become regular subscribers.

After about six months and growth to some 70 subscribers, he realized that other similar products could be represented in the country. As subscriptions started to pick up, delivery was handled by delivery boys on motorcycles and an assistant was hired to keep the administrative routines up to date. Oscar played a key role not only in generating ideas but also in helping establish contacts and writing letters to foreign publishers offering them representation in Columbia.

Craig divided his time between his full-time undergraduate degree in economics, and I.I. In two years I.I. had grown to two part-time employees and two delivery men and represented three different publications. By the end of 1982, Craig decided to take time out of school and devote full time to the business. He spent six months in Canada taking an intensive English course in order to be able to adequately interact with I.I.'s suppliers. As a Canadian citizen born abroad

(his father was born in Canada and had emigrated to Columbia many years before), Craig wanted to become more familiar with the country. During this time, Oscar took charge of the business as a part-time activity. Upon returning to Columbia in June 1983, Craig spent the next 1 1/2 years working exclusively with I.I. During this time, major representations were obtained and the company started growing and gaining a name in the market. New products included The International Hearld Tribune, the distribution of The New York Times (not by contract) and The Economist magazine. Once the business was established, Craig again divided his time between I.I. and school, in order to finish his economics degree. He would go to the office daily, from Monday through Saturday, and finished school not by attending classes, but going only when he had exams.

In 1984, I.I. became incorporated and all family members were included. Oscar had 52% of the shares, since he funded the initial investment (see Exhibit 1).

ORGANIZATION AND OFFICE LAYOUT

Although everyone had specific tasks, cooperation amongst employees was a way of getting things done. Sales were closed by phone by Anna or Craig, without sales or telemarketing people, but based on press ads and direct mail campaigns. Anna acted as secretary and handled distribution, an outside

accountant kept track of the records, and a young computer science student kept the databases updated and printed labels and direct mail promotions. Anna also took care of the finances and supervised all the activities. Distribution was handled by delivery people who were paid according to the number of issues delivered, and reported directly to Anna and Craig.

I.I. had always had a very informal environment. Everybody was called by his or her first name, as opposed to Mr. or Mrs., which was more common in the Columbian marketplace. There were no formal reporting structures except for the family members, who were seen as holding authority over the rest of the employees. Jokes and hard work were combined in the office. Cooperation amongst company members despite their tasks and ranks was a tacit rule. The office layout helped keep all the administrative staff together, sharing tasks and information (see Exhibit 2).

CRAIG ROBBINS 1986-1993

Just after completion of his economics undergraduate degree in September of 1986, Craig left I.I. and joined with his university professor to start up a financial leasing company. Craig had wanted I.I. to become a big company and felt that without rigorous planning it would always be a small family business. Upon failing to convince Oscar to allow him to manage the business that way, he left. He felt that his interests were in conflict with those of his father, who seemed more interested in having a permanent good source of cash for the family and personal needs than in making the company grow.

Although Craig had no contact with I.I.'s day-to-day operations, he maintained a keen interest in watching I.I. develop and kept up with the changes in personnel and the financial health of the business. He also intervened in I.I. when asked for an opinion, or when he saw an opportunity that the business could take advantage of.

In 1993, Craig decided to pursue an MBA. He thought the MBA training would not only give him a broader perspective on several business areas, but would also enable him to do business with North American companies. He felt that, for him, Canada was a good choice and he entered the Western Business School MBA program in September 1993.

INTERNATIONAL INFORMATION LTD. 1986-1993

After Craig left the company, Oscar took charge, although it did not seem to be his first priority. Between 1986 and 1991, the business did well; it grew continuously with the addition of other product lines to the existing ones. However, little emphasis was placed on the administrative structure or on sales and marketing. In 1991, Craig's younger brother, Andrew, graduated with a B.A. in

political science and joined the company as marketing manager. He soon took charge of the administration as well.

Oscar was busy managing two other businesses: a construction company which he had decided to considerably decrease in size after being very active in the market for many years, and a real estate agency. Although they were small businesses, there was enough activity to keep him busy. In the last few years, he seemed to Craig to view the I.I. business as a source of cash, not only for personal purposes but also for funding new business ventures. His involvement in the company was not really in the day-to-day activities, but in setting and maintaining contacts with government and suppliers.

Aside from the family members, only one employee was a professional; another had two years of school left to become a computer engineer. With one exception, administrative staff was composed of women, who lunched together almost every day and sometimes shared social activities outside of the office. Employees worked on five areas: distribution, marketing and sales, customer and supplier relations, accounting and systems. People did not hold titles or positions, but instead developed with time certain areas in which they worked. Nobody had responsibilities or functions assigned; things got done when clients, suppliers or an employee found a need for doing them.

The most respected person in administration seemed to be

Anna, who had joined the company in 1984, and knew the ins and outs of the operation better than anyone. She was often consulted by everyone in order to assist or direct in any task. Although she did not hold any special title, everyone saw this middle-aged woman as a source of cooperation and authority.

In 1992, a new separate sales and telemarketing structure had been created within I.I at the request of an American magazine, in order to comply with the corporate customer service and reporting standards. Sales and telemarketing personnel had been hired from the previous representative, and they brought their expertise and client knowledge to I.I. (see Exhibit 3).

The distribution was carried out by 34 delivery men, four of whom had full-time contracts with I.I. The remaining 30 were paid based on the number of magazines/newspapers distributed. They had no direct supervisor exclusively in charge of distribution, but instead reported to Anna, and to Claire, who handled the magazine's administrative issues. Some delivered only one or two major titles and worked two or three days a week, while others delivered almost every product and worked six days a week.

Claire was 32 years old and had been with I.I. for two years, bringing with her six years' experience in a similar organization. Her knowledge of the customers and products was useful in supporting the telemarketing and sales people, and she always helped to set up the promotion booths at trade shows and special events.

Marketing was done by Andrew, and sales were closed by salespeople or telemarketers. Andrew also had to deal with every area in the organization, since he was seen as its head after coming to the business in 1991. He made bulk sales to big corporations, while small orders were taken by sales people. Andrew spent most of his time dealing with suppliers at the highest level and his work included extensive travelling and public relations. As a major North American publisher put it,

"We are very happy with I.I. as our representative, because we know we have the right people. As you know, we have had many problems in Latin America in the past, when some of our representatives cheated us on commissions. But I.I. is different. They have been in the business for so long that there is no way something like this could happen with them. In addition, Oscar's contacts and marketing experience plus Andrew's conception of the business are a great asset. We invited Andrew to our yearly convention in London this year, and when he was presenting how he closes the big sales for corporations, everybody was listening. They learned so much from him! Of course, we know that sales could be higher, but there is no perfect situation in business."

Sales people were paid a basic salary, plus a 10% commission on new subscriptions and a 6% commission on renewals. If they worked only on a commission basis as most of them did, they had no obligation to go to the office daily or to work exclusively for I.I., and were simply paid a 20% commission on new sales or 10% on renewals. I.I. had three telemarketers and one full-time salesman, plus five part-time sales people, who split their time amongst I.I.'s titles and others from similar companies.

Customer claims and inquiries were handled by whomever answered the phone. The person would look for the information and solve the problem on the phone, or get back to the customer later. Most of the newspaper inquiries ended up on Anna's desk, while inquiries about magazines were very often dealt with by Claire.

Airlines and suppliers of newspapers and magazines were contacted by Anna, whose basic English was sometimes a limitation. However, this middle-aged woman managed to build strong ties with them over time, and therefore always obtained their best cooperation. Anna was also the person to whom the family members (all seven of whom were I.I. partners), delegated personal affairs such as bank accounts, record keeping, tax form due dates, credit card payments, air tickets and travel reservations.

THE SUMMER OF 1994

During his first year of the MBA program, Craig gave a lot of thought to what his professional activity should be upon graduation. Every week he kept in touch with Andrew and Oscar, and was updated on how I.I. was doing. They all agreed that it would be a good idea if Craig went back and worked at I.I. during the summer.

Craig agreed, as he felt that going back to I.I. would be a great opportunity to apply everything he had just learned in his first year of the MBA. "I am going to do some fine tuning in some areas," he thought. "What a privilege: I can walk into the company and pick the areas I am going to concentrate on improving for the next two months." Craig also wondered what he was going to do upon graduation from the MBA program. He was considering pursuing a career in consulting in Columbia for a few years and then going into business on his own. He had some savings set aside for the purpose of establishing such a business. But now he was asking himself why working for somebody else was a good idea. If I.I. was already there, he could possibly work there full time. He was also excited about seeing his family, friends, and Anna.

Craig spent his first evening having dinner with his parents and brothers, and the next day, July 4, 1994, he went to the office at 8 a.m. After saying hello to everybody, he chatted with Anna and the rest of the staff for about 30 minutes. Although the greetings were brief, he felt that the employees saw him as the company again. Fortunately, Oscar and Andrew had agreed that he would have total autonomy to do whatever he considered needed to be improved.

When Andrew finished with an early morning phone call, he invited Craig into his office in order to give him an update on the business. Andrew described the new product lines, but was concerned about administrative issues like delegation, clarity of objectives, and the match between the needs of the partners and the needs of the business. In his opinion, the business had grown too much to be managed like a corner store, but he found no support to do it another way. He told Craig that early in 1994, I.I. had concluded an agreement to represent a well-read American magazine, and would be the only Latin American dealer to handle sales, distribution and advertising for this publication, with three different contracts.

Andrew told him that although I.I.'s product line was excellent, the company had been unable to maintain a permanent sales force and therefore he was handling sales himself. Since he had a lot of things to take care of, he spent his time closing bulk sales for big corporations, and bringing in new products.

He felt a bit frustrated because the partners' requirements had not allowed him to implement a successful cash management system, and that prevented I.I. from growing and consolidating. Although I.I's cash flow was positive, over time it had become tighter. There was no established budgeting process and the company had always been seen as a source of cash for family members. All types of personal expenses from car repairs to phone bills and personal credit cards were usually paid by the company in lieu of distributing dividends. The lack of planning made it difficult to pursue long-term investments or plans. Nevertheless, since subscriptions had continued growing over time and were paid for in advance, I.I. always had a positive cash balance.

Competition was increasing the pressure to spend in advertising and promotion, but there was really no budget for that or for sales force training or bonus programs (see Exhibit 4).

The core of Andrew's time was spent on the phone keeping in touch with publishers, negotiating promotional budgets from them and coordinating booths and contacts at special events like trade shows or conferences. He was also in charge of all administrative issues.

Andrew told Craig that in the last four months he had been spending a lot of time as a member of a presidential campaign committee which dealt with communications and the candidate's image. Moreover, he had just received an offer from a newly appointed cabinet minister to be his full-time advisor, and he was very tempted to go and work in this field for a while. If he took the offer, he would have to leave I.I. in 10 days.

After a three-hour conversation with Andrew, Craig went into Oscar's office. Oscar told him that as far as he knew, everything was going well, with no major changes or problems, but also reminded him that he was not in touch with the day-to-day activities. He had heard about some small operational details that needed to be looked into in the distribution side, but he did not know exactly what they were. He was more concerned about establishing new contacts for the real estate agency, which was an easier business to run, and had better profit margins. Over lunch, Craig wanted Oscar to expand on some of the issues, but very soon the conversation switched to Craig's summer in Europe. After lunch, Craig decided it was time to get firsthand information from the employees.

Back at the office, he called Anna and talked with her for the rest of the afternoon. Anna was overwhelmed by work. Although very seldom did she work after hours, it was clear that not everything was getting done and the range of tasks that she was asked to do varied from solving a customer's complaint, to keeping records of some of I.I.'s bank accounts. When in doubt about what to do, all employees turned to her either for an opinion or an immediate solution. Managing 34 distributors plus all the administrative tasks seemed too much for her. In addition, she felt that no one had time to stop and think what they were doing or how they were doing it, and that I.I. was spending too much effort on new businesses without consolidating the core ones. She felt that although people were working hard, their motivation level was very low, and there were no mechanisms in place to improve performance. Turnover was very high and functions were not clear at all. She had the feeling that the business was already too big to be managed like in the good old days.

At the end of the afternoon, Craig approached the accounting clerk, and asked for time with her first thing next morning. When he told her that he wanted to review the financial statements, she said that the last ones available were from March 1994. They booked an appointment for the next morning. The accounting clerk had been with the company since last May. In the last year and a half, three people had been hired for that job, but none had remained. The accounting clerk kept track of the cash inflows and outflows, and registered the transactions on the original documents. Since the company did not have a computerized accounting system, everything was done manually, and at the end of the month the documents were sent to Leslie, an outside accountant. She input the documents into a PC application, and returned the financial statements to I.I. after two weeks. The Balance Sheet and the Income Statement were usually ready two or three weeks after month closing. No auditing was being performed at I.I. While the accountant reported to Andrew, the clerk reported to both of them.

The accounting clerk also answered the switchboard and transferred the calls across the organization; she took messages when somebody was busy, and also managed the daily cash

payments to the delivery persons.

After having a sandwich in the office going over the numbers, Craig spent the afternoon with Rose. Rose was a 26-year-old part-time computer engineering student, who was in charge of maintaining client databases, printing stickers and renewal forms, and keeping track of newsstand billings and returns. She also handled customer complaints, and occasionally did statistics jobs for Oscar's real estate studies, some of which took up to 45 days. When this happened, her tasks were split amongst the rest of the staff. Craig learned that Rose had applied for a job at Nestle. Although she enjoyed the job very much and liked the company, she was the lowest earner among her classmates. In two years, when she graduated, she wanted to work in IS. Rose worked overtime at least three days a week, and she was not being paid for those extra hours. She had managed to convince Oscar to buy six brand new PCs in order to replace the old ones, but she really had no time to think about installing or maintaining software. As she said:

"I do not mean to interfere in what is none of my business, but I really think I.I. is investing too much in new businesses that take a lot of resources and people's time and are not profitable. I do not know who my boss is and I don't think anybody does. One day I am filling customer complaint forms, and the next one I am calculating statistics for the

real estate agency. Next month I could be doing any small or big task, without knowing why. Customer service and distribution are not being tracked at all, and we are at the mercy of the distributors' words. I am so busy, that I haven't had time to invoice the newsstands for the last four months, and since it is our fault, we have to keep on sending them the publications. I like I.I. and its people. The atmosphere is great. When I came, I was learning a lot, but not anymore. In addition, my salary is the lowest of all my classmates. As much as I like I.I., I might have to leave if the interviews with Nestle go well."

The next day Craig spent the morning observing the distribution process: the 34 delivery men arrived from the airport and amongst themselves sorted out the routes, labelled the publications, wrapped them, and went to deliver them. There was no inventory control and no one kept track of the number of publications each one delivered. When they left, over 240 magazines were left at the office, stacked in a big pile. When Craig asked why those were not being sent to customers or to prospective clients, Anna told him that they were receiving too many, and the newsstands were already getting the quantities they wanted. They had been too busy and had forgotten to ask for a reduction in the shipment.

Just after noon, Craig dropped by Claire's office and listened to her as she said:

"We have good products. The magazines and newspapers are sold because people look for them. We have good and reliable delivery and that is what people want. But sales could be much higher, if only we had more resources, including training. In the last company I worked at, we had sales meetings every morning and that kept people focused. I understand we are bringing in more than 500 different titles for distribution right now, but I would like to see emphasis on main products. Andrew's marketing ability is tremendous: his contacts and the way he sells have allowed us to fulfill the quotas from the publishers, but very little individual sales have been done. As for myself, I was very happy here until two months ago, when I learned that the new accounting clerk has a higher salary than mine. Can you imagine? I have been here for two years and just because she said she was leaving, they raised her salary so that she would stay. I have also wanted to continue my education, but it is so busy here that there is no time and no money for that. I'm keeping my eyes open for a job outside I.I."

By mid-afternoon Craig had a snack while he was waiting for Antonio to come and chat. Antonio was a 25-year-old friend of Andrew who had been with I.I. for the last three months. His duties had nothing to do with newspapers or magazines, but instead he had been hired to manage a new venture at I.I. Craig had learned from Andrew that I.I. was importing book collections from Japan and the U.S. and for that purpose had set up a completely different organization under I.I.'s legal arm. It had been operating in a different office in which a sales manager and 25 sales people were working. They were planning to hire as many as 60 sales people within the next two months. The profile of book sales people was different from that of the newspaper and magazine sales force. In the four months that the book business had been running, no sales had been made, and the inventory held represented about 6% of I.I.'s total sales, without including orders in process. So far, the losses accounted for 8% of I.I.'s yearly sales. Since this was an independent operation, neither Andrew nor Oscar appeared to be on top of things and neither seemed very keen on following up.

Antonio seemed very energetic and enthusiastic, but as he said:

> "I have every intention of doing things right, but this is my first job, and although I have done very well at school, there is a difference between theory and practice. I really need direction in order to perform better and deliver the results that I.I. is looking for. We have been in this book business for four months and we have lost money. I do not know what my job is and I find myself working one day for the book business, the next one for the magazines and the next one I could be doing anything from finding information for the real estate agency, to printing marketing research studies for the development company. I am a professional and I need a job in which I can have some direction and learn at the same time. I think autonomy is great, and here at I.I. everybody has 100% of it. But sometimes it can be too much."

Antonio told Craig that since he was interested in marketing and felt his job at I.I. was not really training him as he expected, he was interviewing with one of the largest world-wide consumer product companies.

CONCLUSION

As Antonio walked out of the office and the evening approached, Anna entered Craig's office. She seemed very happy. "I just learned that you are coming back from Canada for the Christmas break. The timing could not be better. In December, we will celebrate 14 years of the company, as well as my 10th anniversary of being here. But what keeps me more happy is the thought that you will be here with us celebrating those dates as part of the company again. That is the biggest thing to celebrate."

While the overall situation ran through his mind, Craig did not know what to answer. Not only was it possible that he would not be attending the celebration, but there might be no celebration at all if the company was not able to resist the current crisis.

In the long term, the alternative of moving ahead with his initial plans and accepting a job with a consulting company in Columbia was still there. He wondered if it would be wise to reconsider I.I. as part of his future plans. The next two months seemed full of challenges and Craig wanted to get started.

Exhibit 1
I.I. STOCKHOLDERS IN 1994

Name	Relation To Craig	Occupation	Age	Place of Residence	Marital Status	% of Shares
Oscar	Father	President Owner of a construction co.	50	Bogota, Col.	Married	52
Helen	Mother	Housewife	47	Bogota, Col.	Married	8
Nicole	Sister	Graduate Business Student	26	Chicago, Ill.	Married	8
Mark	Brother	Graduate Engineering Student	25	Toronto, Ont.	Married	8
Craig	--------	Under grad Economics Student	22	Bogota, Col.	Single	8
Brian	Brother	Computer Science Student	20	Vancouver, BC	Single	8
Andrew	Brother	Political Science Student	18	Boston, MA	Single	8

Exhibit 2
OFFICE LAYOUT

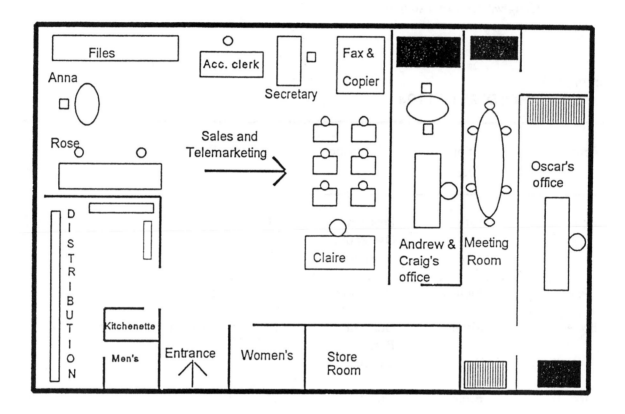

Exhibit 3
ORGANIZATION CHART

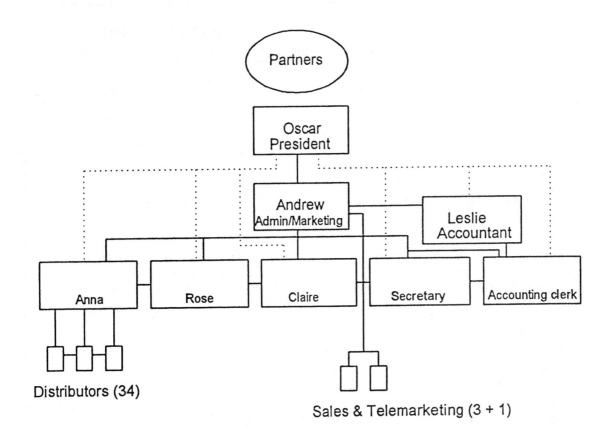

Partners

Oscar
President

Andrew
Admin/Marketing

Leslie
Accountant

Anna

Rose

Claire

Secretary

Accounting clerk

Distributors (34)

Sales & Telemarketing (3 + 1)

Exhibit 4
INTERNATIONAL INFORMATION LIMITED
INCOME STATEMENT ($000's US)

	(Twelve Months Ended)			
	Jun-93		Jun-94	
REVENUE				
Subscriptions	498	79%	675	81%
Newsstands	75	12%	85	10%
Distribution	12	2%	45	5%
Sales Commissions	19	3%	31	4%
Advertising Fees	25	4%	0	0
Total Revenue	629	100%	836	100%
COST OF GOODS SOLD				
Subscriptions	145	23%	204	24%
Newsstands	8	1%	9	1.7%
Distribution	1	0	2	.3%
Sales Commissions	0	0	0	0
Advertising Fees	0	0	0	0
Total Cost of Goods Sold	153	24%	215	26%
GROSS PROFIT				
Subscriptions	353	56%	471	57%
Newsstands	68	11%	77	8%
Distribution	11	2%	43	5%
Sales Commissions	19	3%	31	4%
Advertising Fees	25	4%	0	0
Total Gross Profit	476	76%	621	74%
EXPENSES				
Administrative	104	17%	187	22%
Selling	38	6%	52	6%
Salaries (1)	136	22%	164	20%
Other Partners Expenses	124	20%	143	17%
Communications (2)	67	10%	59	7%
Total Expenses	469	75%	605	72%
EARNINGS BEFORE INTEREST & TAXES	7	1.1%	16	1.9%
Interest Expense	3	0.5%	6	0.7%
PROFIT BEFORE TAX	4	0.6%	10	1.2%
Taxes	1	0.2%	3	0.4%
NET INCOME AFTER TAX	3	0.8%	7	0.8%

Exchange Rate Col./US$ 784 (1993)   818 (1994)
Devaluation Last 12 Months   4%
Inflation (Est.) last 12 Months   26%
NOTES:
(1) Includes partners salaries/fees which account for about 77% of the total
(2) 56% of total is partners related for purposes different than the business

Appendix A
COLUMBIA - COUNTRY ENVIRONMENT 1993 - 1994

a) ECONOMIC

Columbia is the sixth-largest economy in Latin America including Mexico, with a GNP of US$48 billion and an average per capita income of $1.600. In the last four years, the government has instituted a series of structural reforms aimed towards the liberalization of the economy. They included substantial reductions in tariffs, elimination of non-tariff barriers for imports, simplified import and export procedures, and access to foreign exchange markets and foreign investment across most of the sectors in the economy. The expected GDP growth rates for 1994 and 1995 were 5.3% and 6.3% respectively.

The country had a reputation amongst the international financial community for being conservative in terms of its macroeconomic policy.

Columbia played a key role in the G3 group of which Mexico and Venezuela were also part, and within this set of negotiations the three countries had opened their markets. In the Columbian marketplace, 40% of tariff items were duty free, including newspapers, and the average tariff was 12%. Even part of the agricultural sector had been opened to foreign competition under a system of international price bands.

The economy was based on manufacturing, oil, mining and agriculture. The services and financial sector had increasingly gained importance in the last years. Coffee production, which accounted for almost 50% of exports in 1970, represented only 19.7% of exports to major trading partners in 1993, whereas petroleum products accounted for 28.5%.

b) SOCIAL AND POLITICAL

The country was a democracy, with a strong executive power. Unlike parliamentary systems, the president was also the head of state, and presidential elections were held every four years.

The president appointed the cabinet amongst non-Congress members and could introduce bills for Congress approval. The third arm of the power structure was the Judicial, which was currently being transformed in order to fight drug cartels and corruption.

Although there were more than five political parties, only the Liberals and the Conservatives were really strong. The third force was the M19, a guerrilla group that was dismantled and converted into a political party as a result of negotiations with the government, about five years earlier.

Drug processing and trafficking were crucial in the dynamics of the relations between Columbia and the U.S. Since the U.S. had a very strong influence in the economy as a major purchaser of Columbian exports and as the largest foreign investor, usually the business community was eagerly trying to anticipate government measures against drug dealers and U.S. reactions to those, which could sometimes mean changes in trading agreements or preferences, or shifts in the flows of foreign investments.

Guerrilla groups had been around for almost 50 years, but after the breakup of the USSR, many groups had lost their political ideals and turned into delinquency groups. Negotiations had been going on with them for many years, and although not totally successful, over the last years some groups had become political parties. As of December of 1993, 51% of Columbians favoured negotiations with guerrilla groups, whereas 39% wanted strong military solutions to the problem.

c) PEOPLE AND CULTURE

Although drug processing and guerrilla groups represented threats to stability, Columbians worried more about the implications for their daily lives than the political consequences of instability. A major poll conducted at the end of 1993 asked which was the most important problem for Columbians, and insecurity ranked #1, with 26% of answers. Insecurity, violence, and the guerrilla issue together accounted for 50% of the answers. Other issues of concern for Columbians were unemployment (15%), corruption (5%), poverty (4%), inflation and economic conditions (3% each) and drug consumption (3%).

Cultural differences were seen all over the country. While Bogota and three other major cities were considered as business centers, people's practices varied a lot depending on the geographical location of the business. Although hard to generalize, people from the coasts (Atlantic and Pacific) were generally more relaxed and gave a lot of importance to personal relationships and contacts while doing business. In the interior, but outside major cities, agriculture and trading were very informal and sometimes deals were closed by the word of the parties. Bogota was a busy, fast paced city, with intense activity in all areas. Since there were too many cars and traffic jams due to insufficient roads and streets, business people spent a lot of time on their cellular phones, or just going from one appointment to the next. Probably due to its relative closeness to the U.S., Columbian business people loved and managed to keep up with the latest gadgets and technology.

MAP OF COLUMBIA

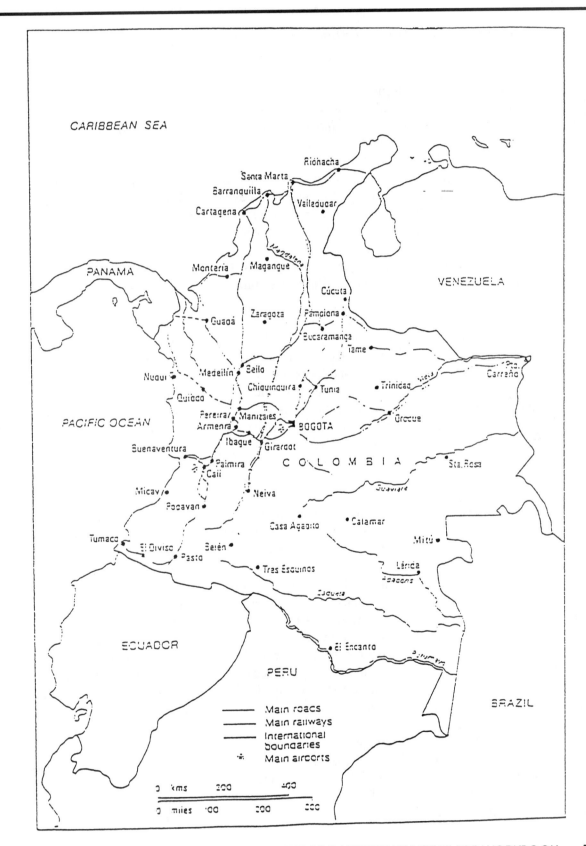

CASE 11
Finova
· · · · · · · ·

Developed by Mark Osborn, Arizona Chamber of Commerce

The $600 billion corporate lending market, traditionally dominated by large banks and finance companies, is highly competitive. With only $5.8 billion in assets, Finova Corporation does not seem to be the type of company that could excel in this market, but they have experienced a 32% annual per-share growth in earnings since 1993. In order to compete with large international institutions and local banks with strong community networks, Finova has developed a specialized niche in markets that are underserved by these traditional financiers. The core of Finova's markets are customers whose financing needs are too small to be of interest to the large financial institutions, but too large and complex for local banks. The strategy has worked for Finova as it gained more than $1.8 billion in new business in 1994.

The company "Finova" is a combination of the words "Financial" and "Innovators." The name is indicative of the culture and atmosphere that helps this small company compete in a market that is not traditionally suited for smaller players. One area in which they are clearly at a disadvantage is the cost of the funds: Finova interest rates are higher than larger banks and financial institutions. One of the mechanisms that is used to reduce costs is to create an innovative compensation system for its sales staff. In most banks, ten to twenty percent of potential loans brought in by the sales staff are accepted for financing. This creates increased costs for internal process and review. At Finova, the sales staff is only compensated for loans that are acceptable to the company and the life of these loans. If a loan defaults, then the sales person loses his or her compensation.

As a result, higher quality prospects are created. Innovation is a significant part of the culture and focus at Finova. Most banks are frequently known for their conservative orientation, but Finova has developed formal mechanisms to reward and increase innovations by its employees. In order to hold on to this standard, Finova must have staff engaged in continual education and have access to a quality communication system. With the goal of an educated and committed work force, Finova offers a generous tuition reimbursement policy for continued education. It includes a partnership with the Karl Eller Graduate School of Management at the University of Arizona.

The focus of the tuition reimbursement program is to provide specific education in the employee's area of interest. With the Eller Graduate School Finova also created another

educational opportunity titled the Finova Institute to build internal cohesion and culture. The Institute does work to improve standard business skills, but it is also designed to build the culture of Finova. Building teamwork and enhancing the interaction within the organization are traditional areas of focus within the Institute. Since Finova is a growing company which has been aggressive in acquisitions of other companies, the Institute provides opportunities to address the impact of these unions and inculcurate the employees of newly acquired companies. The Institute only accepts about 35 employees annually from all business units and functions, therefore, acceptance to the Institute is prestigious and competitive among employees. The combination of associates from different business functions increases the interaction among staff who traditionally would not work together.

Education is just a portion of the culture of innovation at Finova. Improving employees' ability to interact with each other and brainstorm is crucial to foster new ideas, and maximizing the use of innovative technology is an important part of this process. The Finova Interaction Center allows for groups to interact electronically to solve problems and address issues. Through 14 interactive PC's, groups can work together and provide anonymous comments, as well as vote on issues. The proceedings are all electronically recorded so groups can build upon their work. Many employees who may not actively engage in normal meetings because of intimidation of public speaking can speak their mind in the interactive system. The principal goal is to reduce the barriers to idea generation and discussion.

Providing opportunities and the tools to develop new ideas is a strong component of creating a culture of innovation but employees often need tangible incentives. The Chairman Club "Event of Excellence Program" creates rewards for both teams and individuals who exceed organizational expectations. While outstanding performance in day-to-day operations is rewarded at the end of the year through merit raises and bonuses, the "Event of Excellence Program" rewards significant achievements by groups and teams.

CASE 12

Sterling: Managing Out-sourcing of Employee and Human Resource Functions

Developed by Mark Osborn, Arizona Chamber of Commerce

Human resources is a broad field that incorporates a diversity of subjects areas including: staffing, payroll, benefit administration, training, workers' compensation, placement and others. Larger businesses often consolidate these functions into one centralized department. Human resource's departments are designed to work with other units in the organization to help ensure that the qualified individuals are properly placed to meet the needed roles. In addition, HR departments historically managed the administrative aspects for a company's labor force. These departments are seen as a cost to the organization since they produce no direct revenue to the company nor do they provide additional value-added service to customers.

Out-sourcing many of the HR functions often involves many complex issues. Suppliers of these services must be adaptive to a diversity of needs from clients wishing to outsource all or part of their HR functions. The Sterling company is one such supplier of HR services that addresses not only a diversity of clients but does so in a number of different cultures. This international corporation with offices in Arizona, Florida and several in Asian countries has been successful at assisting corporations in effectively outsourcing many traditional HR functions. As a competitive supplier of services, Sterling has a natural incentive to keep costs down for their clients while keeping the quality of their service high.

One of the most significant benefits to out-sourcing in this area is the increased flexibility that subscribing companies receive from these services. For

example, one of the services that Sterling provides is employee leasing. In many cases, Sterling will recruit employees for use a client's facility and assume much of the responsibility for the administration of benefits. Sterling pays the employees and administers their benefits and then bills the client company. The client company retains managerial control over Sterling's leased employees. Generally, when recruiting and placement is requested, Sterling provides the initial screening and the contracting company makes the final approval before successful applicants start on the job.

One of the reasons many of Sterling's clients contract with them is because it provides a better accounting of the personnel costs of a project. Contracts can be structured on a flat rate basis so the client pays only one fee for all personnel costs. Workers' compensation, payroll,

and recruiting, are some of the items that can be incorporated to the flat-rate contract. The client provides salary and benefit ranges for the employees with the contract but the total cost, including the Sterling fee, is billed to the client. This enables the client to make a line item budget for labor that accounts for not only the direct labor costs but the costs of administering the program. This contracting mechanism allows for companies who act as subcontractors to produce an accurate accounting of total labor costs.

The recruiting process is often expensive and requires significant expertise to be completed effectively. Many HR departments are not structured to engage in thorough recruitment and their contacts in the labor market are often limited. One of Sterling's principal clients are high-tech companies. These corporations typically require a highly-skilled labor force, and their demand for labor changes continually as market demands shift. In many cases, high-tech corporations will be required to hire a large number of technical staff people for projects of varying durations. Once the contracts are completed, there may not be new projects to continue the full employment for the newly-hired workers. Under more traditional in-house hiring practices, a company in this situation would be required to maintain a large HR department that would experience wide swings in work loads as demand shifts. In addition, this company would experience large shifts in the size of its labor force which could pose many administrative as well as legal concerns from displaced workers. By internalizing many of these functions the flexibility the company needs to address the work place is greatly reduced.

Rural/Metro

Developed by Mark Osborn, Arizona Chamber of Commerce

Cities and counties across the United States are under increasing fiscal pressure as tax revenues are decreasing and the demands for high quality services are increasing. Fire, emergency services, and police generally make up the majority of a city's budget. Elected officials and city managers are looking to keep costs down in every budget category, especially major budget items like emergency services. Privatization of emergency services is an option that many communities have begun to utilize as they seek to meet citizen demands for low taxes and high quality services.

The Rural/Metro Corporation is a progressive company that has developed a service which keeps the costs of fire and emergency services down while developing mechanisms to ensure community satisfaction. Rural/Metro has operations all across the United States including in states like New York, Nebraska, Arizona, Florida, and Texas. Every community in these areas has diverse needs and Rural/Metro can customize its services and its billing format to meet community needs. The contracts that Rural/Metro enters into often have strict performance criteria and accountability mechanisms to assure the public they are receiving the services for which they have paid. Performance-based contracts are often subject to high levels of public review and in many cases Rural/Metro must compete with other private providers and even public providers. The market place is competitive, but when communities have the option of reducing service costs from 10% to 50%, the interest is always there.

Fire and emergency services are labor intensive industries where employee salaries and benefits drive as much as 70% of the cost service. Typically, city-owned fire and emergency service departments are heavily unionized. Strict work rules, salary schedules, and benefit packages are extremely costly items for the city that often reduce productivity. The unions often have strong political support in the community because they are active in civic and political events. Firefighters are regarded highly by the community, and increases in benefits are often not as politically unpopular for them as increases in other departments. Rural/Metro's firefighters are not unionized, but like their unionized brothers, they have a strong stake in the community.

Understanding that the communities which Rural/Metro services demand highly trained firefighters, Rural/Metro's management have to devise mechanisms to keep the good firefighters at Rural/Metro while competing with other city fire departments and their high benefits schedules. It was important for management to keep turnover low because firefighter quality was key to maintaining citizen confidence. Executives knew that the company could not remain profitable if it offered its firefighters the same benefits as the unionized departments. So management needed to develop performance-based incentives for their employees.

In response to these concerns, Rural/Metro implemented an innovative employee ownership program where the firefighters have a direct stake in the company's profitability. If the company is financially successful, the benefits paid to Rural/Metro employees could potentially out-earn the municipal firefighters. The Employee Stock Ownership Program (ESOP) is available to most employees who have completed 200 hours of work per year and have reached the age of 21. "Each participant's account vests 20% after three years of service and an additional 20% each year thereafter." (Annual Report page #38) Employee ownership helps to reduce turnover and played an important role in building a team spirit among the firefighters and management. For example,

Rural/Metro's ambulance division has only an 8% attrition rate. This is extremely low for an industry that traditionally reports much higher turnover. The community received highly-trained employees who have a solid stake in the success of the community and their company.

The cost of simply providing the service is not the only cost to the community. Prevention and reduction of the number of fires in a community can reduce the costs of not only providing the service, but it can reduce the costs of insurance, and the amount of property damage. In Scottsdale, Arizona, Rural/Metro has developed a solid partnership with community leaders. Through aggressive zoning measures that included sprinkler requirements, the average amount of fire damage has been reduced as well as the number of fatalities. These ordinances have been credited with saving 52 lives and over $300 million in property damage.

Patagonia
. . . .

Developed by Mark Osborn, Arizona Chamber of Commerce

Few companies exemplify social responsibility like the outdoor clothing manufacturer Patagonia. The Ventura, California-based company is more focused on producing quality products and improving the environment than on increasing profit margins. Patagonia's social responsibility is so entrenched that Patagonia has recently stated that slow-growth is a fundamental corporate goal. In addition to social responsibility, Patagonia has unique HR approaches that encourage employees to surf, play volleyball, and mountain bike during their lunch hour. The concept behind these policies is that a company that sells outdoor apparel should allow its employees to enjoy the outdoors for which their products are designed. The culture of social responsibility is dominant throughout the company and it has created management successes as well as problems as Patagonia has grown from an entrepreneurial specialty retailer to an apparel powerhouse.

The operating style within Patagonia is truly unique. As part of a goal of social responsibility, Patagonia employees receive benefits and flexibility that is unusual in the apparel industry. Patagonia subsidizes the employee cafeteria and provides expansive day care facilities as well as other generous benefits. The result is that the cost of production of Patagonia's products and the profit margins for these products are lower than under more structured and disciplined organizations. This is not a significant concern of the corporate leadership because acting as a responsible employer is part of the company's mission. As part of the commitment to social responsibility, Patagonia contributes 1% of sales to various causes. The protection of the environment is paramount among these causes. The mission and the programs that are designed to meet this mission help form the foundation of Patagonia'a corporate culture.

The unique culture of Patagonia is clearly focused with the attitudes and philosophy of its founder, Yvon Chouinard. The story of Chouinard is legendary in the industry and with employees. In 1957 Chouinard, an avid extreme outdoorsman, founded a small company in a tiny tin shed to design and build mountain climbing supplies. Unlike traditional entrepreneurs, Chouinard did not recruit experts in business to build his vision; instead he recruited fellow outdoorsmen, or "dirt bags," as they are commonly known in the company. An outdoor supply company was a perfect for the Chouinard who would spend countless hours field researching products and creating new ideas. Even today with Patagonia as a 125 million dollar company, Chouinard is in the field researching products as much as eight months out of the year. Clearly the day-to-day management is not the focus of Patagonia's founder. Chouinard clearly disdains business as he sees himself, not as a businessman, but as a craftsman. Chouinard is commonly quoted as saying, "I thought most businessmen were grease balls. I considered myself a craftsman-blacksmith."

During the eighties, Chouinard's unconventional approach led Patagonia down a path of great success. The outdoor apparel market during the eighties was blooming, and Patagonia's approach to high quality and innovation was extremely successful. The design teams with Patagonia were made up of "dirt bags" who were allowed to exercise their creativity almost unrestrained. Creativity and innovation characterized many of their products, and profits were fuels on the backs of some of their breakthrough products. Patagonia combined basic lines of outdoor apparel with specialty lines for the adventurous outdoor specialist. Clearly, Patagonia had developed the image as a clothier for the extreme adventurer. The exploits of the founder were well-known and the reputation for high quality allowed Patagonia to spend less than .5% of their sales on advertising. Consumers in the 80's were thrilled with this wide variety of products.

The growth of the 80's was not spurred by dramatic increases in outdoor adventurism, but rather the growth in popularity of these products for daily use. The products were not being used to climb snow-packed peaks but were more commonly used at the weekend barbecue. This market reality always aggravated Chouinard. At one time Patagonia had 375 different styles, with many of them competing against each other in the marketplace. Chouinard was more concerned with innovation and quality than marketing. Developing proper accounting and finance procedures was accepted with open arms. Patagonia had a difficult time determining where the cost centers were and which products were cannibalizing each other. In fact, the distance from traditional business is so distinct that the finance and accounting departments are housed outside of the main compound. During the 80's the loose structure was not a significant problem, but as the leaner 90's were approached, the need for change would become evident.

In 1991, Patagonia hit bottom as the culture and structure that brought the success in the 80's proved to be unresponsive to the leaner markets of the 90's. When Bank of America reduced Patagonia's line of credit and inventory backed up, Patagonia was forced to downsize. Layoffs and a reduction in the number of product lines was clearly needed. The socially responsible company was forced to discharge workers and rethink their approach for the future. Chouinard took the top staffers to a retreat in Patagonia, Argentina to discuss the next 100 years.

Out of that session, an action plan of slow growth and more responsible financial management was developed. The freehand that designed had to create product lines reduced by eliminating the number of styles that were offered by Patagonia. In 1991, Chouinard announced these reforms to customers in an essay titled "Reality Check." With this statement Patagonia announced how they would reexamine their future but still maintain their commitment to quality, the environment, and social responsibility.

CASE 15
Carpax Company and Phyllis Copeland

oug Singer sat back in his chair and reflected on how so much had gone so terribly wrong in such a short period of time. Only 3 months earlier, the opportunity at Carpax, a rapidly growing manufacturer of specialty steel products, had seemed to provide just the kind of boost his career needed. He had not thought twice about tendering his resignation at Tenntex, even though he had spent 10 very good years there. The position of advertising director with young, rapidly growing Carpax was exactly what Doug had been looking for. Or so he thought. Now he wasn't at all sure he had made the right decision.

He was sure that the cause of his current problems originated with one person—Phyllis Copeland—but his best course of action was not at all obvious. Doug had been told by some of his coworkers that in spite of Phyllis's blatantly poor job performance, she was known to wield a lot of power. A few had expressed the opinion that if either Doug or Phyllis had to leave the company, Doug might very well be the one to leave.

As Doug tried to identify alternatives for dealing with the situation, he reflected on Carpax's corporate culture. The "good-old-boy" atmosphere seemed to be a throwback to an earlier era. He smiled as he remembered his wife's reaction the first time he mentioned what he termed the "Bubba Boys" to her. But the more he told her, the less amused she had been.

Doug realized that most of what he knew about Phyllis was based on heresay, but when he considered the number of apparently objective and reliable sources who had said essentially the same things, he concluded that at least some if it had to be true. Doug's new colleagues were candid in sharing what they knew about Phyllis's work history. With this information, Doug compiled the following summary of Phyllis's association with Carpax.

Background

About 6 years earlier, Mr. Rodney Hauck (owner of a local CPA firm and personal friend of Carpax Company's CEO and founder, Justin Broadrick) had phoned Broadrick about a personal problem. It concerned Phyllis Copeland, Rodney Hauck's receptionist and secretary, who had been in his employ for about a year and a half.

Phyllis Copeland, an attractive woman in her late twenties, was a single parent and sole support of an adolescent daughter. She had been deserted by her second husband and her emotionally charged divorce provided a compelling opportunity for an affair with her close associate at work. In fact, Doug Singer was told that Copeland and Rodney Hauck had become the talk of East Ridge and the country club set.

East Ridge was a small town of 25,000. The word going through the rumor mill at Hauck's CPA firm was that Mrs. Hauck had issued an ultimatum to her husband: "Get rid of Phyllis Copeland or else." Rodney Hauck leveled with Phyllis Copeland and set the stage for her dismissal. Unfortunately for Hauck, Phyllis did not accept discharge quietly. Rumor had it that she sensed an opportunity to use the situation to enhance her career, and she took it. It was a common assumption that Phyllis had issued a thinly veiled threat: "Make me a better deal, or I'll make this termination tough" (translation: "Look out for a sexual harassment complaint and its attendant publicity").

Founded some 10 years before Singer joined the company, Carpax was experiencing major growth. The company had been started by a small group of entrepreneurs utilizing imported technology that, until then, had not been precisely duplicated in the United States. Sales-driven and free-spirited, the company was taking advantage of an open market and enjoying extraordinary success, both financial and in terms of market share. Carpax was now the largest employer in East Ridge, employing over 2000, with corporate offices at three different sites in the community. In addition to the manufacturing facility in East Ridge, there was another on the west coast and one in Europe. Carpax maintained numerous regional sales offices in the United States and Europe.

To the average East Ridge resident, the high-profile Carpax seemed to provide a golden opportunity to get on a fast-track career path. It was *the* place to work, even for secretarial, clerical, and production employees, since there were few other attractive employment opportunities locally. Carpax's senior management (the founding group) were the social elite

Source: NACRA. The authors' names and affiliations are withheld from publication in order to assure anonymity to the company and managers described here. All events and individuals are real, but names have been disguised. Faculty members in nonprofit institutions are encouraged to reproduce this case for distribution to their students without charge or written permission. All other rights reserved jointly to the authors and the North American Case Research Association (NACRA). Copyright 1995 by the *Case Research Journal* and the authors. This case was originally presented at the 1993 North American Case Research Association annual meeting.

of East Ridge; quick money had catapulted them to that position. Carpax was also a model of a high-tech environment: impressive offices, corporate jets, and generous expense accounts.

Carpax's founding group effectively managed the business, but stories of their excesses and indiscretions in personal matters were legendary. As local gossip had it, almost every Carpax senior officer, and many other managers, had affairs with their secretaries and other female associates. In fact, the word in East Ridge was that Carpax considered it a corporate perk to have an affair with your secretary. Doug Singer had heard of these personal entanglements for years prior to joining Carpax. It seemed to be common knowledge that the firm had a very macho, sexist culture. There were no women in the firm above middle management, nor were there any known plans for recruiting or promoting women to those positions. Doug was concerned about the firm's reputation, but the opportunity for professional advancement at Carpax seemed too good to pass up.

Justin Broadrick had been a friend of Rodney Hauck's for many years. The Haucks and the Broadricks frequently socialized with each other. Justin and Rodney had graduated from East Ridge High School together and had remained in the community ever since. They had even engaged in some early business ventures together. When Rodney Hauck confessed his plight regarding Phyllis Copeland, Justin Broadrick rallied to the

aid of his friend. Of course he would provide a position for Ms. Copeland.

Phyllis Copeland was hired at Carpax and assigned to the senior vice president of marketing, John Barker, whose executive secretary had recently moved to another city. This was quite a promotion for Phyllis from her former receptionist-secretary position in Mr. Hauck's small CPA firm. Copeland, who possessed few credentials, seemed to realize that the new position was an unusual opportunity. She commented to a coworker in an adjoining office that for the first time in her life, she might be able to buy a little house.

Phyllis Copeland was assigned routine secretarial and administrative duties. But from the outset, it was clear to everyone in the department that she was not qualified; she lacked the education and the experience to handle the job. Even very basic tasks were confusing to her, and customers as well as coworkers were struck by her obvious incompetence. Correspondence for which she was responsible routinely contained grammatical, spelling, and punctuation errors. Her telephone communication skills were equally deficient; she handled calls in an unprofessional, even bored manner. Although Copeland's responsibilities were soon absorbed by her more competent fellow employees (John Baker just bypassed her when he handed down work assignments), she retained her executive secretarial position. To no one's surprise, it was soon widely reported that Baker and Phyllis were having an affair.

Although the Carpax culture was tolerant of their personal relationship, Phyllis's coworkers found it difficult to tolerate Phyllis's own attitude and behavior, which were causing an acute morale problem. The situation was compounded by Phyllis's introverted personality—she appeared almost aloof to everyone in the department, operating in isolation from every other person with the exception of John Baker, on whom she lavished extraordinary attention. Casual peer exchanges were rebuffed with icy indifference. Even the simplest request from anyone other than Baker was ignored, giving her coworkers the impression that she regarded her relationship with Baker as the last word in job security.

In time, it became obvious to even the most casual observer that Phyllis had no real duties left. She read books and wandered about the halls. Several times, coworkers found her taking a nap in Justin Broadrick's office when he was away. At the same time, her relationship with John Baker developed an openness that seemed flagrant to her coworkers, even by Carpax standards. Extended trips with Baker in his car and long personal lunches became the rule. Additionally, the two occasionally spent the entire afternoon behind the closed doors of John Baker's office. The crowning blow was John Baker's own contentious divorce, exacerbated by detailed testimony regarding Phyllis

Copeland's role. Embarrassing details of the company culture and atmosphere at Carpax became part of the court records. An incensed Justin Broadrick called John Baker in for a conference. In the interest of department morale, John Baker agreed to end the affair. In addition, the two concurred on the necessity of transferring Phyllis to another area of the company, preferably to another location in town, away from the main headquarters office.

Baker and Broadrick also agreed that the transfer had to be perceived as a promotion, because they felt that there was no way to predict what action Phyllis might take—even an embarrassing sexual harassment complaint was not out of the question. Following considerable deliberation, they decided to make Phyllis a manager in the advertising department, located

several blocks away from Baker's office.

Wallace Baird, the advertising director, reported to John Baker. Wallace was not originally hired by John Baker, but was assigned to him as the result of a corporate restructuring. Wallace had started with Carpax several years earlier, when the company was still quite small. Wallace's performance as advertising director proved to be more troublesome with each passing year. His reputation was that of an underachiever at the limit of his promotability. His organizational skills and productivity were poor.

John Baker was beginning to feel some pressure from top management as a result of Wallace's poor performance. But John confided to a colleague that even though Phyllis wasn't capable of bringing out any improvements in the advertising department, at least she could

Figure 1
Advertising Department Relationships under Wallace Baird

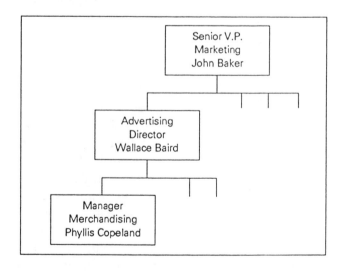

funnel inside information from the department to him—maybe even disclose some of Wallace's more spectacular failures. As stated to his colleague, he also believed that she could not significantly damage the department, since it was already performing poorly. At any rate, she would be out of his way. And with Baird insecure in his position, he would be unlikely to resist the assignment of Phyllis to his staff. So Phyllis was appointed manager of merchandising (see Figure 1).

Soon after Phyllis Copeland's promotion to management status, it became apparent to those in her new department that she had no understanding of the work requirements of her new position. She acted as though "management" was synonymous with indolence, as though she no longer had to do anything. Unmanageable and untouchable, Phyllis proceeded to establish herself in the advertising department. By using veiled threats to exercise her connections with John Baker and, if need be, Justin Broadrick, she thwarted even mild attempts by Wallace Baird to discipline or direct her.

Shortly after Phyllis's arrival, Wallace Baird's morale began a perceptible decline. Subsequently, everyone in the department noticed that he had begun to completely defer to Phyllis Copeland. He seemed to have turned over the departmental reins to her. In less than a year, the advertising department was in shambles. (Baird would later tell friends that he thought letting Phyllis run the depart-

Figure 2
Advertising Department Relationships under Doug Singer

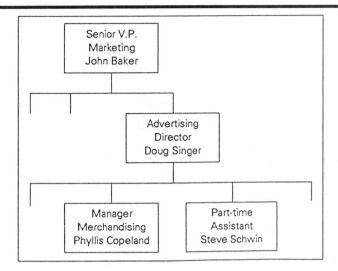

ment would be a sure prescription for her failure.)

Finally, John Baker was called to a conference with Justin Broadrick. This time, the good-old-boy network was showing signs of wear-and-tear. The confusion in the advertising department was beginning to cost the company considerable market share. John Baker received his ultimatum: "Get the advertising department straightened out, or else." A search was begun for a new advertising director. John Baker, who knew that his own reputation—and possibly even career—had been damaged by the situation, told a confidant that he realized he needed to hire a no-nonsense person to replace Wallace Baird. The question remained, however: "How would Phyllis fit into the new picture?"

The Current Situation

Doug Singer, the new advertising director, came to Carpax

from Tenntex, a major customer of Carpax's. With 10 years of related experience under his belt, Doug viewed the position with Carpax as a major career opportunity. His first week on the job, however, revealed some frightening realities. First and foremost, Doug realized the organizational structure was practically nonexistent. He would have to rebuild from scratch. Since Phyllis had joined the department, three key employees had left, apparently demoralized and disgusted with the whole situation, according to those who remained.

Phyllis Copeland quickly sensed potential trouble as a result of the appointment of her new boss, Doug Singer. Having had no performance demands placed on her throughout her employment at Carpax, Phyllis was now suddenly expected to become a productive employee. Her first response, apparently in hopes of securing him as an ally, was an overt sexual advance. Doug was unresponsive.

Although John Baker was no longer having an affair with Phyllis, they continued to have extended telephone conversations at work, with Phyllis making no attempt to conceal this contact. Doug realized he had a major personnel problem.

Desperate to make headway in the rebuilding of the advertising department, Doug Singer decided to look for a part-time employee, someone to run interference while he dug through the reams of undone and botched projects. He wanted an outsider who wasn't suffering from the poor morale that permeated the department.

Steve Schwin, a junior marketing major at East Ridge College, was a bit older and more mature than most of his classmates. One of Steve's fraternity brothers who was employed at Carpax part time alerted him to the opening. Steve joined Doug Singer's department (see Figure 2) and made immediate and significant contributions. Young and career-oriented, he worked hard and performed well beyond his credentials. Doug recognized Steve's talents and sensed an opportunity to groom a key manager.

Within a few weeks, Steve was given projects that would have normally been assigned to the merchandising manager. They were completed promptly and accurately. Steve's performance did not go unnoticed by Phyllis. Her reaction to Doug's increasing reliance on his new, young assistant was to do even less work than she had previously. Before long, Phyllis's attendance began to fall drastically. In one month she was absent 11 days, without bothering to call in. It was clear to Doug that Phyllis had no intention of performing even the most routine of tasks.

Morale in the department continued to fall. The other workers in the department resented Phyllis's very presence. Doug often overheard cutting remarks made about Phyllis. He was certain the remarks were usually meant for him to hear and that his associates in the department expected something to be done very soon. As an experienced manager, Doug knew that he had to resolve this crisis by taking definite action.

Doug did not expect the human resource department to provide much assistance to him. Carpax had emphasized sales and, to a lesser extent, manufacturing functions during its years of rapid growth. The human resource function was not well developed, providing few guidelines and little expertise to operating managers. In fact, modern human resource management techniques were presently nonexistent at Carpax. Doug knew this situation would have to change if Carpax was to survive.

Knowing Phyllis's history in the company, it was unclear what course of action had the best chance of success. Well aware of Phyllis's role in the departure of his predecessor, Wallace Baird, Doug was determined not to let the same thing happen to him.

CASE 16
ADEQ Mission Impossible
· ·
Developed by Mark Osborn, Arizona Chamber of Commerce

Arizona Department of Environmental Quality (ADEQ) was an agency under fire when Ed Fox took over as the new director. The legislature and regulated communities were constantly criticizing the department for a lack of stability and effectiveness. Strangely, environmentalists had joined with the business community and begun placing pressure on the agency to enforce the law more aggressively. Complying businesses wanted their noncomplying competitors to meet the standard regulations, while the environmentalists merely saw the noncompliers as responsible for deteriorating the environment. The agency was clearly wedged between two groups with extremely divergent opinions. Environmentalists and the business community were frequently at war in the state legislature, and, to make matters worse, the media frequently scrutinized the activities of the ADEQ.

Fox had clearly entered a hornets' nest of controversy. If he was to be successful, he would need to balance the conflicting policy options of the business community, the legislature, and the environmentalists, while improving and, in many cases, creating effective management structures. To many outsiders, Fox appeared to be the perfect candidate. He was a leader who had credibility with both the environmentalists and the business community, and he had significant experience as a regulator. While outspoken and committed to protecting the environment, before joining ADEQ, he had represented private sector clients as an attorney.

During the first years of his tenure, Fox greatly improved policy implementation. Environmental permits were processed faster, and customer service improved enormously. Despite all of Fox's efforts, however, the business community and many individuals in the legislature believed that more significant reforms were needed. The legislature had become increasingly conservative since Fox became the ADEQ director, and the business community was increasing pressure for reforms and modification to the environmental statutes. Fox clearly felt like he was in a no-win situation—when he addressed the concerns of the business community in the legislature, the environmentalists attacked him strongly using the press.

In 1995, the pressure grew to its highest level as the business community and the legislature presented the most ambitious series of environmental reforms in years. The most controversial of these bills was the environmental audit legislation. Fox was personally opposed to many of the provisions of the bill, but he received a great deal of pressure from the governor and the business community to work out a solution. The environmentalists were clearly opposed to the bill and convinced influential reporters to trash it in the local papers.

Fox lobbied against the bill through friendly legislators and the governor, but he never publicized his actions or had direct meetings with the business community regarding his position. Despite strong efforts to modify the key provisions of the bill, the environmental audit bill found its way to the governor's desk. The Governor, understanding his ADEQ director's opposition to many of the provisions of the bill, vetoed it. The business community was incensed at Fox's torpedoing of the bill. Despite Fox's efforts on the environmental audit, many environmentalists felt that Fox had betrayed them because he had negotiated deals with the business community on other issues. The end of the 1995 legislative session saw true polarization of issues, and the trust among all stakeholders was virtually nonexistent.

CASE 17
Malden Mills
· · · · · · · · · · · · · ·

Developed by Mark Osborn, Arizona Chamber of Commerce

Aaron Feuerstein, CEO and a major shareholder in Malden Mills does not describe himself as a hero, just a smart businessman. In the last decades of this century, spinning and weaving operations moved from their historical homes in the heavily unionized Northeast to cheaper nonunionized labor in the rural south and then the Caribbean. That is, all but Malden Mills and Aaron Feuerstein.

Feuerstein thought that the constant chase for cheaper labor was just plain foolish. About the time employees were trained and operating effectively, it was time to move the machinery and open a whole new plant with all new untrained individuals. On the surface, most jobs in a spinning and weaving operation appear quite simple. This was one of the last industries to abandon child labor because children were said to have nimble hands and quick feet- the so-called necessary skills to operate in a mill. Feuerstein rejected the notion that mill jobs were simple as he noted the subtle but important adjustments more experienced workers would make to the machines to prevent problems and defects. Over years of experience, employees had developed a tacit knowledge of their jobs. Tacit knowledge is difficult to communicate and is the type of knowledge and skill possessed by skilled artists and craftspersons. Feuerstein figured that with a highly trained, experienced and dedicated workforce, Malden could effectively compete in the speciality markets where quality

and innovativeness were the key to success. Instead of building a new plant in the South, Malden Mills invested in new equipment, new products and employees.

The success story came to an abrupt halt in the late fall of 1995 with a fire that destroyed the main Malden Mills plant. In their small New England town the middle-aged workforce of Malden Mills was ready for a bleak Thanksgiving when Feuerstein called all of his employees together. He shocked them all in the era of short term profits and downsizing by making two simple announcements. The plant would be rebuilt. All employee benefits would be continued until Christmas and training on the new equipment for the new plant would begin for key employees.

Feuerstein was an instant town hero and soon received national TV coverage for his decision. On public TV he stated his philosophy in very simple terms. The difference between Malden Mills and its competitors is its people and their willingness, hard work and innovativeness to make the

business a success. While labor cost is a small proportion of total manufacturing costs, the benefits from dedicated employees can make all the difference to the success of the firm. We do not use human resources, we engage individuals to share their work, their skills and their brains with us.

CASE 18
Confused Leadership at the Children's Advocacy and Charity Foundation

Developed by Mark Osborn, Arizona Chamber of Commerce

The Children's Advocacy and Charity Foundation had been an active charity in the community for many years. The goal of the Foundation was to promote children's issues in the community and implement a number of programs for disadvantaged children. The Foundation had a small staff of eight, and utilized approximately 500 volunteers from its member companies. The Foundation was funded by businesses in the community through formal memberships and other fundraisers. It was governed by a board of directors that seated about 30 members and an executive committee of five associates.

Membership on the board was achieved by one of two ways. The vast majority of the board were executives in local businesses who contributed significantly to the Foundation's effort. The rest of the board was made of community activists who had been invited. Their principal contribution was not revenue, but effort. Three out of the five on the Executive Committee were citizen activists because a majority of the business members did not have the time to become active with the executive committee. The executive committee was responsible for assisting the CEO in addressing the day-to-day operations, while the board took care of larger policy issues.

The Foundation was noted in the community for its successful implementation of very innovative children's programs. Dan Maxwell, Vice President of Charity Programs, had been credited with much of the success of these innovative programs. Maxwell had a low-key style and as a result, the Foundation received little credit in the media for these achievements. However, within the charity community, the foundation was well respected. Mr. Maxwell was often asked to provide advice on other community programs as a result of his 12 years of experience with the Foundation. He also had membership on many other charity boards, because many people in the community sought his input on their projects. Many on the Foundation's board felt that without Dan, the Foundation would collapse.

Dan Maxwell was somewhat frustrated with the leadership at the Foundation, for they had gone through three CEO's in the last eight years. The fundraising efforts had suffered significantly and the membership rosters were at an all-time low. During the last CEO search, Mr Maxwell had applied for the position, but the Executive Committees opted for a former Washington politician who had extensive experience working with the media. Maxwell was prepared to quit after being passed up, but members of the Board made sure they increased his pay and stated that the new CEO was 60 years old and would be retiring within five years. After three years, the Foundation experienced no increases in media coverage and the CEO was terminated.

Maxwell always believed that he was passed up for the CEO position because he had disagreements with members of the Executive Committee who were more focused on getting their names in the paper and not focused enough on the Foundation's programs. The Jackson Group, another local charity, always seemed to trump any efforts their organization did in the community by receiving more press. Most of the community leaders knew the Foundation was responsible for the substantive children's programs, but the Jackson Group's aggressive public relations campaign created a public perception that they were the leaders in community programs. To Maxwell, public exposure was immaterial as long as the Foundation had the revenue to keep its programs growing.

Even though the membership numbers were down, the programs were still successful and Maxwell hoped to translate this success into a position as the new CEO. When the executive committee terminated the Washington politician, they failed to get the approval of the full board. Although after the termination the board agreed with the decision, some of the larger members expressed displeasure with the lack of consultation. Many on the Board believed that Dan Maxwell was the obvious choice for the available CEO position and they decided not to play an active role during recruitment.

Children's Advocacy and Charity Foundation: What Happened

The recruitment was managed by an executive committee who chooses a candidate for the new position and that decision would be ratified by the Board. Immediately, Maxwell knew that his candidacy was in trouble when the Executive Committee contracted an executive search firm to find a new CEO. He hoped that this was just a procedural step, but his concerns grew greater as he saw the job description and the candidates' qualification list. The list clearly reflected the public relations focus of the Executive Committee. It was almost as if the job description was designed to exclude Maxwell. The search firm was to review all of the candidates and prepare a ranking based upon the informa-

tion found in the job description and five finalists would be interviewed by the Executive Committee. Maxwell had made the final cut during a previous search and he was confident that he would make the final list.

During the present search, the executive committee had engaged in negotiations with the Jackson Group regarding the possible merging of the two organizations. Proposals had been floated by the Foundation to the Jackson Group's executive committee. Neither board knew about these talks, but final proposals were developed and were to be presented to each board. Both executive committees believed they could effectively combine the substantive programs of the Foundation with the exposure of the Jackson Group. The flamboyant CEO of the Jackson Group could help translate the hard work of Maxwell's group into more exposure. One of the biggest problems for the Foundation's Executive Committee was how to finesse the CEO search process when the need for the position might actually be eliminated.

When the Foundation's Executive Committee presented the merger proposal to the Board, the reaction was extremely negative. Many of the larger members agreed that a merger with the Jackson Group would bring more exposure in the media, but the culture and history of the Foundation should be preserved. Many of the board liked the low key and productive image of the Foundation, and with the implementation of a

more successful media strategy, the Foundation's exposure could be increased appropriately. Many on the board were adamant that the only purpose of media exposure was to increase the ability to raise funds and implement the Foundation's program. After the highly charged board meeting, the Executive Committee retreated and withdrew their position for a merger. The animosity between the larger Board members and the activist Executive Committee ran high.

The Executive Committee had purposely stalled the hiring of a new CEO until the negotiations with the Jackson Group reached a conclusion. The three citizen activists who were most upset with the Board were still determined to find a way to get more exposure for the foundation. Based on the criteria provided to the search firm, the firm finally produced a list of five names. Dan Maxwell was not one of the names listed, but the firms's director made a note that Maxwell should be included on the final list. The Executive Committee, ignoring the suggestion, only interviewed the five candidates and recommended a former news reporter for the position. No mention of Maxwell was provided to the Board. When the new CEO was recommended, many on the board expressed outrage that Maxwell was not the candidate. Others on the board approved of the new CEO, not because he was the best choice, but to appease the Executive Committee after the failure of their merger proposal.

When the new CEO was announced, Dan Maxwell was outraged and tenured his resignation. Maxwell's supporters on the Board decided to revaluate their commitment to the organization and concluded the Executive Committee needed to be kept in check. The Foundation was clearly at a crisis. The new CEO had excellent experience at working with the media, but he had no management experience. He faced a situation where the Board was uncertain and the most critical staff person had left the organization.

CASE 19
Elite Electric Company

Developed by Barry R. Armandi, SUNY-Old Westbury

Elite Electric Company is a moderately small manufacturing subsidiary of a large European conglomerate. The company manufactures electric components supplied to its parent company for sale to consumer retail outlets as well as commercial distribution. Sales in 1978 were approximately $10 million and grew to $35 million in 1982. Elite Electric Company has two plants, one in Pennsylvania and the other in Massachusetts. The plant in Pennsylvania is relatively new and can manufacture three times the amount of units as the Massachusetts plant. The Massachusetts plant was established in the early 1920s and is on a large, beautifully manicured estate. The buildings are quite old, and the machinery is antiquated. However, the company headquarters is at the Massachusetts plant, and the company's president is insistent upon keeping both plants active. (See Table 1 for the five-year production history of both plants.)

In order to cope with the growth of the company administratively, additional staff were hired. However, there was no organized plan to establish systems and procedures for training, mechanization, etc., in anticipation of the increased work load and specialization of activities and functions that would eventually arise. People who had been with the company for a long period of time knew their assignments and, by and large, carried the company through its day-to-day activities. When many of these people left suddenly during a personnel reduction, an information void was created because there was little in way of written procedures to guide those who remained and the replacement staff who were hired.

Another significant factor in the company's history was employee turnover. An administrative employee organization chart shows that 40% of the people employed as of 1982 are no longer associated with the company. Of those remaining, 90% have different assignments today. Many of the losses in staff were in important positions, and all levels were affected. (Figures 1 and 2 show the organization charts for the company and the Massachusetts plant, respectively.)

THE MASSACHUSETTS PLANT

The president of the company, Mr. William White, originally came from LTV, which is located in Dallas, Texas. From there he was recruited to be Plant Operations Manager in Massachusetts. When the original owners sold out to the European concern, Mr. White was made president. In early 1980, he opened the Pennsylvania plant.

As president, Mr. White developed an extensive operational philosophy. The components of this philosophy are listed below:
1. Make product quality and customer service a top priority;
2. Foster a human-oriented working atmosphere;
3. Maximize communication, interaction, and involvement;
4. Minimize the layers of organizational structure and control the growth of bureaucracy;
5. Value and respect our form of company organization, and
6. Strive for excellence in our business performance.

Upon being appointed president in 1979, White promoted Peter Johnson to the position of Plant Operations Manager from his previous position of Production Manager. White told Johnson that he (Johnson) had a lot to learn about running a plant and to go easy with changes until he got "his feet wet." He also indicated that with the projected operation of the new plant the following year, Johnson should expect some reduction in production demand, but White felt this would be temporary. Further, White emphatically reminded Johnson of the company's operational philosophy.

While Mr. White was Plant Operations Manager, he initiated daily operations meetings with the following people: the Purchasing Manager (Paul Barbato); the Production Manager (Brian Campbell); the Quality Control Manager (Elizabeth Schultz); the Engineering Manager (David Arato); the Safety Manager (Martin Massell); the Personnel Manager (Jane Wieder); a representative from Customer Service (Michael St. John); and an Accounting representative (Harvey Jones).

When Mr. Johnson took over, he decided to continue the daily meetings. In 1979, after discussing problems of the company at an open meeting, it was decided that individuals from various other line and staff areas should attend the daily meetings. The transcript of a typical meeting is given below.

PETER JOHNSON: O.K. everybody, it's 9:00, let's get started. You all know what the agenda is, so let's start with safety first.

MARTIN MASSELL (Safety Manager): Well Peter, I have a number of things to go over. First, we should look into feedback from maintenance. The other day we had an incident where the maintenance crew was washing down the walls and water leaked into the electrical wiring. Nobody was told about this, and subsequently seepage began Friday and smoke developed.

PETER JOHNSON: O.K., we will have maintenance look into it and they will get back to you. What else, Marty?

MARTIN MASSELL: We found out that the operators of the fork lifts are operating them too fast in the plant. We are sending out a memo telling them to slow down.

DAVID ARATO (Engineering Manager): Why don't we just put some bumps in the floor so they can't speed over them.

MARTIN MASSELL: Well, we are looking at that. We may decide to do it, but we have to get some cost estimates and maintenance will have to fill us in.
PETER JOHNSON: By the way, where is the representative from Maintenance...well, I will have to contact Irving (Maintenance Manager). Anything else, Marty?

MARTIN MASSELL: Oh yeah, I forgot to tell you yesterday the entire loading dock has been cleaned. We shouldn't be having any more problems. By the way, Brian, make sure you contact Irv about the spill in the area.

BRIAN CAMPBELL: Oh, I forgot to tell you, Peter, but Irv said that we would have to close down machines 1 and 6 to get at the leak that is causing the oil spill. I have already gone ahead with that.

PETER JOHNSON: Gee, Brian, I wish you would clear these things with me first. How badly will the affect our production?

BRIAN CAMPBELL: Not badly, we should be able to get away

with a minimum of overtime this weekend.

PETER JOHNSON: Customer Service is next. Mike, how are we doing with our parent company?

MICHAEL ST. JOHN (Customer Service): Nothing much. We are starting to get flack for not taking that Japanese order, but the guys at the parent company understand. They may not like it, but they can deal with it. Oh, Paul, are you going to have enough transistors on hand to complete that order by next Tuesday?
PAUL BARBATO (Purchasing Manager): Sure, Mike, I sent you a memo on that yesterday.

MICHAEL ST. JOHN: Sorry, but I haven't had a chance to get to my morning mail yet. I was too busy with some visitors from Europe.

PETER JOHNSON: Are these people being taken care of Mike? Is there anything we can do to make their stay here more comfortable?

MICHAEL ST. JOHN: No, everything is fine.
PETER JOHNSON: O.K. let's move on to Employee Relations, Jane.

JANE WIEDER (Personnel Manager): I would like to introduce two guests from Training Programs, Inc. As you know, we will be embarking upon our final training program shortly. The grievance with Al Janow has been resolved. At the

TABLE 1
Five-Year Production History for Elite Electric Company (in units)

	1978	1979	1980* Mass.	1980* Penn.	1981 Mass.	1981 Penn.	1982 Mass.	1982 Penn
Transistors (K)	800	600	500	400	475	535	452	629
Large integrated circuit boards (K)	475	479	325	201	300	227	248	325
Small integrated circuit boards (K)	600	585	480	175	250	212	321	438
Large-capacity chips (millions)	1.2	1.1	700	506	600	700	571	927
Small-capacity chips (millions)	1.8	2.0	500	1.3	170	2.0	276	2.7
Cathode-ray tubes (K)	325	250	210	22	126	46	147	63
Percent with defects	0.1	0.15	0.9	4.2	1.6	2.5	2.5	1.2

*New plant begins operations.

Source: Reprinted from *Journal of Management Case Studies,* 1987, Vol. 3, pp. 348-354. Address reprint requests to: Barry R. Armandi, State University of New York, College at Old Westbury, Long Island, NY 11568.

Management/Employee Meeting last week, an agreement was reached that a representative from each department would attend. As you are aware, this meeting is once a month. It's funny, the biggest complaint at the meeting was an extra chair for the conference room (laughter). The Interview Workshop memo is done, Peter, and here it is. Also, Peter, we have to work on a posting of dates for the Annual Family Get-Together. I don't know if July will work out.

MICHAEL ST. JOHN: July does not look that good. We have a great deal of overtime since that Australian order is due the beginning of August. Can we push it up to June?

HARVEY JONES (Accounting Representative): Don't forget that in June, revised budgets are due. (The meeting continues to discuss the best date for the Annual Family Get-Together for another 15 minutes.)

JANE WIEDER: One more thing, please notify us of any changes in marital status, address, etc. We have to keep our records up to date. Also, please be advised that the company cars can be purchased by employees. Sales will take place through a lottery system.
DAVID ARATO: Will we get a memo on this?

JANE WIEDER: Yes, I will have one out by the end of the week.

PETER JOHNSON: Let's move on to Quality Control. Elizabeth?

ELIZABETH SCHULTZ (Quality Control Manager): Our number 1 and 8 machines have been throwing out bent transistor leads. Over the weekend, these two machines will be down. Irv and Brian are aware of this. We have to straighten out this problem before we do the order from IBM. I have also noticed that the last gold shipment had some other metals in it. Paul, can you check this out to see what was the problem?

PAUL BARBATO: What amount of extraneous metals was present?

ELIZABETH SCHULTZ: We didn't do complete tests of the material, but it seems 5 ounces per 100 pounds.

PAUL BARBATO: That doesn't seem to be a significant amount.

ELIZABETH SCHULTZ: Well, it is according to our estimates, and I would like it to be checked out.

FIGURE 1
Elite Electric Company organization chart (1982).

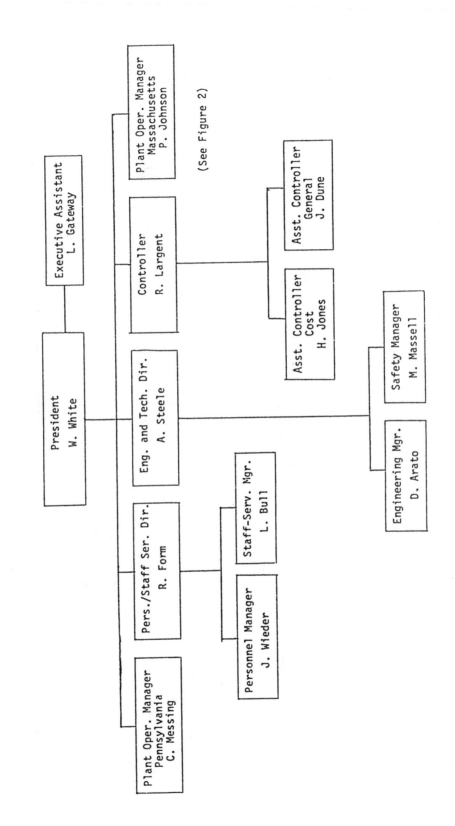

FIGURE 2
Massachusetts' plant organization chart (1982).

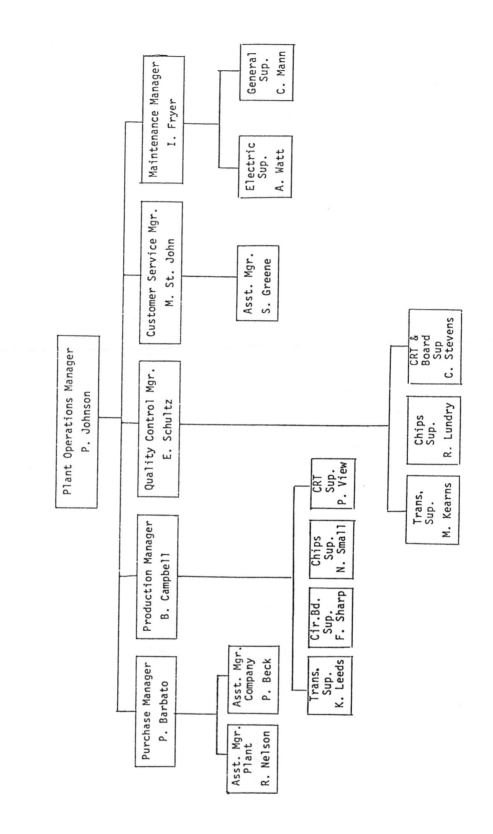

PETER JOHNSON: O.K., Elizabeth, Paul will look into it. Now let's turn to production.

BRIAN CAMPBELL: Last Monday we manufactured 3,000 transistors. Machines 1, 2, and 8 did 300, machines 2 and 4 were down, and the rest of the production was done by the remaining machines. On Tuesday we had to change to produce the larger integrated circuits that were needed by Control Data. We had two hours of down time to change the machines. Machines 6 and 7 did 20% out of the total production run of 5,000 boards. Machine 1 continued to manufacture the small transistorized chips, with machines 2 and 5 completing the rest of the integrated circuit board runs (at about this time, two people got up and walked out of the room as Brian was talking). Wednesday we switched back to the transistor runs on all machines. Unfortunately, machine 2 was down for the entire day, and machine 7 was up for preventive maintenance. We manufactured 2,700 transistors. Machines 4,5, and 8 did approximately 60% of the work (a number of people started yawning). Thursday we produced only 1,000 transistors and had to ship part of our run to the cathode-ray tube production for Digital Equipment Corp. We produced 500 units for Digital. Machines 3,4, and 5 were used for the DEC run, and machines 1,2, and 8 were kept on the transistor production. Machine 7 was down. On Friday we had half a day and in the morning we had a blackout and were only able to get 100 transistors and 22 cathode-ray tubes done.

PETER JOHNSON: Brian, do you think you will be able to make up the rest of the order this week without much overtime?

BRIAN CAMPBELL: I don't know. I think we should talk to Harry (Harry Brown was the union representative).

PETER JOHNSON: That may be difficult since Harry is on vacation, but I will try to get in touch with him. If I can't, let's go ahead with it anyway and we will take the consequences. All right, let's go around the room and see what anybody has to say.

PAUL BARBATO: Nothing.

MARTIN MASSELL: I just wanted to let everyone know that we had a problem in one of the machine wells. It appears that while they were pouring some concrete around the well, some slipped in and it took us a couple of days to get it cleaned up.

JANE WIEDER: Paul, see me on Mary Bernstein's problem.

MICHAEL ST. JOHN: Just wanted to let you know we may be getting a very big order from Grumman.

HARVEY JONES: The following people have not reported their exempt status to payroll (he lists about 12 individuals). Remember this was from Jane's memo about three weeks ago.

PETER JOHNSON: Brian, I want to take a tour with a couple of people from the university next week. I will call you and set something up. O.K.? Good meeting. See you tomorrow, same time, same place.

CASE 20
Dell Computers
· · · · · · · · · · · · · · · · ·

Developed by Mark Osborn, Arizona Chamber of Commerce

Dell is one of the most successful computer firms in the emerging global personal computer market. It does not produce components for its machines, but rather is at the hub of a network of firms, each of which concentrates on one or two areas of expertise. The companies that provide services are modular units to Dell, and vice versa.

More traditional, vertically integrated companies handle all aspects of their business, from the conception of an idea to the manufacturing and distribution of the product. Because they own and operate their own plants and factories plus plants providing key components, vertically integrated companies put a great deal of capital into establishing and maintaining their manufacturing bases. Vertically integrated firms establish long production runs with very specialized equipment supported by a stable management structure to capture economies of scale. When the final product and components are based on rapidly changing technology, vertically integrated firms can't keep up.

In contrast, Dell purchases almost all of its parts from a network of suppliers around the world. Dell does lease two small factories in which the outsourced parts are assembled into computers. It also specializes in combining new components with new technology into workable customized machines. This outsourcing of non-core activities has two primary financial advantages. First, it minimizes the investment needed to roll out new products quickly and, in this way, holds down the unit costs. Second, it frees up Dell's capital so that more of it can be used in the actual development of the products. This translates into more funds for marketing research, designing new products, hiring top quality people in the field, and training both sales and service employees.

By purchasing globally and using its expertise to find compatible components, Dell is able to outstrip IBM or Apple by offering customized PCs rather than a standard machine. Customers have a variety of choices when purchasing a Dell computer. They may choose a color monitor made by Mitsubishi, or an extremely powerful microprocessor made by Intel, or one of hundreds of other choices.

Using a network strategy, companies can grow more rapidly on less capital and maintain a smaller and more efficient management group. Some companies, such as Dell, have been able to develop fast-growing enterprises on surprisingly small initial investments. Because they are lean, nimble structures, instead of towering corporate giants, they can change as rapidly as their customers' interests change.

SOURCE: Adapted from Dell 1992 annual report: R. Osborn, *The Evolution of Strategic Alliances in High Technology*, working paper for Department of Management, Wayne State University, 1993; and Shawn Tully, "The Modular Corporation," *Fortune* (February 8, 1993).

CASE 21
Negotiating Contracts for the National Hockey League

Developed by Mark Osborn, Arizona Chamber of Commerce

With teams in both Canada and the United States, the National Hockey League is truly international. In addition, it is diversifying itself. Once dominated by Canadian players, the NHL is now seeing a host of Europeans become major stars. Even the Japanese are getting involved; a group of Japanese investors has purchased one of Florida's expansion teams. The expansionism and internationalism of the NHL is a deliberate strategy by league president John Ziegler, who believes that everyone will benefit from this expansion into new markets.

As part of his plan to popularize hockey, Ziegler has sought both national and international television contracts. In the past, NHL coverage was limited to league cities and selected areas in the North. By expanding the league into Florida, California and Arizona, Ziegler hopes to move hockey into the national spotlight. Recent contracts with ESPN and Sports Channel have helped hockey gain some of the national recognition it needs. With national coverage comes an increase in profits and advertising for league owners.

In 1992, the National Hockey League Players' Association voted in a new president, Bob Goodenow. Goodenow had been a player representative for several NHL superstars and had negotiated some of the first mega-contracts in pro hockey. He was known throughout the league as a tough bargainer. As the new NHLPA president, Goodenow wanted the players to assert their rights and increase their percentage of the growing hockey market.

Goodenow and the players' union had an opportunity to assert their new unity. Their contract had expired, and a new deal needed to be negotiated. The players wanted a contract that allowed for a less restrictive free agent system, with arbitration suits to be resolved by independent judges instead of league officials. The owners wanted to hold salaries down.

While the players' union was relatively unified under Goodenow, the owners were fairly disorganized. Some owners were dead set against giving the players any significant concessions, while others wanted to work with the players to help the game of hockey grow. Goodenow had to find a way to develop a consensus among the owners to get the changes he wanted.

The NHLPA waited until two weeks before the 1992 playoffs to begin their strike.

This was a time when the owners made a large portion of their profits, as playoffs meant increased attendance and television revenues. If the 1992 playoffs were canceled because of the strike, the owners would definitely feel the pinch. The players, on the other hand, made little financially from the playoffs and had less to lose.

After a 10-day players' walkout, Goodenow and Ziegler shook hands on a compromise deal, saving the NHL's 75th anniversary season. Players settled for a two-year instead of a three-year contract but won new financial rights, including a doubling of playoff bonus money. A joint player--management committee was inaugurated to examine the problems and promises of the hockey business

The strike showed just how much bad blood existed between the players' union and the owners, but it also demonstrated how much love both sides had for the game. The final negotiations were held well after a deadline to end the season because neither Goodenow nor Ziegler would give up.

CASE 22
New Age Hooey?

By Beth Mattson

Old-world unionism clashes with new-age thinking at Whole Foods

On a steamy summer day, Glen Ruiz walks the picket line outside the new Whole Foods Market on Grand Avenue in St. Paul, Minnesota. Like his brother, father, and grandfather, Ruiz has spent his entire adult life working in the grocery industry, striving to maintain the standards of pay and benefits workers have achieved.

Inside the air-conditioned store, upbeat employees go about their daily work, laughing and joking with customers and co-workers as the hock Whole Foods' all-natural grocery fare. Ironically, many of these workers are earning $5.50 an hour, while members of the United Food & Commercial Workers Local 789 are being paid $6 an hour to stand on the picket line outside.

Local 789 has been picketing Whole Foods since the non-union store opened here May 17. The union claims that it is trying to educate consumers rather than organize labor at Whole Foods. Their signs politely ask customers to refrain from shopping the store; newsletters explain their position.

But beneath this rather tranquil scene is an example of one of the nation's most perplexing conflicts: unionism and its old-world ways vs. socially responsible companies that claim to treat employees exceptionally well.

Whole Foods Market Inc. adopted its unique labor structure in 1980 when its first store opened in Austin, Texas. Today, the publicly traded corporation (OTC: WFMI) operates the largest natural foods supermarket chain in the country, with 1994 sales reaching $402 million. The corporation owns thirty-five natural foods stores in eight states under the names Whole Foods Market, Bread & Circus, Mrs. Gooch's, and Wellspring Grocery.

Throughout its rapid development, Whole Foods has stood by its original labor structure and "team member happiness" philosophy. "It's not that we don't like unions, it's that we're building off them to make something better," says Dan Blackburn, associate store team leader in St. Paul. Whole Foods touts the team approach and stands behind its banner of job fulfillment, empowerment, and equality in the ranks. "It's one of those things where the freedom of choice really sets this company apart," he says.

But Whole Foods' non-union practices continue to be targeted by the United Food & Commercial Workers. Its California members picketed a Whole Foods Market in Berkeley for eighteen months during the early 1990s. Later they targeted another California store in Los Gatos. And now, they've surfaced again to fight the company at its St. Paul location.

"This is about power. This is about control. This is about monopoly," says Whole Foods CEO John Mackey. "I think Whole Foods has a different way of doing business than the unions, and that's why we're getting attacked."

Mackey published his own nineteen-page position statement, "Beyond Unions," as a response to the California pickets. In it he defends Whole Foods' philosophy and refutes claims of sub-standard wages and benefits as union rhetoric. Unions perceive Whole Foods' labor model as "new age hooey," he says. But the employee/management partnership structure not only works, it has generated inquiries from hundreds of interested companies across the country. As to union charges of lower wages, Mackey says it's simply not true, and points the finger back to unions

Source: This originally appeared in *Business Ethics*, September/ October

as the ones "exploiting" workers.

Part of the controversy stems from Whole Foods' more ambiguous pay scales, compared with the union's pay standards. According to Local 789 labor contracts, entry-level workers earn $4.90 to $5.30 an hour at stores it represents. Part-timers start at $5.40 an hour and reach $9.70 an hour after 5,200 hours (that's five years at twenty hours a week); and full-time employees after five years on the job earn as much as $12.70 to $16.26 an hour. Union employees also receive a full benefits package. "We're trying to preserve these types of benefits," says Bill Pearson, president of Local 789.

On the other side of the aisle at Whole Foods, officials talk about profit percentages, formulas, and raises based on team performance, rather than concrete numbers. But according to Mackey, Whole Foods' wage and benefits package is equal or greater than union standards. Current wages at the St. Paul store are likely to be lower than other stores in the corporate system, he adds, because of the short amount of time that it's been open. Wages are based in part on duration of employment and a stores's performance, and the St. Paul store has been performing 30 percent below projected sales because of road construction, slower sales during the summer season, and the picketers, Mackey says.

About one-third of the store's one hundred employees started at a minimum of $5.50 an hour - slightly more than union level. And regular pay increases of 50 cents to $1.50 an hour are the norm. Blackburn started out at the minimum level at a Whole Foods Market in North Carolina as a vitamins stocker. Within two years he was promoted to assistant store manager. "In Whole Foods the philosophy is to push people up," he says.

Whole Foods employees enjoy advantages that most grocery store employees don't have. Workers can transfer to other stores. They also receive 20 percent off on purchases made at Whole Foods stores, can participate in an employee stock ownership plan, and receive bonuses for taking on additional training.

"It seems like it's a good company, and a growing company," says Joseph Woods, who works in the meat and seafood department and is a former union member. Another employee, who declined to give her name, splits her time between Whole Foods' cheese department and her job at the United Postal Service, where she is a member of a union. She sees benefits from both non-union and union approaches. The union helps secure solid wages and benefits, but Whole Foods offers incentive programs such as career development. And her career development bonus amounts to an additional $1.05 an hour, bringing her hourly wage to $6.55.

Local 789 hopes to use Whole Foods as a stepping stone to what it sees as a larger concern, Pearson says. The union is taking advantage of the exposure to kick-off efforts to organize retail workers elsewhere, and rally opposition to low-paying jobs. "Our system, our society can't survive on $6 to $7 an hour jobs," he says.

The union plans to continue its picketing at Whole Foods into the fall. And in early 1996, it plans to start an advertising campaign to promote labor. "I think this really boils down to a grass roots issue," Pearson says. "We're going to move forward: Whole Foods is just the beginning of the process."

Officials at Whole Foods, meanwhile, address the issue with the same upbeat attitude for which the grocery chain has earned its reputation. "The union being out there has allowed us - in a really positive way - to educate out team because the questions from our employees have been more open," Blackburn says "It has allowed us to shine as a model of what Whole Foods is all about."

EXPERIENTIAL EXERCISES

What Managers Do

Preparation

Think about the questions that follow. Record your answers in the spaces provided.

1. How much of a typical manager's time would you expect to be allocated to these relationships?

   (total should=100%)

   _____ %   of time working with subordinates

   _____ %   of time working with the boss

   _____ %   of time working with peers and outsiders

2. How many hours per week does the average manager work? _____hours

3. What amount of a manager's time is typically spent in the following activities? (total should=100%)

   _____ %   in scheduled meetings

   _____ %   in unscheduled meetings

   _____ %   doing desk work

   _____ %   talking on the telephone

   _____ %   walking around the organization/work site

Instructions

Talk over your responses with a nearby classmate. Explore similarities and differences in your answers. Be prepared to participate in class discussion led by your instructor.

EXERCISE 2

In-Class Management Essay

Preparation
Students spend part of one class period (about twenty minutes) writing an essay describing either an outstanding manager they have worked for or a poor or ineffective manager. No names are mentioned. Simply describe what this person was like, how they acted, etc.

Instructions
Form groups (4 or 5 students) by finding others who wrote about the same type of manager. Discuss the common characteristics of outstanding and poor managers. Share with the entire class. Outstanding managers tend to share common characteristics such as "treat employees fairly" or "set high standards of performance." Likewise poor managers tend to share similar characteristics such as "technically incompetent" or "play favorites."

Source: Adapted from Bonnie L. McNeely, Murray State University, "Make Your Principles of Management Class Come Alive"

Graffiti Needs Assessment:
Involving Students in the First Class Session

Contributed by Barbara K. Goza, Visiting Associate Professor, University of California Santa Cruz and Associate Professor California State Polytechnic University, Pomona.
From *Journal of Management Education*, 1993.

Instructions for Students

Preparation
Complete the following sentences with as many endings as possible.

     1. When I first came to this class, I thought...

     2. My greatest concern this term is...

     3. In 3 years I will be...

     4. The greatest challenge facing the world today is...

     5. Organizational behavior specialists do...

     6. Human resources are...

     7. Organizational research is...

     8. The most useful question I've been asked is...

     9. The most important phenomenon in organizations is...

    10. I learn the most when...

Instructions
Your instructor will guide you in a class discussion about your responses. Pay careful attention to similarities and differences in students' answers.

EXERCISE 4

Cross-Cultural Awareness

Objectives

1. To assist you in establishing a better awareness of differences among various cultures.
2. To explore different cultural norms and values.
3. To enhance your awareness of the demands of global competition.

Time

60 to 90 minutes

Procedure

1. Form a group of four to five people and choose a specific country to target for this exercise.
2. In your group, develop a profile on the country you have selected. Profiles may include such things as:
   a. What the local people look like.
   b. Climate and geographic characteristics.
   c. Socioeconomic structure.
   d. Expected roles for various persons in this society.
   e. Moral/ethical beliefs and traditions.
   f. Competitive strength/advantages in the global marketplace.
   g. Greatest weaknesses/needs.
3. Your group will present a brief overview of the country's profile to the rest of the class.
4. After the group presentations, your instructor will pair your group with another group. You are to assume the role of manager in a company in your profiled country that has recently experienced a corporate merger with a company represented by your paired group. Managers from both companies are assigned to a special task force to address the merger. Specific issues to be discussed include:
   a. What problems will the new management team have?
   b. What can be done to make it work effectively?
   c. What major cultural issues may be cause for concern?
5. Following your task-force discussion, you will be asked to share your findings with the entire class.

EXERCISE 5

Men and Women as Allies:
Exploring Egalitarian Relationships

Contributed by Mark Maier, Ph.D., Organizational Leadership Program Director, Chapman University

Advance Preparation Questions (Homework):

1. a. Think of someone with whom you have had a relationship that you could characterize as "truly equal." How did you *know* it was "equal?" What qualities made it such? What does it mean to say that two people relate in this way?

2. a. Think of the things that members of *the other sex* do in work situations that *inhibit* you from relating to them as equals.

   b. List the things that *you* do in work situations that *inhibit* the establishment and maintenance of egalitarian relationships between the sexes.

3. a. List the things that members of the other sex do (or could do) to *promote* the establishment and maintenance of egalitarian relationships.

   b. List the things the *you* do (or could do) to *promote* the establishment and maintenance of egalitarian relationships.

In Class (Session 1)

1. The Qualities of Egalitarian Relationships. 10 min.

   (Total group sharing and posting of results from question #1).

2. *Inhibitors* of Egalitarian Relationships between the Sexes. (Single-sex groups)

   a. "In-group" summary and recording of results from question #2 (newsprint). 10 min.

   b. Sharing and posting of summaries. (2 x 2 chart; on newsprint) 15 min.

   Women (as seen by men);   Women (as seen by themselves)

   Men (as seen by women);   Men (as seen by themselves)

3. Discussion of results. 15 min.

In Class (Session 2)

1. Review of results from previous session.

2. *Enhancers* of Egalitarian Relationships. (*Mixed-sex groups of 6-10 members*)

   a. In group summary and recording of results from question #3 (newsprint). 10 min.

   b. Sharing and posting of summaries from various groups (newsprint). 15 min.

      i. What *Women* do (or can do)

      ii. What *Men* do (or can do)

3. Sharing of overall conclusions and insights. (10-20 minutes.)

OB Work Setting Observations

Objectives

1. To draw inferences from information in an OB work setting.
2. To compare and contrast these inferences with those of other people.
3. To develop OB insights from this comparison and contrasting process.

Total Time

45 to 70 minutes

Procedure

1. Form six groups: two all-male groups; two all-female groups; and two mixed male-female groups.
2. Follow the instructions in the vignette below after receiving additional information from your instructor.
3. *Each individual* in the group read the description of the character in the setting and jot down a brief explanation of each of the nine statements listed (about 5 minutes).
4. Using each *individual's* explanations prepared above, *collectively* construct a reasonable explanation for each of the descriptions (about 15 minutes).
5. Record the group's conclusions either on flipchart paper or so they can be recorded on a chalkboard or equivalent.
6. Once your instructor has so indicated, answer the following three questions as a group (about 5 minutes).
a. How would you rate the performance of Burroughs on a 10-point scale?
b. How would you rate this person's satisfaction on a 10-point scale?
c. How much would you want this person as a boss?
7. Be prepared to present and defend your group's explanations and answers to questions, if called upon by the instructor.
8. Follow through as indicated by the instructor.

Burroughs is employed as the chief pathologist and supervisor of the pathology lab of Central Catholic Hospital, a major medical center in the core of a major city. Burroughs holds several advanced degrees, is licensed as a pathologist, and has been employed at the lab for 5 years. You have recently observed this chief pathologist and supervisor at work, as part of your investigation of how the principles of organizational behavior apply in the work setting.

You found the following information about Burroughs. Briefly explain each of these pieces of information.

1. There is a family picture on Burroughs' desk.
2. The desk is usually cluttered.
3. Burroughs is often seen talking to coworkers.

OB Work Setting Observations, (continued)

4. Several times when you went to Burroughs' office there was no one at Burroughs' desk.

5. Several times you found that Burroughs simply was not in the office.

6. Burroughs lunches with the boss several times a week.

7. Burroughs is excited about the expected arrival of a new baby in the family.

8. Burroughs is going on a business trip.

9. In six weeks Burroughs is leaving for a better job.

The Women as Managers Scale (WAMS)

INSTRUCTIONS

The following items are an attempt to assess the attitudes people have about women in business. The best answer to each statement is your *personal opinion*. The statements cover many different and opposing points of view; you may find yourself agreeing strongly with some of the statements, disagreeing just as strongly with others, and perhaps uncertain about others. Whether you agree or disagree with any statement; you can be sure that many people feel the same way you do.

Using the numbers from 1 to 7 on the rating scale, mark your personal opinion about each statement in the blank that immediately precedes it. Remember, give your *personal opinion* according to how much you agree or disagree with each item. Please respond to all 21 items. Thank you.

RATING SCALE

1 = Strongly Disagree

2 = Disagree

3 = Slightly Disagree

4 = Neither Disagree nor Agree

5 = Slightly Agree

6 = Agree

7 = Strongly Agree

_____ 1. It is less desirable for women than men to have a job that requires responsibility.

_____ 2. Women have the objectivity required to evaluate business situations properly.

_____ 3. Challenging work is more important to men than it is to women.

_____ 4. Men and women should be given equal opportunity for participation in management training programs.

_____ 5. Women have the capability to acquire the necessary skills to be successful managers.

_____ 6. On the average, women managers are less capable of contributing to an organization's overall goals than are men.

_____ 7. It is not acceptable for women to assume leadership roles as often as men.

_____ 8. The business community should someday accept women in key managerial positions.

_____ 9. Society should regard work by female managers as valuable as work by male managers.

_____ 10. It is acceptable for women to compete with men for top executive positions.

_____ 11. The possibility of pregnancy does not make women less desirable employees than men

_____ 12. Women would no more allow their emotions to influence their managerial behavior than would men.

The Women as Managers Scale (WAMS), (continued)

_____ 13. Problems associated with menstruation should not make women less desirable than men as employees.

_____ 14. To be a successful executive, a woman does not have to sacrifice some of her femininity.

_____ 15. On the average, a woman who stays at home all the time with her children is a better mother

_____ 15. than a woman who works outside the home at least half time.

_____ 16. Women are less capable of learning mathematical and mechanical skills than are men.

_____ 17. Women are not ambitious enough to be successful in the business world.

_____ 18. Women cannot be assertive in business situations that demand it.

_____ 19. Women possess the self-confidence required of a good leader.

_____ 20. Women are not competitive enough to be successful in the business world.

_____ 21. Women cannot be aggressive in business situations that demand it.

SCORING GUIDE FOR THE "WOMEN AS MANAGERS SCALE."

1. _Circle_ each of the following items on the scale after you have finished responding to all 21 items:
1, 3, 6, 7, 15, 16, 17, 18, 20, 21. (i.e., you should have circled 10 numbers)

Example: 1. It is less desirable for women than men to have a job that requires responsibility.

2. Before calculating your TOTAL SCORE (on all 21 items), you must first _convert_ your scores _on the items just circled._ (This is so that the direction of the scoring remains consistent and that a higher value always represents a more favorable attitude towards women as managers).

CONVERT the scores on items 1, 3, 6, 7, 15, 16, 17, 18, 20, and 21 as follows:

	IF YOUR SCORE WAS:			...CROSS IT OUT AND REPLACE IT WITH:
	1	=	7	
	2	=	6	
(OLD SCORE)	3	=	5	(NEW SCORE)
	4	=	4	
	5	=	3	
	6	=	2	
	7	=	1	

(New Score)

Example: 6 ~~2~~ 1. It is less desirable for women than men to have a job that requires responsibility.

(Old Score)

The Women as Managers Scale (WAMS), (continued)

3. *NOW* add up your total on *all items, 1-21*, and enter it here: _____
(Note: The minimum score would be 21, and the maximum could be 147! *DOUBLE-CHECK YOUR ARITHMETIC!!!)*

Name: _____ Sex: M F Age: _____

Date: _____

Student ID#: _____

Source: L. H. Peters, J. T. Terborg, and J. Taynor, "Women as Managers Scale (WAMS)" (ms. no. 585), *Journal Supplement Abstract Service* (APA), 1974.

Essentials of Motivation

Objectives

1. To stimulate personal analysis of social and academic motivators.
2. To contrast and compare social and academic motivators.
3. To provide insight into a variety of motivators for you and other people in groups.

Total Time

45 to 70 minutes

Procedure

1. Make a list for each category of worker below in response to the question "What are the five most important 'turn-ons' or things that motivate you in your job?"

    a. You
    b. A skilled worker.
    c. A white-collar manager.
    d. A professional (e.g., physician, attorney).

2. Form a group of five to seven individuals, share your lists, and reach agreement as to the top five motivators for each worker listed above.
3. Discuss as a group whether any conflicts were discovered among the workers, and if so, why?
4. Compare and contrast each worker's motivators. Emphasis should be placed on differences and reasons for differences.
5. Await further class discussion led by your instructor.

EXERCISE 9

Compensation and Benefits Debate

Preparation

Consider the following statements.

On *compensation*: "A basic rule of thumb should be - pay at least as much, and perhaps a bit more, in base wage or salary than what competitors are offering."

On *benefits*: "When benefits are attractive or at least adequate, the organization is in a better position to employ highly qualified people."

Instructions

Form groups as assigned by the instructor. Each will be given *either* one of the prior position statements, *or* one of these alternatives.

On *compensation*: Given the importance of controlling costs, organizations can benefit by paying as little as possible for labor.

On *benefits*: Given the rising cost of health-care and other benefit programs, and the increasing difficulty many organizations have staying in business, it is best to minimize paid benefits and let employees handle more of the cost on their own.

Each group should prepare to debate a counterpoint group on its assigned position. After time allocated to prepare for the debate, each group will present its opening positions. Each will then be allowed one rebuttal period to respond to the other group. General class discussion on the role of compensation and benefits in the modern organization will follow.

Job Design Preferences

Preparation

Use the left column to rank the following job characteristics in the order most important *to you* (1=highest to 10=lowest). Then use the right column to rank them in the order you think they are most important *to others*.

_____ Variety of tasks _____

_____ Performance feedback _____

_____ Autonomy/freedom in work _____

_____ Working on a team _____

_____ Having responsibility _____

_____ Making friends on the job _____

_____ Doing all of a job, not part _____

_____ Importance of job to others _____

_____ Having resources to do well _____

_____ Flexible work schedule _____

Instructions

Form work groups as assigned by your instructor. Share your rankings with other group members. Discuss where you have different individual preferences and where your impressions differ from the preferences of others. Are there any major patterns in your group--for either the "personal" or the "other" rankings? Develop group consensus rankings for each column. Designate a spokesperson to share the group rankings and results of any discussion with the rest of the class.

Interviewing Job Candidates

Preparation

Make a list of the "generic" questions you think any employment interviewer should ask any job candidate, regardless of the specific job or situation. Then, place an X next to those of the following items you think represent additional important questions to ask.

_____ How old are you?

_____ Where were you born?

_____ Where are you from?

_____ What religion are you?

_____ Are you married, single, or divorced?

_____ If not married, do you have a companion?

_____ Do you have any dependent children or elderly parents?

Instructions

Form work groups as assigned by your instructor. Share your responses with other group members, and listen to theirs. Develop group consensus on a list of "generic" interview questions you think any manager should be prepared to ask of job candidates. Also develop group consensus on which of the items on the prior list represent questions that an interviewer should ask. Elect a spokesperson to present group results to the class, along with the reasons for selecting these questions.

The Case of the Contingency Workforce

Preparation

Part-time and contingency work is a rising percentage of total employment in the United States. Go to the library and read about the current use of part-time and contingency workers in business and industry. Ideally, go to the Internet, enter a government data base, and locate some current statistics on the size of the contingent labor force, the proportion that is self-employed and part-time, and the proportion of part-timers who are voluntary and involuntary.

Instructions

In your assigned work group, pool the available information on the contingency workforce. Discuss the information. Discuss one another's viewpoints on the subject, as well as its personal and social implications. Be prepared to participate in a classroom "dialog session" in which your group will be asked to role-play one of the following positions:

(a) Vice president for human resources of a large discount retailer hiring contingency workers.

(b) Owner of a local specialty music shop hiring contingency workers.

(c) Recent graduate of your college or university, working as a contingency employee at the discount retailer in (a).

(d) Single parent with two children in elementary school, working as a contingency employee of the music shop in (b).

The question to be answered by the (a) and (b) groups is: "What does the contingency workforce mean to me?" The question to be answered by the (c) and (d) groups is: "What does being a contingency worker mean to me?"

Setting Work Objectives

Objectives

1. To help you develop and refine your skills for objective development and analysis.
2. To develop a realistic assessment framework for your personal objectives.
3. To develop logical thinking and structure as a means of analysis.

Total Time

45 to 70 minutes

Procedure

1. Identify a specific objective that you would not mind sharing with others in the class. An appropriate objective might be targeted at something important for you during the current academic session (a short-range objective) or an important issue in your social, family, or career plans (a longer-range objective).
2. Next, you should identify three to five "goals" or areas that are linked to the accomplishment of your goal.
3. For each goal you should next develop three to five action steps, or "personal strategies," that would contribute to accomplishing the objective.
4. Briefly describe your objective statement with its goals and strategies on one sheet of paper.
5. Pair up with a partner to evaluate each other's objective model:
   a. Is it achievable?
   b. Is it in an appropriate time frame?
   c. What resources are needed?
6. Discuss how items can be improved or better targeted.
7. Await direction from your instructor regarding class discussion.

EXERCISE 14
Creative Solutions

Instructions

Complete these five tasks while working alone. Be prepared to present and explain your responses in class.

1. Divide the following shape into four pieces of exactly the same size.

2. Without lifting your pencil from the paper, draw no more than four lines that cross through all the dots below.

     .   .   .

     .   .   .

     .   .   .

3. Draw the design for a machine that will turn the pages of your textbook so you can eat a snack while studying.

4. Why would a wheelbarrow ever be designed this way?

5. Turn the following into words.

    a. _____program

Creative Solutions, (continued)

b. r\e\a\d\i\n\g

c. ECNALG

d.   j
         u
    yousme
       t

e. stand
  i

Optional Instructions

After working alone, share your responses with a nearby classmate or with a group. See if you can develop different and/or better solutions based on this exchange of ideas.

Source: Ideas 2 and 5 found in Russel L. Ackoff, *The Art of Problem Solving* (New York: Wiley, 1978); ideas 1 and 4 found in Edward De Bono, *Lateral Thinking: Creativity Step by Step* (New York: Harper & Row, 1970); source for 5 is unknown.

EXERCISE 15

Groups in Organizations

Preparation

For this exercise, select a specific group you work with or have worked with. It can be a group from college or work. Answer the following questions as they relate to the group.

1. Is the group a work group? Explain why or why not.
2. Is the group a formal or informal group? Explain why.
3. Is the group a psychological group? Explain why or why not by discussing the four criteria of a psychological group.
4. Is the group an open system? Explain why or why not by discussing its inputs, throughputs, and outputs.
5. Describe the organizational setting (resources, technology, spatial arrangements, reward systems and goals, structure, size, and culture), nature of the group task, general membership characteristics (interpersonal compatibilities, membership homogeneity-heterogeneity, status), and group size.
6. Describe some of the required and emergent behaviors of the group, activities, interactions, and sentiments.
7. Is the group a self-managing work team, quality circle, or worker involvement group? Explain why the group is or is not each of these three types of groups.

Objective

To better understand the basic attributes of groups.

Total Time

15 to 30 minutes

Procedure

The class will share their answers to the preparation in groups of four to six members or as a class.

EXERCISE 16

Decision Making

It is generally agreed that the trend is toward increasing levels of participative management. The big problem facing managers today is determining when to make the decision alone, when to use participation, and when to let the group make the decision. This exercise will give you practice as a manager at determining when to use participation and when not to.

Preparation

For the ten situations described below, decide which of the three styles you would use for that unique situation. Place the letter A, P, or L on the line before each situation's number.

        A—autocratic; make the decision alone without subordinate input.

        P—participative; make the decision based on subordinate input.

        L—laissez-faire; allow the group to which you belong to make the decision.

_____ 1. You have developed a new work procedure that will increase productivity. Your boss likes the idea and wants you to try it within a few weeks. You view your employees as fairly capable and believe that they will be receptive to the change.

_____ 2. The industry of your product has new competition. Your organization's revenues have been dropping. You have been told to lay off three of your ten employees in 2 weeks. You have been the supervisor for over 1 year. Normally, your employees are very capable.

_____ 3. Your department has been facing a problem for several months. Many solutions have been tried and failed. You finally thought of a solution, but you are not sure of the possible consequences of the change required or the acceptance of the highly capable employees.

_____ 4. Flex time has become popular in your organization. Some departments let each employee start and end work whenever they choose. However, because of the cooperative effort of your employees, they must all work the same 8 hours. You are not sure of the level of interest in changing the hours. Your employees are a very capable group and like to make decisions.

_____ 5. The technology in your industry is changing faster than the members of your organization can keep up. Top management hired a consultant who has given the recommended decision. You have 2 weeks to make your decision. Your employees are capable, and they enjoy participating in the decision-making process.

_____ 6. Your boss called you on the telephone to tell you that someone has requested an order for your department's product with a very short delivery date. She asked that you call her back with the decision about taking the order in 15 minutes. Looking over the work schedule, you realize that it will be very difficult to deliver the order on time. Your employees will have to push hard to make it. They are cooperative, capable, and enjoy being involved in decision making.

Decision Making, (continued)

_____ 7. A change has been handed down from top management. How you implement it is your decision. The change takes effect in 1 month. It will personally affect everyone in your department. The acceptance of the department members is critical to the success of the change. Your employees are usually not too interested in being involved in making decisions.

_____ 8. You believe that productivity in your department could be increased. You have thought of some ways that may work, but you're not sure of them. Your employees are very experienced; almost all of them have been in the department longer than you have.

_____ 9. Top management has decided to make a change that will affect all of your employees. You know that they will be upset because it will cause them hardship. One or two may even quit. The change goes into effect in 30 days. Your employees are very capable.

_____ 10. A customer has offered you a contract for your product with a quick delivery date. The offer is open for 2 days. Meeting the contract deadline would require employees to work nights and weekends for 6 weeks. You cannot require them to work overtime. Filling this profitable contract could help get you the raise you want and feel you deserve. However, if you take the contract and don't deliver on time it will hurt your chances of getting a big raise. Your employees are very capable.

Objective

To gain a better understanding when and when not to use groups in decision making.

Total Time

5 to 30 minutes

Procedure

The instructor will give the class the answers to the ten preparation situations. Groups and/or the class may discuss the answers.

EXERCISE 17

Empowering Others

Instructions

Think of times when you have been in charge of a group--this could be a full-time or part-time work situation, a student work group, or whatever. Complete the following questionnaire by recording how you feel about each statement according to this scale.

1=Strongly disagree

2=Disagree

3=Neutral

4=Agree

5=Strongly agree

When in charge of a group I find:

_____ 1. Most of the time other people are too inexperienced to do things, so I prefer to do them myself.

_____ 2. It often takes more time to explain things to others than to just do them myself.

_____ 3. Mistakes made by others are costly, so I don't assign much work to them.

_____ 4. Some things simply should not be delegated to others.

_____ 5. I often get quicker action by doing a job myself.

_____ 6. Many people are good only at very specific tasks and so can't be assigned additional responsibilities.

_____ 7. Many people are too busy to take on additional work.

_____ 8. Most people just aren't ready to handle additional responsibilities.

_____ 9. In my position, I should be entitled to make my own decisions.

Scoring

Total your responses; enter the score here [_____].

Interpretation

This instrument gives an impression of your *willingness to delegate*. Possible scores range from 9 to 45. The higher your score, the more willing you appear to be to delegate to others. Willingness to delegate is an important managerial characteristic; it is essential if you--as a manager--are to "empower" others and give them opportunities to assume responsibility and exercise self-control in their work. With the growing importance of empowerment in the new workplace, your willingness to delegate is well worth thinking about seriously.

Source: Questionnaire adapted from L. Steinmetz and R. Todd, First Line Management, ed. 4 (Homeword, IL: BPI/Irwin, 1986), pp. 64–67. Used by permission.

Identifying Group Norms

Objectives

1. To help you determine the norms operating in an organization.
2. To assess the strength of response to particular norms.
3. To help clarify the importance of norms as influences on individual and group behavior.

Time

60 minutes

Procedure

1. Choose an organization you know quite a bit about.
2. Complete the questionnaire below, indicating your responses using one of the following:

   a. Strongly agree or encourage it.

   b. Agree with it or encourage it.

   c. Consider it unimportant.

   d. Disagree with or discourage it.

   e. Strongly disagree with or discourage it.

Instrument

If an employee in your organization were to...*most other employees would:*

1. Show genuine concern for the problems that face the organization and make suggestions about solving them...
2. Set very high personal standards of performance...
3. Try to make the work group operate more like a team when dealing with issues or problems...
4. Think of going to a supervisor with a problem...
5. Evaluate expenditures in terms of the benefits they will provide for the organization...
6. Express concern for the well-being of other members of the organization...
7. Keep a customer or client waiting while looking after matters of personal convenience...
8. Criticize a fellow employee who is trying to improve things in the work situation...
9. Actively look for ways to expand his/her knowledge to be able to do a better job...
10. Be perfectly honest in answering this questionnaire...

Identifying Group Norms, (continued)

Scoring

A= +2, B= +1, C= 0, D= -1, E= -2

   1. Organizational/Personal Pride   Score _____

   2. Performance/Excellence   Score _____

   3. Teamwork/Communication   Score _____

   4. Leadership/Supervision   Score _____

   5. Profitability/Cost Effectiveness   Score _____

   6. Colleague/Associate Relations   Score _____

   7. Customer/Client Relations   Score _____

   8. Innovativeness/Creativity   Score _____

   9. Training/Development   Score _____

 10. Candor/Openness   Score _____

Work Team Dynamics

Preparation

Think about your course work group, a work group you are involved in for another course, or any other group suggested by the instructor. Indicate how often each of the following statements accurately reflects your experience in the group. Use this scale:

1= Always   2= Frequently   3= Sometimes   4= Never

_____ 1. My ideas get a fair hearing.

_____ 2. I am encouraged for innovative ideas and risk taking.

_____ 3. Diverse opinions within the group are encouraged.

_____ 4. I have all the responsibility I want.

_____ 5. There is a lot of favoritism shown in the group.

_____ 6. Members trust one another to do their assigned work.

_____ 7. The group sets high standards of performance excellence.

_____ 8. People share and change jobs a lot in the group.

_____ 9. You can make mistakes and learn from them in this group.

_____ 10. This group has good operating rules.

Instructions

Form groups as assigned by your instructor. Ideally, this will be the group you have just rated. Have all group members share their ratings, and make one master rating for the group as a whole. Circle the items on which there are the biggest differences of opinion. Discuss those items and try to find out why they exist. In general, the better a group scores on this instrument, the higher its creative potential. If everyone has rated the same group, make a list of the five most important things members can do to improve its operations in the future. Nominate a spokesperson to summarize the group discussion for the class as a whole.

Source: Adapted from William Dyer, *Team Building*, ed. 2 (Reading, MA: Addison-Wesley, 1987), pp. 123–125.

EXERCISE 20
Organizational Analysis

Objectives

1. To develop and refine your understanding of the basic attributes and characteristics of various organizations.
2. To explore differences and similarities among organizations.
3. To enhance your research and analysis skills.

Total Time

60 to 90 minutes

Procedure

1. Choose an organization you know quite a bit about. Develop a list of its basic attributes, including its goals, culture, structure, and specialization.
2. In groups of five members, select one organization and thoroughly assess its attributes. It is best to develop a matrix to record all discussion on each of the attributes.
3. Also address the five concerns listed below:
   a. *Product:* Are its products of real social value? Are they critical elements in machines or elements of mass destruction?
   b. *Workplace:* Is the workplace safe? Is the business finding ways to involve workers in the decision-making process?
   c. *Environment:* If you have chosen a manufacturer, does the business protect air, water, and so on? If you have chosen a financial business, does it use environmental responsibility when investing or underwriting?
   d. *Community:* What kind of commitment does it have to local and national community? Does it apply some standards to overseas workers?
   e. *Ownership:* Are workers brought in to ownership through employee stock options?
4. In groups, discuss the implications of what was observed in developing the matrix (i.e. similarities, differences, types of attributes common to a variety of organizations).
5. Choose a group representative to present the highlights of the discussion and analysis to the entire class.

The "Rational" Organization

Objectives

1. To assess an organization's ethical culture.
2. To understand the importance and relevancy of ethical issues in the modern business world.

Total Time

60 to 75 minutes.

Procedure

1. Choose an organization you know.
2. Complete the following questionnaire as candidly as possible regarding that organization.

Instrument

Indicate whether you agree or disagree with each of the following statements about the company you have chosen. Use the rating scale below to represent your answer to what extent the following statements are true about your company.

0 Completely False   1 Mostly False   2 Somewhat False

3 Somewhat True   4 Mostly True   5 Completely True

_____ 1. In this company, people are expected to follow their own personal and moral beliefs.

_____ 2. People are expected to do anything to further the company's interests.

_____ 3. In this company, people look out for each other's good.

_____ 4. It is very important here to follow strictly the company's rules and procedures.

_____ 5. In this company, people protect their own interests above all other considerations.

_____ 6. The first consideration is whether a decision violates any law.

_____ 7. Everyone is expected to stick by company rules and procedures.

_____ 8. The most efficient way is always the right way in this company.

_____ 9. Our major consideration is what is best for everyone in the company.

_____ 10. In this company, the law or ethical code of the profession is the major consideration.

_____ 11. It is expected that employees will always do what is right for the customer and the public.

The "Rational" Organization, (continued)

3. Score your responses to the above statements by adding your totals on the grid below.

4. In groups of three to five compare your results and share your reactions to the findings. Which of the criteria or levels of analysis do you believe is most revealing of your company?

5. Await further instruction from your instructor.

LEVELS OF ANALYSIS

	INDIVIDUAL	LOCAL	COSMOPOLITAN
EGOISM	Self-Interest	Company Profit	Efficiency
	#5 Score	#2 Score	#8 Score
ETHICAL CRITERIA	Friendship	Team Interest	Social Responsibility
BENEVOLENCE	#3 Score	#9 Score	#11 Score
PRINCIPAL	Personal Morality	Rules and Standard Operating Procedures	Laws and Professional Codes
	#1 Score	#4 + #7 Score	#6 + #10 Score

Machiavellianism

Objectives

1. To assess individual Machiavellianism (Mach) scores.
2. To explore the dynamics of power in a group environment.
3. To develop an understanding of the rewards and frustrations of held power.
4. To analyze behaviors of various Mach personality types.

Total Time

45 to 60 minutes

Procedure

1. Complete the 10-item Mach Assessment Instrument below.
2. Follow directions for scoring your instrument individually.
3. Form a group of five to seven persons and designate one individual as the official group "observer." The observer will not participate in any of the discussion but will take notes on the activities of the group and later report to the class.
4. Your instructor will announce the topic to be discussed. The topic should be highly controversial and stimulating and one that encourages different viewpoints.
5. The observer will begin by handing a specific textbook or magazine to one member of the group. Only that member of the group may speak. The textbook or magazine will be held by that person until another member of the group signals, *nonverbally*, that he or she wishes to have it. The person with the textbook or magazine may refuse to relinquish it, even when signaled. A time limit of 15 minutes should be placed on the group discussion.
6. Following the controversial discussion period, the group observer should lead a group discussion on what they observed and learned: power phenomena, frustrations, feedback, and so on.
7. Each group observer will then present what their group has learned to the entire class.

Machiavellianism, (continued)

Mach Assessment Instrument

For each of the following statements, circle the number that most closely resembles your attitude.

Statement	DISAGREE a lot	a little	neutral	AGREE a little	a lot
1. The best way to handle people is to tell them what they want to hear.	1	2	3	4	5
2. When you ask someone to do something for you, it is best to give the real reason for wanting it rather than reasons that might carry more weight.	1	2	3	4	5
3. Anyone who completely trusts someone else is asking for trouble.	1	2	3	4	5
4. It is hard to get ahead without cutting corners here and there.	1	2	3	4	5
5. It is safest to assume that all people have a vicious streak, and it will come out when they are given a chance.	1	2	3	4	5
6. One should take action only when it is morally right.	1	2	3	4	5
7. Most people are basically good and kind.	1	2	3	4	5
8. There is no excuse for lying to someone else.	1	2	3	4	5
9. Most people forget more easily the death of their father than the loss of their property.	1	2	3	4	5
10. Generally speaking, people won't work hard unless forced to do so.	1	2	3	4	5

Scoring Key and Interpretation

This assessment is designed to compute your Machiavellianism (Mach) score. Mach is a personality characteristic that taps people's power orientation. The high-Mach personality is pragmatic, maintains emotional distance from others, and believes that ends can justify means. To obtain your Mach score, add up the numbers you checked for questions 1, 3, 4, 5, 9, and 10. For the other four questions, reverse the number you have checked, so that 5 becomes 1; 4 is 2; and 1 is 5. Then total both sets of numbers to find your score. A random sample of adults found the national average to be 25. Students in business and management typically score higher.

The results of research using the Mach tests have found: (1) men are generally more Machiavellian than are women: (2) older adults tend to have lower Mach scores than do younger adults; (3) there is no significant difference between high Machs and low Machs on measures of intelligence or ability; (4) Machiavellianism.

EXERCISE 23

Analysis of Personal Power

PURPOSE:

(1) To help you explore the typical ways that you interact with people.

(2) To help you think about the meaning of power to you, in terms of your relations with other people.

(3) To identify those individuals in the learning environment who have more or less power, and to understand how this power is derived.

ADVANCE PREPARATION: At discretion of group leader.

GROUP SIZE: Unlimited group size; three-to four-person groups may be used to discuss the results.

TIME REQUIRED: Part I, 1 hour; Part II, 1 hour

SPECIAL MATERIALS: None.

SPECIAL PHYSICAL REQUIREMENTS: None.

RELATED TOPICS: Motivation: basic concepts, Managers as leaders.

INTRODUCTION

The first part of this exercise is designed to help you explore some aspects of your relations with other people. You will do this by responding to a questionnaire. That questionnaire will be scored in class, and the group leader will explain the concepts needed to help you interpret your scores. The second part of this exercise will help you to explore the different ways that power can be used, and the impact of that approach on behavior.

PROCEDURE

Step 1: 10 Minutes

Read the following description.

The questionnaire in this section is based on a theory called FIRO. FIRO was developed by Dr. William Schutz as a measure of an individual's basic interpersonal needs. Schutz proposed that individuals differed in the strength of their interpersonal needs along three major dimensions: inclusion, control, and affection. For each of these three needs, individuals also differed in the degree to which an individual was comfortable expressing each need toward others, and the degree to which individuals wanted others to express that need toward him. His theory led him to develop a questionnaire that measured individual differences on the three major dimensions (inclusion, control, and affection), and the strength of each need on both expressed (toward others) and wanted (from others).

Inclusion refers to your need to establish and maintain contact with other people. Some people have high needs for inclusion—that is, they like to be with other people, to be part of a group, to be included in a lot of formal and informal social groups and events, and to be around people a great deal. Some other people have low needs for inclusion—that is, they prefer to be alone, to do things by themselves, to have only a few friends, or to avoid groups and social gatherings. Finally, still other people have moderate

Analysis of Personal Power, (continued)

needs for inclusion. Individuals can differ in the degree to which they express this need for inclusion to others, *and* to the degree that they want others to express inclusion to them. These two orientations can vary independently. For example, it is not uncommon for a somewhat shy person to express very little inclusion toward others, but want others to express a lot of inclusion toward her.

Control refers to the need to have influence or control other people, or have them influence and control you. Some people have high needs for control—that is, they like to have influence over others, to be in charge, to tell other people what to do. Other people have low needs for control—that is, they have little or no interest in whether they have influence or not, or whether they are in charge, or whether someone is giving direction and orders. Finally, still other people have moderate needs for control. Individuals can also differ in the degree to which they express this need for control over others, and the degree to which they want others to express control to them. These two dimensions can also vary independently. For example, it is not uncommon for an individual to want someone else to make the decisions and control him, but have little or no interest in controlling others.

Affection refers to the need to have a close, personal relationship with other people, to be comfortable in expressing affection, and in having it expressed to you. Some people have high needs for affection—that is, they like to have close and personal relationships with other people. Other people have low needs for affection—that is, they prefer to be have rather cool and distant relationships with people. Finally, still other people have moderate needs for affection. Individuals can also differ in the degree to which they express this need for affection to others, and the degree to which they want others to express affection toward them. These two orientations can also vary independently. For example, it is not uncommon for an individual to be very comfortable in expressing affection, but very uncomfortable in receiving it.

The questionnaire below is designed to have you estimate the strength of your own needs along two scales for each of six dimensions: expressed inclusion, want inclusion, expressed control, want control, expressed affection, and want affection. You are to select one number from 0 (very low) to 9 (very high) for each of the 12 scales. Several descriptive statements and phrases are placed along each dimension to help you pick the number that best identifies the strength of your need.

Before you make your ratings, we want to offer two statements of caution:

1. Please be as candid as you can. Do not try to answer this questionnaire as you think you "should." *There are no right answers! No one set of answers makes you appear healthier or unhealthier, better or worse than somebody else! You will not be required to share your answers with anyone, so please try to describe yourself as you really think you are!*

2. As you read this description of the major needs, you may recognize that your needs vary. For example, sometimes you may want to be around people and sometimes you don't. That's true! You will note that there are two scales for each dimension. One asks you to rate yourself on the strength of your need in terms of how often it occurs, while the other asks you to rate yourself on the number of other people with whom you feel this need.

Analysis of Personal Power, (continued)

Step 2: 10 Minutes

Below you will find two scales for each of the six dimensions. Rate yourself along each of the scales. Circle *one* number, from 0 to 9, indicating your best guess as to the strength of your need on that particular scale. Then find the *average* of your two scale scores for each of the six dimensions.

Expressed Inclusion

| 0 | 1 | 2 | 3 | 4 | 5 | 6 | 7 | 8 | 9 |

Most often try to be alone, not include others in activities and social events

Sometimes; Occasionally

Most often try to include others in activities and social events, not be alone

| 0 | 1 | 2 | 3 | 4 | 5 | 6 | 7 | 8 | 9 |

Most often don't include anybody in activities and social events, want to be by myself

Some people; a few people

Most often try to include one or more people in activities and social events, want to be with someone.

Average score of two scales = _____

Want Inclusion

| 0 | 1 | 2 | 3 | 4 | 5 | 6 | 7 | 8 | 9 |

Most often want to be alone, not included by others in activities and social events

Sometimes; Occasionally

Most often want others to include me in activities activities and social events; don't want them to leave me alone

| 0 | 1 | 2 | 3 | 4 | 5 | 6 | 7 | 8 | 9 |

Don't want anybody to include me in activities and social events, want to be alone

Some people; a few people

Want most people to include me in their activities and social events; want to be included by a lot of people

Average score of two scales = _____

Analysis of Personal Power, (continued)

Expressed Control

| 0 | 1 | 2 | | 3 | 4 | 5 | 6 | | 7 | 8 | 9 |

Most often avoid influencing others; avoid trying to be dominant, avoid taking charge

Sometimes; Occasionally

Most often try to influence others, try to be dominant, try to take charge

| 0 | 1 | 2 | | 3 | 4 | 5 | 6 | | 7 | 8 | 9 |

Don't try to influence anybody, don't try to be dominant or take charge over most people

Some people; A few people

Try to influence most people, try to be dominant of or take charge over most people

Average of two scale scores = _____

Want Control

| 0 | 1 | 2 | | 3 | 4 | 5 | 6 | | 7 | 8 | 9 |

Usually don't want to be influenced by others, don't want to be dominated, usually avoid others taking charge of me

Sometimes; Occasionally

Usually want to be influenced by others, want to be dominated, want others to take charge of me.

| 0 | 1 | 2 | | 3 | 4 | 5 | 6 | | 7 | 8 | 9 |

Usually do't want anyone to influence me, don't want anyone to dominate me, don't want anyone to take charge of me

Some people; A few people

Want lots of other people to influence me, dominate me, take charge of my activities

Average of two scale scores = _____

Analysis of Personal Power, (continued)

Expressed Affection

0	1	2	3	4	5	6	7	8	9

Never want to act close and personal to others; usually want to act cool and distant to others

Sometimes; Occasionally

Usually want to act close and personal to others; never want to act cool and distant to others

0	1	2	3	4	5	6	7	8	9

Never want to act close and personal to anyone; want to act cool and distant to most people

Some people; a few people

Want to act close and personal to most people; never want to act cool and distant to anyone

Average of two scales = _____

Want Affection

0	1	2	3	4	5	6	7	8	9

Never want people act close or personal with me; usually want people to act cool and distant

Sometimes; Occasionally

Usually want people to act close and personal with me; never want people to act cool and distant

0	1	2	3	4	5	6	7	8	9

Don't want anybody act close and personal with me; want most people to act cool and distant to me

Some people; a few people

Want most people to act close and personal with me; never want anyone to act cool and distant to me

Average of two scales = _____

Analysis of Personal Power, (continued)

Step 3: 5 Minutes

Enter the averages from the six scales in the appropriate spaces below. In each box, you should have a number between 0 and 9:

	Inclusion	*Control*	*Affection*
You give (express to others)	$e^i =$	$e^c =$	$e^a =$
You get (want from others)	$w^i =$	$w^c =$	$w^a =$

Each of these scores, individually and together with the others, can tell you something about yourself and your relations with others. As you read the brief description below, and think about your scores, compare that against your own feelings and beliefs about yourself. When you have read the description you may want to share your scores with others who know you well, to verify their accuracy.

Remember that each individual, if he makes his ratings honestly, will probably have a different profile of scores. There is no "right" answer to this questionnaire, except that it is "right" for your impressions about yourself.

Step 4: Interpreting the Questionnaire, 10 Minutes

The *inclusion* scales are designed to measure your needs to establish and maintain contact with other people. How might some people behave, based on their scores? A person who has a high score on *expressed* inclusion, and a low score on *wanted* inclusion (e.g. 9,0) will be very outgoing toward others. He will be continually making gestures toward others to include them in group activities—sports, parties, work activities, going out to lunch, and so on. However, he probably has no strong needs for others to include him in their groupings. On the other hand, a person who has a high score (e.g. 0,9) on *expressed* inclusion and a low score on *wanted* inclusion (e.g. 0,9) will seldom make invitation gestures toward others, but desperately wants others to include him. People who have strong scores in both categories will both want and express a lot of inclusion, and a person with two low scores on inclusion will be more of a "private" person, who neither wants to include a lot of people in his activities nor be included in theirs.

More interesting problems occur when you explore the needs of two people and their "compatibility" based on inclusion scores. Two people who are strong on both *expressed* and *wanted* will probably see a lot of one another, since each want to involve the other and get satisfaction from being involved. Similarly, people with "complementary needs" may also find their relationship satisfactory, since one is always initiating inclusion and the other wants to receive it. (The 9,0 says, "Hey, let's go to the movies," and the 0,9 says, "I thought you'd never ask.") Difficulties arise where both people are high in *expressed* inclusion, but low in *wanted* inclusion ("Hey, let's go to the movies." "No I really don't want to, but would you like to go to the ball game tomorrow?") or when both are high in *wanted* but low in *expressed*. (Each thinks, "I wish he would invite me to go to the movies.") People low on both inclusion scales will probably

Analysis of Personal Power, (continued)

be very comfortable spending a lot of time by themselves, rather than in group situations.

The *control* scales are designed to measure your needs to control or be controlled by other people.

A person with a high *expressed* power score (e.g. 9,0) will like to be in charge. When he encounters another 9,0 person, there is likely to be a strong battle for leadership in the group. The high want control person likes to be controlled, and will make an excellent subordinate for any 9,0. (In addition, he probably will not understand the conflict between two 9,0s—"How could anyone get that concerned about wanting to run things?") However, when the 0,9 person meets another 0,9 person, there is a "power gap" in which each waits for the other to take over and run things—there is usually no action, and no productivity. The 0,0 person withdraws from power, having no strong needs either to be controlled or to control others.

The 9,9 individual may seem "enigmatic"—how can a person both like to be controlled and control others at the same time? However, when we explore the role of middle management in most organizations, we find that the 9,9 thrives on his dual responsibilities of (1) taking orders and direction from above, and (2) at the same time managing and controlling those below him. The 9,9 is really the "perfect second lieutenant" in the military, completely willing and able to be a good subordinate to his superiors and a good superior to his subordinates.

Comparing inclusion to control, we can say that individuals with strong inclusion needs want to be on the team, regardless of what it is doing and how it is performing. The person with strong control needs wants to be a winner, regardless of what team he is on or who the people on it are.

The *affection* scales are designed to measure your needs to express love and affection to others, or have it expressed to you. A person with a high *expressed* affection score (9,0) will be likely to show others how much he cares for them. He has strong needs for (and will be very comfortable) being warm, caring, and demonstrating his liking. The person with the high *wanted* affection score (0,9) will be drawn to this expression, and so we can expect that a 9,0 and a 0,9 could form a very strong relationship, but in which the affection goes all one way. Similarly, two 9,9 individuals, high on both *expressed* and *wanted* affection, will constantly be preoccupied with showing their liking for one another, and receiving those gestures. Obviously, two 0,0 people will neither show much affection for the other, nor really need it for themselves.

Again, problems may occur when two individuals have mutually strong *expressed* scores without want (9,0s), or mutually strong *wanted* scores without expression (0,9). In the first case, the two individuals probably offer the other individual a lot of liking and attraction, yet they are uncomfortable about receiving it. Each may come to see the other as "gushy" and overly affectionate because they can't manage the receiving end of the affection. Similarly, two 0,9s will be attracted to one another but very seldom express it, and draw away from one another *not* because of their feelings but because of their low need to or ability to express their feelings for the other person.

Overall Pattern of Scores

We may look at the six overall scores, and also make the following inferences:

Analysis of Personal Power, (continued)

1. Obtain the *total* for each column (inclusion, control and affection); this should indicate how much inclusion, power or affection are important to you and the ways you spend your time.
2. Obtain the *discrepancy* for the scores in each column (inclusion, control and affection); this should indicate how much more you express things toward others than they express them toward you (or the reverse).
3. Obtain the *total* of all six scores. This will be a number from 0 to 54, and should give you some strong indication of the relative information of people in your life. The higher the total score, the more important your relations with people are.

Step 5: Discussion, 15 to 30 Minutes

The previous steps asked you to rate yourself on the "magnitude" of your concern for personal power in relation to interpersonal needs for inclusion in social groupings and affection with others. As you review these scores, consider the following:

1. Think about examples or situations from your experience that reflect your scores—for example, instances where you wanted to be included or wanted to include others, wanted to be in charge, and so on. Which examples confirm your scores, and which ones disconfirm them?
2. Think about a situation in which you had a problem relating to other people in a group—deciding who was a "member" of the group, who was in "charge" or making decisions for the group, or who belonged to subgroups that were very close to one another. Do the ideas of "compatibility" between two or more people's styles help you to understand how people behaved?
3. Try completing this questionnaire several times, each time with respect to a particular social group. That is, try responding to the questionnaire in terms of your family, work group, student friends, fraternity or sorority, and so on. Do the responses differ? What does this say about how your needs vary from group to group?

PART II

Step 1: 5 Minutes

The instructor will divide the class into three equal-size groups. These groups may be subdivided if there are more than six people per group.

Step 2: 5 Minutes

Read the following scenario:

You are the manager of a group of research scientists and laboratory technicians in a chemical research laboratory. The scientists and technicians receive a monthly salary, and are expected to work from 8:30 to

Analysis of Personal Power, (continued)

4:30, 5 days a week. In fact, many of the scientists work late or come into the laboratory on weekends in order to complete their experiments.

Recently, you have become aware that one of your best laboratory technicians is repeatedly late for work, and sometimes goes out for too long a coffee break soon after getting to work. The technician seems to be satisfied with his salary and his overall performance is good, but you would like to see him come in on time, work harder in the morning, and thus do even better in his job performance. You even feel that the technician might get turned on to starting research experiments of his own, and perhaps be promoted to a project leader position.

As a manager, you are respected and liked by the others in the lab, and it irritates you that this person treats your dedicated management with such a cavalier attitude. You want to influence the technician to start work on time.

Step 3: 15 Minutes

Each group has the task of preparing an *actual influence strategy* to be used by the manager in correcting the technician's behavior. This strategy will be role-played in class; therefore, you must:

1. Specify exactly what the manager will do with the technician.
2. Select one member of your group to role-play the manager.
3. Select one member of your group to role-play the technician with a manager from another group.
4. Decide on the "environment" in which the role play will take place (the manager's office, coffee shop, chemistry laboratory, etc.)

Step 4: 15 to 20 Minutes

The instructor will select several groups. Each group will role-play the strategy developed.

Analysis of Personal Power, (continued)

Step 5: Discussion

1. As each group role-plays each influence attempt, think of yourself on the receiving end of the influence (i.e., as the technician). Record your own reaction.

	Group 1	Group 2	Group 3	Group 4

a. As a result of the influence attempt, I will. . .

    1   2   3   4   5   ____   ____   ____   ____

    definitely

                        definitely

    comply   not comply

b. Any change that does come about will be. . .

    1   2   3   4   5   ____   ____   ____   ____

    temporary   permanent

c. My own personal reaction is. . .

    1   2   3   4   5   ____   ____   ____   ____

    resistant   acceptant

d. As a result of this influence attempt, my relationship with the manager of the laboratory will probably be. . .

    1   2   3   4   5   ____   ____   ____   ____

    worse   better

2. Look at your reactions to these questions for each influence attempt. Compare them to the reactions of others when the instructor asks for the information.

   a. Which group designed the influence attempt that would most likely result in immediate change of the technician's behavior?

   b. Which group's strategy will have the most long-lasting effects?

   c. Which strategy do people find the most acceptable?

3. By now, your instructor will have told you how the groups were composed at the beginning of the activity. What difference did you observe in the ways that the groups worked together to plan their role play? What implications does this have for considering individual member "styles" in the formation of the task groups?

Analysis of Personal Power, (continued)

GENERALIZATIONS AND CONCLUSIONS

Concluding points:

1. FIRO-B is an instrument with three scales (inclusion, control and affection) and two subscales for each scale (expressed and wanted). Describe the behavior patterns of a person scoring high on each of the six scales.

2. Which scales on the FIRO-B would be most related to the ability to:

   a. Work with others on a team project?

   b. Follow the direction of a leader?

   c. Reorganize a department in a company?

   d. Develop good relationships in a marriage?

3. (For Part II) Identify the types of influence strategies that are developed when people of a similar style work together, as well as the problems that may occur in these groups as a result of all members having similar styles.

Participant's Reactions

Analysis of Personal Power, (continued)

READINGS AND REFERENCES

Jacobsen, W., *Power and Interpersonal Relations* (Belmont, Calif.: Wadsworth Publishing Co., 1972).

French, J. R. P., and Raven, B. H., "The Bases of Social Power," in D. Cartwright (Ed.), *Studies in Social Power* (Ann Arbor, Michigan: Institute for Social Research, 1959)

Schutz, W., *The Interpersonal Underworld* (Palo Alto, Calif.: Science and Behavior Books, 1966).

Winter, D., *The Power Motive* (New York: The Free Press, 1973)

Source: Adapted by Roy J. Lewicki from FIRO: *A Three Dimensional Theory of Interpersonal Behavior* by William C. Schutz (New York: Rinehart & Co., 1958). Part II is adapted from "An Exercise in Social Power" by Gib Akin, Exchange, Vol. 3, No. 4 (1979).

Power In Management: Correcting Performance

PURPOSE:

(1) To demonstrate the use of power in superior-subordinate relations

(2) To explore techniques for improving performance

ADVANCE PREPARATION: Role scenarios may be assigned and prepared in advance.

GROUP SIZE: Any number of dyads or trios (observers may be assigned to each pair).

TIME REQUIRED: 90 minutes total for preparation, role playing, and debriefing.

SPECIAL MATERIALS: None.

SPECIAL PHYSICAL REQUIREMENTS: None

RELATED TOPICS: Applied Motivation, Interpersonal Communication, Negotiation and Conflict, Managers as Leaders

INTRODUCTION

The performance appraisal process in superior-subordinate interaction and managerial strategies for performance improvement have typically been treated by organizational behavior as problems of motivation and goal setting. Yet motivation and goal-setting perspectives on this process typically ignore the power differences and power dynamics between managers and their subordinates. Managers have the formal authority and power to critique and correct a subordinate's performance; the way they exercise this power and authority can have a significant impact on the willingness of the subordinate to change his or her behavior and the future relationship between them. Subordinates have power, too, and can exercise it in different ways. The purpose of this exercise is to examine power dynamics in superior-subordinate interaction.

PROCEDURE

Step 1: 15 Minutes

The instructor will give an introductory lecture on types of power and their use in organizations.

Step 2: 5 Minutes

The instructor will divide the class in half. All students in one group will be designated to play the role of the supervisor, Jan Summers. The other group will play the role of the subordinate, Lee Nolan.

Step 3: 10-20 Minutes

Each student should read his or her role and prepare for the meeting between Nolan and Summers. Instructors may also assign all Nolans to meet together (as a group) and all Summers to meet together (as a

Power In Management: Correcting Performance,

(continued)

group) to prepare. Each Nolan and Summers should prepare individual goals that they want to attain from the meeting.

Step 4: 20-30 Minutes

Each Nolan and Summers will pair up as instructed. Conduct the role play. Be prepared to report to the class on the specific outcome of your meeting and how the outcomes were achieved.

Step 5: 20-30 Minutes

Discussion of role play results and procedures.

DISCUSSION QUESTIONS

1. What were the actual outcomes of the meetings?
2. How did the actual outcomes match what each party wanted to achieve?
3. What kinds of power were used by each party?
4. Which power tactics were likely to be most effective in getting the other to change his or her behavior? Which power tactics were least effective? Why?

READINGS AND REFERENCES

Bell, C. R., *Influencing: Marking the Ideas that Matter.* (Austin, TX: Learning Concepts, 1982)

Lewicki, R. J., and Litterer, J., *Negotiation* Chapter 11. (Homewood, IL: Richard D. Irwin, 1985)

Source: The original "Joe Summers/John Nolan" role play was created by Prof. Henry P. Sims, The Pennsylvania State University. Used with permission of the author. Adapted and developed in this context by Roy J. Lewicki.

Analysis of Personal Power

OBJECTIVES

1. To explore the individual's self-perception of the strength of his needs to control others, and be controlled by others, in relation to his needs for inclusion in groups and attraction to others.
2. To explore the participant's understanding of how individuals with different needs for control use that control in social settings.
3. To explore different styles of exerting influence and their impact on the targets of influence.

WHAT TO EXPECT

Part I of this activity requests the individual's candid self-analysis of his own needs for inclusion with other people, control over other people, and affection toward other people. In order to be meaningful, the individual must be willing to stand back from himself and "realistically" answer the questions, and explore the meaning of the responses. Total acceptance of the results without some questioning, or total rejection of the results without similar exploration of their potential occurrence, will make the instruments useless as learning devices. Part II employs the French and Raven bases of power to understand how power relates to effective influence.

ADVANCE PREPARATION

To understand the nature of the concepts being measured, a prereading of the exercise materials is necessary. It would also be helpful to read the descriptive materials on FIRO, as well as French and Raven's (1959) bases of power.

You should complete the questionnaire yourself before giving it to others. Sharing your scores with the class, and asking them to draw a profile based on their scores, is often a useful bridge to help participants evaluate and compare their own profiles.

You should also decide on the best use of class time. If time is limited, have students complete the questionnaire as homework, and devote the class period to the interpretation and meaning of the scores. If you have additional time, Part II of the exercise can be done.

OPERATING PROCEDURE, HINTS, AND CAUTIONS
OPTIONS FOR PROCEDURE

1. Have participants complete the instrument in Part I before coming to the first class. Class time can be used for scoring, interpreting scores, and relating the different scores to other concepts and approaches to power.

2. Have participants complete and score the instrument in Part I before coming to class; have students

Analysis of Personal Power, (continued)

submit their scores as they enter the classroom. The instructor may then use the scores to compose the subgroups for Part II of the exercise (see below).

HINTS AND CAUTIONS: PART I

Instructors who have used this exercise before will note that the questionnaire in this edition is an adaptation of the original FIRO-B instrument. (Instructors who wish to use the original instrument can obtain copies directly from Consulting Psychologists Press). Because our new version asks individuals to "estimate" their scores on each of the six dimensions rather than derive them from the full questionnaire, scores are likely to be less precise and more subject to an individual's desire for impression management. This may have the following consequences:

1. We would predict that individuals would be less likely to report "extreme" scores (i.e., very high or low values on any of the dimensions), and particularly less likely to report high power scores. However, even scores which are relatively high or low can be compared and discussed.

2. We also suspect that individuals with less self-awareness will have a difficult time estimating the strength of their interpersonal needs. In these cases, it may be useful to encourage a student to share and discuss his/her self-estimates with a close friend, roommate, etc. as they are being made. This will give the individual some opportunity to get some feedback and a more realistic picture of how their needs come across to others. Keep these elements in mind while using this version.

OPERATING PROCEDURE: PART II

1. Students should be divided into three groups based on their Express Control Scores of the FIRO-B. You may either collect their scores in advance and assign them to groups, or organize the groups in the classroom. Students in the bottom third of the distribution should be in one group, the middle third in a second group, and the top third in the final group. Groups of larger than six people should be divided into smaller subgroups. The exercise will probably be more fun if students do not initially know how they were assigned to groups, since discovering the rationale and observing the differences in the group dynamics on the task can be an exciting part of the activity.

2. Students should be instructed to read the role scenario, and design an influence strategy as instructed. It will also be more interesting if the "target" of influence (the lab technician) comes from a different group, so that the "target" does not know the strategy. Moreover, individual needs for Want Control will affect how willingly the target "goes along" or "resists" the influence efforts of the laboratory manager.

3. Students should complete the short questionnaire after each role play, to measure different reactions to different strategies. This data can be compared and summarized later to explore differences as a result of different styles.

Analysis of Personal Power, (continued)

ALTERNATIVES AND VARIATIONS

1. The questionnaire explores a person's desire to control others or be controlled. These needs can be contrasted against the actual opportunities available in this book (e.g., Exercises #27, "The Power Game"). That is, it is possible to group students according to similar need profiles, and to explore the impact of such grouping on the activity. *This alternative should be conducted with caution.* For example, in "The Power Game," it is possible to make all of the people with very *low* needs for expressed control into Tops (the high-resource group) and people with *high* needs for expressed control into Bottoms (the low-resource group). The Tops, with low needs for power in a powerful position, often "rise to the occasion" and begin behaving like high-power people—although quite guiltily. The Bottoms, on the other hand, have a strong need to control things but no resources to do so. Under these conditions, frustration and anger can escalate quickly and irrationality may take over much more rapidly, Obviously, if the groups were reversed, (high expressed control as Tops, low expressed control as Bottoms), the Tops would be very satisfied with their position, and unwilling to yield to the lower groups, while the Bottoms would probably be reasonably docile and unconcerned with their low status.

   If the questionnaire is used in conjunction with another power or conflict exercise, it might also be used to balance the groups in terms of distributing power-concerned people in each group. This maximizes the intragroup difference of opinion, and can lead to some interesting discussion about the leaders or high-influence people who emerge in each group, their scores, and so forth.

2. Familiarity with inclusion, control, and affection scores may help you to explore with a group the match between the "needs" of a particular job and the need profile of the person hired for it. What types of jobs in organizations would be best filled by a person with high inclusion needs? High influence and control needs? High affection needs?

3. In observing and evaluating the different styles used by the groups in Part II, students may also be briefed on the French and Raven bases of power, and how these different types of power are used by the managers in gaining the technician's compliance. These are:

   a. *Reward Power:* The ability to meet the needs of another, or control him by giving reward for the desired behavior. Pay, promotions, or bonuses may be ways that organizations exert reward power over their employees.

   b. *Punishment Power:* Coercive power, or the ability to deliver a painful or punishing outcome to another, and hence control him by his desire to avoid the punishment. Firing, ridiculing, or disciplining an individual are common techniques of coercive power.

Analysis of Personal Power, (continued)

c. *Expert Power:* Power based on the ability to understand, use, and deliver information that others need. Engineers or scientists may exert great influence in an organization based on their knowledge of scientific techniques for manufacturing a product.

d. *Legitimate Power:* Control or influence which is exerted by virtue of the person holding a particular position in the organizational structure. The "power" is vested in the rights and responsibilities of the position, not the person. Thus, the president or chairman of the board of a company has the power by virtue of the rights *and* responsibilities given to the persons holding those offices. Compliance with that power occurs because other individuals in the organization respect the organization structure and the rights and responsibilities that accompany particular positions.

e. *Referent Power:* Liking, charisma, or the desire to comply with someone's wishes because you are attracted to him/her are examples of referent power. Control based on referent power will be dependent upon the power-holder's ability to have others like him/her and be attracted to him/her, and to follow his/her leadership because of this attraction.

A complete description of an exercise designed to explore the impact of these power types is described by Akin (1979).

CONCLUDING THE EXERCISE

1. The behavior patterns can be deduced by the student from the subscriptions in Step 3 of EMOB.

2. The following questionnaire scores would be most related to the tasks:

a. *Ability to work with others on a team project:* Moderate or high inclusion scores, demonstrating a desire to be with others and to want to include others; low expressed control scores, unless the individual is to be a leader; moderate want control scores, indicating an ability to work with others and contribute to "teamwork." Affection scores should be unrelated.

b. *Follow the directions of a leader:* Most directly, the want control score.

c. *Reorganize a department in a company:* Most directly, the expressed control score.

d. *Developing good relationships in a marriage:* While the expressed affection scores are the most important, inclusion and control will be very critical. "Mismatches" in terms of people not satisfying one another's needs, or having needs come into direct conflict, will contribute to marital conflict.

Analysis of Personal Power, (continued)

3. When individuals divide into subgroups based on Expressed Control scores, there will be several interesting dynamics that occur:

   a. Individuals will now be in groups of low, moderate, and high expressed control. With the low expressed control group, the discussion will be quiet and low-keyed, with few individuals taking the responsibility for directing the discussion and focusing on a particular strategy. Moreover, the influence strategy that they probably adopt to change the technician's behavior will probably be "mild" and "tame" in its approach, and will probably appear that way to other students when it is role played.

   b. By contrast, individuals in the high expressed control group will probably exercise a lot of discussion and debate as many individuals vie for controlling the group's discussion and dominating the decision as to the strategy they will use with the technician. Again, the strategy they adopt will probably be strong, directive, and "commanding" in its approach, and will also be fairly evident to others when it is role played.

   c. Students in the middle expressed control group will experience dynamics that are intermediate to the low and high groups. Leadership that emerges and strategies that are adopted will probably be more determined by a process of "give-and-take" in the group discussion.

   d. The "want control" needs of the target individuals in the role play will also be a factor in how successful it is. Individuals with strong want-control needs will generally be happy to follow any strategy that is proposed to them: individuals with low want-control needs may be far more resistant, and/or may try to "fight back." Both want control and expressed-control scores between the two role players should be revealed after the exercise, to determine how much these scores reflected their own particular styles and reactions to the role-play scenario.

ADDITIONAL RESOURCES

Akin, G., "An Exercise in Social Power," *Exchange*, 3(4), pp. 38-39.

Winter, D., *The Power Motive* (New York: The Free Press, 1973).

Relating Power and Politics

Your ability to politick effectively will be affected by your possession of and effective use of power. The following exercise will ask you to take the basics you've learned about politics and power and to relate the two.

Exercise

1. Break into groups or 3-5 people to discuss the following questions as they relate to nine politicking guidelines discussed earlier.

   a. Using the information about power found in Table 14.1, what power type(s) does your group believe would be most useful in implementing each guideline? Use the letters for your answers.

   b. Briefly describe how the power type(s) you selected could be used.

2. In completing your exercise, do your best to use all power types at least once.

3. After each group completes the exercise, share your answers with the rest of the class.

Power Source	Power Type
Position	A. Reward
	B. Coercive
	C. Legitimate
	D. Connection
Personal	E. Expert
	F. Referent
	G. Information

1. Frame arguments in terms of organizational goals

   a. _____

   b. _____

   _____

2. Develop the right image.

   a. _____

   b. _____

   _____

Relating Power and Politics, (continued)

3. Gain control of organizational resources.

    a. _____

    b. _____

    _____

4. Make yourself appear indispensable.

    a. _____

    b. _____

    _____

5. Be visible.

    a. _____

    b. _____

    _____

6. Get a mentor.

    a. _____

    b. _____

    _____

7. Develop powerful allies.

    a. _____

    b. _____

    _____

8. Avoid "tainted" members.

    a. _____

    b. _____

    _____

9. Support your boss.

    a. _____

    b. _____

    _____

10. Was your group able to use all seven power types at least once?_____ If not, which one(s) were you unable to relate to a politicking guideline and why do you think you were unable to relate it?

Relating Power and Politics, (continued)

Notes

1. Tom Peters, *The Tom Peters Seminar: Crazy Times Call for Crazy Organizations* (New York: Vintage Books, 1994), pp. 110-111
2. Dan Farrell and James C. Petersen, "Patterns of Political Behavior in Organizations," *Academy of Management Review* (July 1982), pp. 430-442
3. Stephen P. Robbins, *Training in Interpersonal Skills; TIPS for Managing People at Work* (Englewood Cliffs, NJ: Prentice Hall, Inc. 1989), pp. 172-174.

The Power Game

PURPOSE:

(1) To explore the dynamics of power at the individual, interpersonal, group, and system levels.

(2) To create the opportunity for students to examine their personal beliefs about power, power strategies, and reactions to power.

ADVANCE PREPARATION: A thorough understanding of the rules and procedures of the simulation is necessary. The instructor should have identified the physical space to conduct the exercise, and selected instructors or students to work as "observers" (help record events as they occur). Videotape in some rooms is also useful for later analysis. Finally, the instructor should carefully prepare the debriefing session, in order to generate as many different perceptions of events and their meaning as possible. Instructors may do well to consult similar exercises developed by Bolman and Deal (1979), Oshry (1976), and Peabody 1983) to gain a perspective on the issues that need to be observed and processed later.

GROUP SIZE: 15-40 students

TIME REQUIRED: 80-90 minutes for the exercise, 60 minutes for discussion.

SPECIAL MATERIALS: See pages 159–161

SPECIAL PHYSICAL REQUIREMENTS: Three separate rooms or gathering spaces for groups.

RELATED TOPICS: Negotiation and Conflict, Organizational Communication, Organizational Realities, Organizational Structure and Design

INTRODUCTION

The concept of "power" is a complete, elusive, and almost paradoxical one. It is complex because there is a wide variety of definitions of what constitutes power, and how it is effectively accumulated and used. It is elusive because there seems to be very little consensus about the definitions, or the best way to describe power and talk about it in action. Finally, power is paradoxical because it doesn't always work the way it is "expected" to; sometimes those who seem to have the most power really have the least, while those who may appear to have the least power are most in control.

This simulation offers an opportunity to experience power in a wide variety of forms and styles. During the activity, you will become aware of your own power, and the power of others. Your objective will be to determine who has power, how power is being used, and how other's power may be effectively counteracted with your own power in order for you to achieve your goals. This type of analysis is essential to effective negotiations in power-laden situations.

The Power Game, (continued)

1. Briefing Sheet for Group 1 - Top Group

You have been assigned to Group 1, the Top group for this exercise. Your task as a group is twofold:

a. You are responsible for the overall effectiveness of the simulation, and student learning from it. It is your responsibility to discuss, decide, and carry out strategies to maximize these objectives. You may use any means you choose to achieve these goals.

b. Your group has been assigned the responsibility for two-thirds of the total dollars collected in this simulation. It is your decision as to how to use this money.

All groups have been informed about rules regarding communication between groups. Members of the Top group are free to enter the space of either of the other groups, and to communicate whatever they wish, whenever they wish. Members of the Middle group may enter the space of the Bottom group whenever they wish, but must request permission from the Top group to enter the Top group's space—this permission can be denied by the Top group. Members of the Bottom group may not disturb the Top group in any way, unless specifically invited by the Top group. The Bottom group does have permission to request communication from the Middle group by knocking on the door of the room housing the Middle group—the Middle group may refuse permission. Members of the Top group are given authority to make any changes in the rules that they wish, with or without notice.

The Power Game, (continued)

2. Briefing Sheet for Group 2 - Middle Group

You have been assigned to Group 2, the Middle group in this exercise. Your task as a group is twofold:

    a. You are responsible for assisting the Top group in maximizing the overall effectiveness of the simulation, and student learning from it. It is your responsibility to provide any assistance to them or take any action yourselves that may achieve this end.

    b. Your group has been assigned the responsibility for one-third of the total dollars collected in this simulation. It is your decision as to how to use this money.

All groups have been informed about the rules regarding communication between groups. Members of the top group are free to enter the space of either of the other groups, and to communicate whatever they wish, whenever they wish. Members of the Middle group may enter the space of the Bottom group whenever they wish, but must request permission from the Top group to enter the Top group's space—this permission can be denied by the Top group. Members of the Bottom group may not disturb the Top group in any way, unless specifically invited by the Top group. The Bottom group does have permission to request communication from the Middle group by knocking on the door of the room housing the Middle group—the Middle group may refuse permission. Members of the Top group are given authority to make any changes in the rules that they wish, with or without notice.

The Power Game, (continued)

3. Briefing Sheet for Group 3 - Bottom Group

You have been assigned to Group 3, the Bottom group in this exercise. Your task as a group is twofold:

    a. To help the Top and Middle groups maximize overall effectiveness of the simulation, and student learning from it. It is your responsibility to provide any assistance to them, or take any action yourselves to accomplish this end.

    b. To identify whatever resources you have to influence the other two groups.

All groups have been informed about rules regarding communication between groups. Members of the Top group are free to enter the space of either of the other groups, and to communicate whatever they wish, whenever they wish. Members of the Middle group may enter the space of the Bottom group whenever they with, but must request permission from the Top group to enter the Top group's space—this permission can be denied by the Top group. Members of the Bottom group may not disturb the Top group in any way, unless specifically invited by the Top group. The Bottom group does have permission to request communication from the Middle group by knocking on the door of the room housing the Middle group—the Middle group may refuse permission. Members of the Top group are given authority to make changes in the rules that they wish, with or without notice.

The Power Game, (continued)

PROCEDURE

Step 1: 5 Minutes

Your instructor will ask you for a monetary contribution. This money is to be given to the instructor. He will then announce what he will do with it.

Step 2: 5 Minutes

Your instructor will assign you to a group. You will become acquainted with the group that you are assigned to. You will be given a place to meet.

Step 3: 60 Minutes

Your instructor will give you descriptions of the duties and responsibilities of the group that you are assigned to. Please read this information closely. You will have exactly one hour to conduct the exercise, unless your instructor gives you different instructions.

DISCUSSION QUESTIONS

1. What did you learn about power from this experience?
2. Did this experience remind you of events you have experienced in other organizations? If so, what were the similarities?
3. What did you learn about yourself personally, and the way that you react to power or use?
4. What events occurred in your own subgroup? Did you feel satisfied with the amount of power you had? With the way you used it? Why?
5. What did you or your group do to exercise power, or to gain more power? How did it work out?

READINGS AND REFERENCES

Block, P., *The Empowered Manager.* (San Francisco: Jossy Bass, 1987)

Yates, D., *The Politics of Management.* (San Francisco: Jossy Bass, 1985)

Source: Adapted from an exercise developed by Lee Bolman and Terrance Deal, Harvard Graduate School of Education. Previously published in *Negotiation: Readings, Exercises and Cases,* Roy J. Lewicki and Joseph Litterer, Richard D. Irwin, 1985. Used with permission of authors and Richard D. Irwin.

Sources and Uses of Power

Preparation

Consider *the way you behaved* in each of the following situations. This may be from a full-time or part-time job, student organization or class group, sports team, or whatever. If you do not have an experience of the type described, try to imagine yourself in one. In this case, think about how you would expect yourself to behave.

1. You needed to get a peer to do something you wanted that person to do but were worried he or she didn't want to do it.
2. You needed to get a subordinate to do something you wanted her or him to do but were worried the subordinate didn't want to do it.
3. You needed to get your boss to do something you wanted him or her to do, but were worried the boss didn't want to do it.

Instructions

Form into groups as assigned by the instructor. Start with situation 1 and have all members of the group share their approaches. Determine what specific sources of power (see Chapter 12) were used. Note any patterns in group members' responses. Discuss what is required to be successful in this situation. Do the same for situations 2 and 3. Note any special differences in how situations 1, 2, and 3 should be or could be handled. Choose a spokesperson to share results in general class discussion.

EXERCISE 29
Leading Through Participation

Preparation

Read each of the following vignettes. Write in the space to the left of each whether you think the leader should handle the situation by an individual decision (I), consultative decision (C), or group decision (G).

Vignette I

You are general supervisor in charge of a large gang laying an oil pipeline. It is now necessary to estimate your expected rate of progress in order to schedule material deliveries to the next field site. You know the nature of the terrain you will be traveling and have the historical data needed to compute the mean and variance in the rate of speed over the type of terrain. Given these two variables, it is a simple matter to calculate the earliest and latest times at which materials and support facilities will be needed at the next site. It is important that your estimate be reasonably accurate; underestimates result in idle supervisors and workers, and overestimates result in tying up materials for a period of time before they are to be used. Progress has been good, and your five supervisors and other members of the gang stand to receive substantial bonuses if the project is completed ahead of schedule.

Vignette II

You are supervising the work of 12 engineers. Their formal training and work experience are very similar, permitting you to use them interchangeably on projects. Yesterday, your manager informed you that a request had been received from an overseas affiliate for four engineers to go abroad on extended loan for a period of 6 to 8 months. For a number of reasons, he argued and you agreed, this request should be met from your group. All your engineers are capable of handling this assignment, and from the standpoint of present and future projects there is no particular reason that any one should be retained over any other. The problem is complicated by the fact that the overseas assignment is in what is generally regarded in the company as an undesirable location.

Vignette III

You are the head of a staff unit reporting to the vice president of finance. He has asked you to provide a report on the firm's current portfolio to include recommendations for changes in the *selection criteria* currently employed. Doubts have been raised about the efficiency of the existing system in the current market conditions, and there is considerable dissatisfaction with prevailing rates of return. You plan to write the report, but at the moment you are quite perplexed about the approach to take. Your own speciality is the bond market and it is clear to you that a detailed knowledge of the equity market, which you lack, would greatly enhance the value of the report. Fortunately, four members of your staff are specialists in different segments of the equity market. Together, they possess a vast amount of knowledge about the intricacies of investment. However, they seldom agree on the best way to achieve anything when it comes to the stock market. Whereas they are obviously conscientious as well as knowledgeable, they have major

Leading Through Participation, (continued)

differences when it comes to investment philosophy and strategy. The report is due in 6 weeks. You have already begun to familiarize yourself with the firm's current portfolio and have been provided by management with a specific set of constraints that any portfolio must satisfy. Your immediate problem is to come up with some alternatives to the firm's present practices and select the most promising for detailed analysis in your report.

Vignette IV

You are on the division manager's staff and work on a wide variety of problems of both an administrative and technical nature. You have been given the assignment of developing a universal method to be used in each of the five plants in the division for manually reading equipment registers, recording the readings, and transmitting the scoring to a centralized information system. All plants are located in a relatively small geographical region. Until now there has been a high error rate in the reading and/or transmittal of the data. Some locations have considerably higher error rates than others, and the methods used to record and transmit the data vary between plants. It is probable, therefore, that part of the error variance is a function of specific local conditions rather than anything else, and this will complicate the establishment of any system common to all plants. You have the information on error rates but no information on the local practices that generate these errors or on the local conditions that necessitate the different practices. Everyone would benefit from an improvement in the quality of the data as it is used in a number of important decisions. Your contacts with the plants are through the quality-control supervisors who are responsible for collecting the data. They are a conscientious group committed to doing their jobs well but are highly sensitive to interference on the part of higher management in their own operations. Any solution that does not receive the active support of the various plant supervisors is unlikely to reduce the error rate significantly.

Instructions

Form groups as assigned by the instructor. Share your choices with other group members and try to achieve a consensus on how the leader should best handle each situation. Nominate a spokesperson to share your results in general class discussion.

Source: Victor H. Vroom and Arthur G. Jago, *The New Leadership* (Englewood Cliffs, NJ: Prentice Hall, 1988). Used by permission.

Your Leadership Style

Objectives
1. To assess your personal propensity for transformational or transactional leader style.
2. To develop an understanding of leadership characteristics and what makes a person a leader.
3. To aid your understanding of the similarities and differences in leadership styles and types of leaders.
4. To provide a broad perspective of current and historical leaders.
5. To develop and enhance your research and analytical skills and abilities.

Total Time
30 to 60 minutes

Procedure
1. You should begin by individually completing and scoring the leadership questionnaire below.
2. Next, choose a leader (current or historical) whom you know something about.
3. Now, develop a listing of the key characteristics of this particular leader. Write these characteristics down on a piece of paper.
4. Form a group of four to seven persons and share key characteristics of your individual leaders in a round-robin fashion. Designate one member of the group to serve as group reporter, who will later present your findings to the rest of the class.
5. As a group, rank the strongest characteristics (i.e., the characteristics that appeared most frequently on people's lists) and discuss overall generalizations and ideas about leadership.
6. Discuss whether there is any relationship between your personal transformational/transactional score and your evaluation of the leaders above.
7. The group reporter shares results in general class discussion.

Leadership Questionnaire
For each of the following 10 pairs of statements, divide five points between the two according to your beliefs, perceptions of yourself, or according to which of the two statements characterizes you better. The five points may be divided between the A and B statements in any way you wish with the constraint that only whole positive integers may be used (i.e., you may not split 2.5 points equally between the two). Weigh your choices between the two according to the one that better characterizes you or your beliefs.

_____ 1. A. As a leader I have a primary mission of maintaining stability.

B. As a leader I have a primary mission of change.

_____ 2. A. As a leader I must cause events.

B. As a leader I must facilitate events.

Your Leadership Style, (continued)

_____ 3.   A. I am concerned that my followers are rewarded equitably for their work.

             B. I am concerned about what my followers want in life.

_____ 4.   A. My preference is to think long range: What might be.

             B. My preference is to think short range: What is realistic.

_____ 5.   A. As a leader I spend considerable energy in managing separate but related goals.

             B. As a leader I spend considerable energy in arousing hopes, expectations, and aspirations among my followers.

_____ 6.   A. While not in a formal classroom sense, I believe that a significant part of my leadership is that of teacher.

             B. I believe that a significant part of my leadership if that of facilitator.

_____ 7.   A. As a leader I must engage with followers at an equal level of morality.

             B. As a leader I must represent a higher morality.

_____ 8.   A. I enjoy stimulating followers to want to do more.

             B. I enjoy rewarding followers for a job well done.

_____ 9.   A. Leadership should be practical.

             B. Leadership should be inspirational.

_____ 10.   A. What power I have to influence others comes primarily from my ability to get people to identify with me and my ideas.

             B. What power I have to influence others comes primarily from my status and position.

Scoring Key

Transformational	Your Point(s)	Transactional	Your Point(s)
1. B	_____	1. A	_____
2. A	_____	2. B	_____
3. B	_____	3. A	_____
4. A	_____	4. B	_____
5. B	_____	5. A	_____
6. A	_____	6. B	_____
7. B	_____	7. A	_____
8. A	_____	8. B	_____
9. B	_____	9. A	_____
10. A	_____	10. B	_____
Column Totals:	_____		_____

Note: The higher column total indicates that you agree more with, and see yourself as more like, either a transformational leader or a transactional leader.

EXERCISE 31

Movement, Power & Leadership

Contributed by Mark Maier, Ph.D.

Associate Professor and Director, Organizational Leadership, Chapman University

Audience: New and experienced instructors of graduate and undergraduate OB/OD and Management courses. Also relevant for corporate trainers and executive educators. (A great exercise to "have in your pocket," ready to go at any appropriate time, without a moment's notice!)

Length: 50 Minutes.

Special Requirements: None. (Large enough room for participants to move around in.) Flip chart and marker.

Abstract: What happens in groups when individuals have conflicting (or similar) goals is brought vividly to light in this powerful, yet simple, simulation. A unique "twist" is added to this classic from the "human potential movement era," to make it refreshingly contemporary. How can one exercise teach group dynamics, conflict, shared vision, pyramidal politics, empowerment, goal-setting, communication, power, resistance, change, gender issues, organizational structure, leadership, and more…all in less than 6 minutes? This one does it!

Workshop Description: Quick introduction (5 minutes): *"Today, we are going to experience power (and/or leadership) in groups. To do that, I need you to break up into groups of 5-7, and to arrange yourselves in a circle, standing side-to-side, about half-a-step apart."*

"Raise your arms, and hold them so that you are touching palms with the person on either side of you. (Glance around to ensure everyone has got it right.)"

"Now, as I suggested, the purpose of this exercise is to teach each other something about power (and/or leadership) in your groups. What can you learn about power (and/or leadership) from each other today?"

"Look around the room and—CAREFULLY and surreptitiously, so that no one knows what location you're zeroing in on—identify a spot you could move your group to when I give you the signal to begin. There are only two ground rules I forgot to mention: (1) You must at all times remain in contact with the person on your left and on your right. Your hands must remain touching at all times (if you break contact you and the person next to you will be "disqualified" from the exercise). You may not GRASP hands to force contact; simply remain "in touch" at all times. (2) Second, you may not talk—not a word— during the five minutes or so we will take to conduct the actual exercise.

Movement, Power & Leadership, (continued)

"Have all of you identified a spot you can move your group to when I give the signal to start?" (Look around for everyone to nod.)

"OK—BEGIN!" (Observe interactions; record observations on paper.)
(At the end of 3 minutes, announce to the groups:) *"Take a moment to notice what the other members of your group seem to want?"*

(Allow exercise to continue for another minute or two, then stop the exercise and poll the participants:)
"How many of you got to your designated spots?" (Proceed to debrief.)

Determining Your Preferred Communication Style

Objectives

To help you reflect on your preferred communication style and identify your interpersonal communication skills in an organizational setting.

Time

30 to 40 minutes

Procedure

To determine your preferred communication style, select the one alternative that most closely describes what you would do in each of the 12 situations below. Do not be concerned with trying to pick the correct answer; select the alternative that best describes what you would actually do. Circle the letter *a*, *b*, *c*, or *d*.

_____ 1. Wendy, a knowledgeable person from another department, comes to you, the engineering supervisor, and requests that you design a special product to her specifications. You would:

    a. Control the conversation and tell Wendy what you will do for her.

    b. Ask Wendy to describe the product. Once you understand it, you would present your ideas. Let her realize that you are concerned and want to help with your ideas.

    c. Respond to Wendy's request by conveying understanding and support. Help clarify what is to be done by you. Offer ideas, but do it her way.

    d. Find out what you need to know. Let Wendy know you will do it her way.

_____ 2. Your department has designed a product that is to be fabricated by Saul's department. Saul has been with the company longer than you have; he knows his department. Saul comes to you to change the product design. You decide to:

    a. Listen to the change and why it would be beneficial. If you believe Saul's way is better, change it; if not, explain why the original idea is superior. If necessary, insist that it be done your way.

    b. Tell Saul to fabricate it any way he wants to.

    c. You are busy; tell Saul to do it your way. You don't have the time to listen and agree with him.

    d. Be supportive; make changes together as a team.

Determining Your Preferred Communication Style,
(continued)

_____ 3. Upper management has a decision to make. They call you to a meeting and tell you they need some information to solve a problem they describe to you. You:

    a. Respond in a manner that conveys personal support and offer alternative ways to solve the problem.

    b. Respond to their questions.

    c. Explain how to solve the problem.

    d. Show your concern by explaining how to solve the problem and why it is an effective solution.

_____ 4. You have a routine work order. The work order is to be replaced verbally and completed in three days. Sue, the receiver, is very experienced and willing to be of service to you. You decide to:

    a. Explain your needs, but let Sue make the other decision.

    b. Tell Sue what you want and why you need it.

    c. Decide together what to order.

    d. Simply give Sue the order.

_____ 5. Work orders from the staff department normally take 3 days; however, you have an emergency and need the job today. Your colleague Jim, the department supervisor, is knowledgeable and somewhat cooperative. You decide to:

    a. Tell Jim that you need it by three o'clock and return at that time to pick it up.

    b. Explain the situation and how the organization will benefit by expediting the order. Volunteer to help any way you can.

    c. Explain the situation and ask Jim when the order will be ready.

    d. Explain the situation and together come up with a solution to your problem.

_____ 6. Danielle, a peer with a record of high performance, has recently had a drop in productivity. Her problem is affecting her performance. You know Danielle has a family problem. You:

    a. Discuss the problem; help Danielle realize the problem is affecting her work and yours. Supportively discuss ways to improve the situation.

    b. Tell the boss about it and let him decide what to do about it.

    c. Tell Danielle to get back on the job.

    d. Discuss the problem and tell Danielle how to solve the work situation; be supportive.

Determining Your Preferred Communication Style,
(continued)

____ 7. You are a knowledgeable supervisor. You buy supplies from Peter regularly. He is an excellent salesperson and very knowledgeable about your situation. You are placing your weekly order. You decide to:

    a. Explain what you want and why. Develop a supportive relationship.

    b. Explain what you want and ask Peter to recommend products.

    c. Give Peter the order.

    d. Explain your situation and allow Peter to make the order.

____ 8. Jean, a knowledgeable person from another department, has asked you to perform a routine staff function to her specifications. You decide to:

    a. Perform the task to her specifications without questioning her.

    b. Tell her that you will do it in the usual way.

    c. Explain what you will do and why.

    d. Show your willingness to help; offer alternative ways to do it.

____ 9. Tom, a salesperson, has requested an order for your department's services with a short delivery date. As usual, Tom claims it is a take-it-or-leave-it offer. He wants your decision now, or within a few minutes, because he is in the customer's office. Your action is to:

    a. Convince Tom to work together to come up with a later date.

    b. Give Tom a yes or no answer.

    c. Explain your situation and let Tom decide if you should take the order.

    d. Offer an alternative delivery date. Work on your relationship; show your support.

Determining Your Preferred Communication Style, (continued)

_____ 10. As a time-and-motion expert, you have been called in regard to a complaint about the standard time it takes to perform a job. As you analyze the entire job, you realize the one element of complaint should take longer, but other elements should take less time. The end result is a shorter total time for the job. You decide to:

    a. Tell the operator and foreman that the total time must be decreased and why.

    b. Agree with the operator and increase the standard time.

    c. Explain your findings. Deal with the operator and/or foreman's concerns, but ensure compliance with your new standard.

    d. Together with the operator, develop a new standard time.

_____ 11. You approve budget allocations for projects. Marie, who is very competent in developing budgets, has come to you. You:

    a. Review the budget, make revisions, and explain them in a supportive way. Deal with concerns, but insist on your changes.

    b. Review the proposal and suggest areas where changes may be needed. Make changes together, if needed.

    c. Review the proposed budget, make revisions, and explain them.

    d. Answer any questions or concerns Marie has and approve the budget as is.

_____ 12. You are a sales manager. A customer has offered you a contract for your product with a short delivery date. The offer is open for days. The contract would be profitable for you and the organization. The cooperation of the production department is essential to meet the deadline. Tim, the production manager, and you do not get along very well because of your repeated requests for quick delivery. Your action is to:

    a. Contact Tim and try to work together to complete the contract.

    b. Accept the contract and convince Tim in a supportive way to meet the obligation.

    c. Contact Tim and explain the situation. Ask him if you and he should accept the contract, but let him decide.

    d. Accept the contract. Contact Tim and tell him to meet the obligation. If he resists, tell him you will go to the boss.

Determining Your Preferred Communication Style,
(continued)

To determine your preferred communication style, below, circle the letter you selected as the alternative you chose in situations 1-12. The column headings indicate the style you selected.

	Autocratic	Consultative	Participative	Laissez-Faire
1.	a	b	c	d
2.	c	a	d	b
3.	c	d	a	b
4.	d	b	c	a
5.	a	b	d	c
6.	c	b	a	b
7.	c	a	b	d
8.	b	c	d	a
9.	b	d	a	c
10.	a	c	d	b
11.	c	a	b	d
12.	d	b	a	c
TOTAL				

Add up the number of circled items per column. The total column should equal 12. The column with the highest number represents your preferred communication style. There is no one best style in all situations. The more evenly distributed the numbers are between the four styles, the more flexible are your communications. A total of 0 or 1 in any column may indicate a reluctance to use the style(s). You could have problems in situations calling for the use of this style.

Source: Adapted from Robert N. Lussier, *Human Relations in Organizations: A Skill-Building Approach,* Second Edition (Homewood, IL: Richard D. Irwin, Inc., 1993), pp. 153-156.

How to give, and take, criticism

Preparation

The "criticism session" may well be the toughest test of a manager's communication skills. Picture Setting 1—you and a subordinate, meeting to review a problem with the subordinate's performance. Now picture Setting 2—you and your boss, meeting to review a problem with *your* performance. Both situations require communication skills in giving and receiving feedback. Even the most experienced person can have difficulty and the situations can end as futile gripe sessions resulting in hard feelings. The question is: How can such "criticism sessions" be handled in a positive manner that encourages improved performance...and good feelings?

Instructions

Form into groups as assigned by the instructor. Focus on either Setting #1 or Setting #2, or both, as also assigned by the instructor. First, answer the question from the assigned perspective. Second, develop a series of action guidelines that could be used to best handle situations of this type. Third, prepare and present a mini-management training session to demonstrate the (a) unsuccessful and (b) successful use of these guidelines.

If time permits outside of class, prepare a more extensive management training session that includes a videotape demonstration of your assigned criticism setting being handled first poorly and then very well. Support the videotape with additional written handouts and an oral presentation to help your classmates better understand the communication skills needed to successfully give and take criticism in work settings.

Feedback and Assertiveness

Preparation

Indicate the degree of discomfort you would feel in each situation given below by circling the appropriate number:

1, *high discomfort;* 2, *some discomfort;* 3, *undecided;* 4, *very little discomfort;* 5, *no discomfort*

1 2 3 4 5   1. Telling an employee who is also a friend that she or he must stop coming to work late.

1 2 3 4 5   2. Talking to an employee about his or her performance on the job.

1 2 3 4 5   3. Asking an employee if she or he has any comments about your rating of her or his performance.

1 2 3 4 5   4. Telling an employee who has problems in dealing with other employees that he or she should do something about it.

1 2 3 4 5   5. Responding to an employee who is upset over your rating of his or her performance.

1 2 3 4 5   6. An employee's becoming emotional and defensive when you tell her or him about mistakes in the job.

1 2 3 4 5   7. Giving a rating that indicates improvement is needed to an employee who has failed to meet minimum requirements of the job.

1 2 3 4 5   8. Letting a subordinate talk during an appraisal interview.

1 2 3 4 5   9. An employee's challenging you to justify your evaluation in the middle of an appraisal interview.

1 2 3 4 5   10. Recommending that an employee be discharged.

1 2 3 4 5   11. Telling an employee that you are uncomfortable in the role of having to judge his or her performance.

1 2 3 4 5   12. Telling an employee that her or his performance can be improved.

1 2 3 4 5   13. Telling an employee that you will not tolerate his or her taking extended coffee breaks.

1 2 3 4 5   14. Telling an employee that you will not tolerate her or his making personal telephone calls on company time.

Instructions

Form three-person teams as assigned by the instructor. Identify the three behaviors with which they indicate the most discomfort. Then each team member should practice performing these behaviors with another member, while the third member acts as an observer. Be direct, but try to perform the behavior in an appropriate manner. Listen to feedback from the observer and try the behaviors again, perhaps with different members of the group. When finished, discuss the exercise overall. Be prepared to participate in further class discussion.

Source: Feedback questionnaire is from Judith R. Gordon, *A Diagnostic Approach to Organizational Behavior,* Third Edition (Boston: Allyn and Bacon, 1991), p. 298. Used by permission.

Lost At Sea

Consider this situation

You are adrift on a private yacht in the South Pacific when a fire of unknown origin destroys the yacht and most of its contents. You and a small group of survivors are now in a large raft with oars. Your location is unclear, but you estimate being about 1000 miles south-southwest of the nearest land. One person has just found in her pockets five $1 bills and a packet of matches. Everyone else's pockets are empty. The following items are available to you on the raft.

	A	B	C
Sextant	____	____	
Shaving mirror	____	____	
5 gallons water	____	____	
Mosquito netting	____	____	
1 survival meal	____	____	
Maps of Pacific Ocean	____	____	
Floatable seat cushion	____	____	
2 gallons oil-gas mix	____	____	
Small transistor radio	____	____	
Shark repellent	____	____	
20 square feet black plastic	____	____	
1 quart 20-proof rum	____	____	
15 feet nylon rope	____	____	
24 chocolate bars	____	____	
Fishing kit	____	____	

Instructions

1. *Working alone*, rank in Column A the 15 items in order of their importance to your survival ("1" is most important and "15" is least important).
2. *Working in an assigned group*, arrive at a "team" ranking of the 15 items and record this ranking in Column B. Appoint one person as group spokesperson to report your group rankings to the class.
3. *Do not write in Column* C until further instructions are provided by your instructor.

Source: Adapted from "Lost at Sea: A Consensus-Seeking Task," in *The 1975 Handbook for Group Facilitators.* Used with permission of University Associates, Inc.

Conflict Resolution

Preparation

You will be given the opportunity to role play handling a conflict you face or have faced. Select the conflict and write out the information for a class member who will play the role of the person with whom you are in conflict.

1. Define the situation and list pertinent information about the other party (i.e., relationship with you, knowledge of the situation, age, background, etc.)
2. State what you wish to accomplish during the conflict resolution.
3. Identify the other party's possible reaction to your confrontation (resistance to change).
   Plan how you will overcome resistance to change using the problem-solving conflict management style. A good way to open the conflict resolution is the use an X (behavior), Y (consequences), Z (feelings) statement. For example, "When you smoke in my room (behavior), I have trouble breathing and become nauseous (consequence) and feel uncomfortable and irritated (feeling)." Write out an XYZ statement to open your selected conflict resolution. During the role play, open with your XYZ statement, then allow the person to respond as you seek true satisfaction of everyone's concerns by working through differences, finding and solving problems so everyone gains as a result.

Objective

To develop your conflict resolution skills.

Total Time

30 to 40 minutes

Procedure 1

Break into as many groups of three as possible. If there are any people not in a triad, make one or two groups of two. Each member selects the number 1, 2, or 3. Number 1 will be the first to initiate a conflict role play, then 2, followed by 3.

Procedure 2

1. Initiator number 1 gives his or her information from the preparation to number 2 (the responder) to read. Once number 2 understands, role-play (see number 2 below). Number 3 is the observer.
2. Role-play the conflict resolution. Number 3, the observer, writes his or her observation. Focus on what was done and how to improve.
3. Integration. When the role play is over, the observer leads a discussion on the effectiveness of the conflict resolution. All three should discuss the effectiveness. Number 3 is not a lecturer. Do not go on until told to do so.

Conflict Resolution, (continued)

Procedure 3

Same as procedure 2, only number 2 is now the initiator, number 3 is the responder, and number 1 is the observer.

Procedure 4

Same as procedure 2, only number 3 is the initiator, number 1 is the responder, and number 2 is the observer.

EXERCISE 37
Strategic Scenarios

Preparation

In today's turbulent environments, it is no longer safe to assume that an organization that was highly successful yesterday will continue to be so tomorrow-or that it will even be in existence. Changing times exact the best from strategic planners. Think about the situations currently facing the following well-known organizations; think, too, about the futures they may face.

> McDonald's
>
> Texaco
>
> Xerox
>
> Harvard University
>
> United Nations
>
> National Public Radio

Instructions

Form into groups as assigned by your instructor. Choose one or more organizations from the prior list (as assigned) and answer for that organization the following questions:

1. What in the future might seriously threaten the success, perhaps the very existence of this organization?
   (As a group develop at least three such *future scenarios*.)
2. Estimate the probability (0 to 100 percent) of each future scenario occurring.
3. Develop a strategy for each scenario that will enable the organization to successfully deal with it.

Thoroughly discuss these questions within the group and arrive at your best possible consensus answers. Be prepared to share and defend your answers in general class discussion.

Source: Suggested by an exercise in John F. Veiga and John N. Yanouzas, *The Dynamics of Organization Theory: Gaining a Macro Perspective* (St. Paul, MN: West, 1979), pp. 69–71.

EXERCISE 38

Time Management Techniques

Preparation

The better you are at time management, the less stress you will have. Below is a list of 42 ideas that can be used to improve your time management skills. Place the number 1-4 that represents the appropriate response on the line before each technique.

(1) I should do this   (3) I do this now

(2) I could do this   (4) Does not apply to me

Planning and Controlling

_____ 1. Set objectives—long and short term.

_____ 2. Plan your week; how you will achieve your objectives.

_____ 3. Use a to-do list—write all assignments on it.

_____ 4. Prioritize the items on your to-do list. Do the important things rather than urgent things.

_____ 5. Get an early productive start on your top-priority items.

_____ 6. Schedule a quiet hour(s). Only be interrupted by true emergencies. Have someone take a message or ask people to call you back during scheduled unexpected event time.

_____ 7. Establish a quiet time for the entire organization, department, etc. the first hour of the day is usually the best time.

_____ 8. Schedule large blocks of uninterrupted (emergencies only) time for projects, etc. If this doesn't work, hide somewhere.

_____ 9. Break large (long) projects into parts (time periods).

_____ 10. If you don't follow your schedule, ask the priority question (is the unscheduled event more important than the scheduled event?)

_____ 11. Schedule a time for doing similar activities (i.e., make and return calls, write letters, memos).

_____ 12. Keep your scheduled events flexible—allow ____% of time for unexpected events.

_____ 13. Schedule unexpected event time and answer mail, and do routine things between events.

_____ 14. Ask people to see/call you during your scheduled unexpected event time only, unless it's an emergency.

_____ 15. If staff members ask to see you—"got a minute?"—tell them you're busy and ask if it can wait until x o'clock (scheduled unexpected time).

_____ 16. Set a schedule time, agenda, and time limit for all visitors, and keep on topic.

Time Management Techniques, (continued)

_____ 17. Control your time. Cut down on the time controlled by the boss, organization, and your subordinates.

Organizing

_____ 18. Keep a clean desk.

_____ 19. Rearrange your desk for increased productivity (see "your desk" session for how to).

_____ 20. All nonwork-related or distracting objects should be removed from your desk.

_____ 21. Do one task at a time.

_____ 22. With paperwork, make a decision at once. Don't read it again later and decide.

_____ 23. Have calls screened to be sure the right person handles them.

_____ 24. Plan before calling. Have an agenda and all necessary information ready—take notes on agenda.

_____ 25. Ask people to call you back during your scheduled unexpected event time. Ask when is the best time to call them.

_____ 26. Have a specific objective/purpose for every meeting.

_____ 27. For meetings, invite only the necessary participants and keep them only for as long as they are needed.

_____ 28. Always have an agenda for a meeting and stick to it. Start and end as scheduled.

_____ 29. Conclude each meeting with a summary, and get a commitment on who will do what by when.

_____ 30. Call rather than visit, if possible.

_____ 31. Set objectives for travel. List everyone you will meet with. Send (call) them agendas and have a file folder for each with all necessary data for your meeting.

_____ 32. Combine and/or modify activities to save time.

Leadership and Staffing

_____ 33. Set clear objectives for subordinates with accountability—give them feedback/evaluate results often.

_____ 34. Use your subordinates' time well. Do you make subordinates wait idly for decisions, instructions, materials, or in meetings?

_____ 35. Communicate well. Do you wait for a convenient time, rather than interrupt your subordinates and waste their time?

_____ 36. Train your subordinates. Don't do their work for them.

Time Management Techniques, (continued)

_____ 37. Delegate activities in which you personally do not need to be involved.

_____ 38. Don't be a perfectionist—define acceptable and stop there.

_____ 39. Learn to stay calm. Getting emotional only causes more problems.

_____ 40. Reduce socializing without causing antisocialism.

_____ 41. Identify your time wasters and work to minimize them.

_____ 42. If there are other ideas you have that are not listed above, add them here.

Review and prioritize the (1's) should-do techniques. Start by implementing the most important techniques and work your way down the list. Go on to the (2's) could-do techniques next.